Edwina

Stage images and traditions:
Shakespeare to Ford

Stage images and traditions:
Shakespeare to Ford

MARION LOMAX

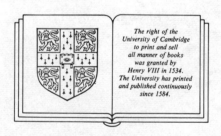

The right of the
University of Cambridge
to print and sell
all manner of books
was granted by
Henry VIII in 1534.
The University has printed
and published continuously
since 1584.

CAMBRIDGE UNIVERSITY PRESS

Cambridge
London   New York   New Rochelle
Melbourne   Sydney

Published by the Press Syndicate of the University of Cambridge
The Pitt Building, Trumpington Street, Cambridge CB2 1RP
32 East 57th Street, New York, NY 10022, USA
10 Stamford Road, Oakleigh, Melbourne 3166, Australia

First published 1987

Printed in Great Britain at
the University Press, Cambridge

British Library cataloguing in publication data
Lomax, Marion
Stage images and traditions: Shakespeare to Ford.
1. English drama – Early modern and Elizabethan, 1500–1600 –
History and criticism   2. English drama – 17th century –
History and criticism
I. Title
822'.3'09   PR651

Library of Congress cataloguing in publication data
Lomax, Marion.
Bibliography.
Includes index.
1. English drama – 17th century – History and criticism.
2. Shakespeare, William, 1564–1616 – Stage history.
3. Shakespeare, William, 1564–1616 – Symbolism.
4. Ford, John, 1586-ca. 1640 – Symbolism.
5. Theater – England – History – 17th century.
6. Symbolism in literature. I. Title.
PR678.S94L6   1987   822'.3'09   86-31062

ISBN 0 521 32659 1

CE

For Michael, William, and Ezra

Contents

List of illustrations   *page* ix

Preface   xi

Acknowledgments   xiii

Introduction   1

1 The development and language of spectacle: Thomas Heywood's *Ages* and Shakespeare's last plays   10

2 The multiple roots of symbolic staging   34

3 The masque and the drama: *Macbeth* and *Lord Hay's Masque*   55

4 *Pericles*: the old and the new   70

5 'Beyond beyond': the multi-layered quality of *Cymbeline*   99

6 Webster and 'The suburbs of hell': *The White Devil* and *The Duchess of Malfi*   127

7 Conventions and improvised rituals in *The Changeling*, *'Tis Pity She's a Whore* and *The Broken Heart*   155

Notes   183

Index   197

Illustrations

page

1 A booth stage set up in an inn yard. Reprinted from *The Revels*   18
   history of drama in English Volume III, 1576–1613, ed. J.
   Leeds Barroll, Alexander Leggatt, Richard Hosley, and Alvin
   Kernan (London, 1975).

2 Jove on an eagle in 'Tempe Restored' (1632). Drawing by Inigo   32
   Jones: Devonshire Collection, Chatsworth. Photograph repro-
   duced by permission of the Courtauld Institute of Art.

3 Symbol of the fecundity of sacrifice: the cross bears fruit (after   41
   an engraving dated 1512). Reprinted from *Dictionary of
   symbols*, ed. J. E. Cirlot, 2nd edn (London, 1971).

4 Emblem of marriage. A woodcut reprinted from Bathelemy   42
   Aneau's *Picta Poesis* (Lyon, 1552). Copyright: the Bodleian
   Library, Douce, C. 123, p. 14.

5 The Cheek by Jowl Theatre Company in *Pericles* (1984): the   86
   vision of Diana. Photo: Peter Mareš.

6 The Cheek by Jowl Theatre Company in *Pericles* (1984): the   88
   statue of Marina at Tharsus. Photo: Peter Mareš.

7 The Cheek by Jowl Theatre Company in *Pericles* (1984):   93
   Marina singing to a shrouded Pericles. Photo: Peter Mareš.

8 The Cheek by Jowl Theatre Company in *Pericles* (1984):   95
   Diana's temple. Photo: Peter Mareš.

9 Romeo with Juliet's body. Sketch by C. Walter Hodges.   101

10 Two possible ways of staging *Othello* v.ii at the Blackfriars   102
   Theatre, where *Cymbeline* was probably performed. Sketches
   by C. Walter Hodges.

11 The Royal Shakespeare Company in *As You Like It* (1985/6):   112
   the dream landscape of Arden. Photo: Joe Cocks Studio.

12 A model of the set by René Allio for *Cymbeline* v.iv at the   122
   Royal Shakespeare Theatre, Stratford-upon-Avon (1962).

13 The National Theatre production of *The Duchess of Malfi*   152
   (1985): the Duchess, Death and Duke Ferdinand. Photo: John
   Vere Brown.

Preface

Our understanding of drama must be limited if we consider texts in isolation from each other and from their age. We can put individual achievements in perspective more effectively if they are considered alongside other works originally performed at the same time, or in the recent past. This inevitably provides a historical context – both in terms of topical knowledge and events – and in relation to their place in the development of drama.

In many ways Shakespeare is the fulcrum of this book, but he is not its sole subject. I began by taking a mixed selection of dramatic works which appeared on different stages from approximately 1607 onwards and set out to explore the traditions behind the ideas which they dramatised – putting Shakespeare with his contemporaries to see whether any sense of development, shared trends, or interdependence was apparent. Even after he had withdrawn from the scene, it is possible to discern his influence in later drama, and it is equally fascinating to move in the other direction and try to trace the influences on which he, himself, drew. Although the starting point is the early seventeenth-century stage, it is hoped that any greater understanding derived from studying these plays in their contemporary context will indicate even more rewarding possibilities for performances in our own time.

Whenever possible, references are made to modern editions of the plays: I acknowledge a particular debt to those in the Arden and Revels series. Where no such editions were available (e.g. certain plays by Thomas Heywood and John Day) the letters 's', 'u', and 'j' have been changed to their modern counterparts for ease of understanding. I thank the staff of the Bodleian Library, the British Library, the Brotherton Library (University of Leeds), the J. B. Morrell Library (University of York), the Library and Audio-Visual Aids Centre, King Alfred's College, Winchester, and the Libraries of the Shakespeare Centre, Stratford-upon-Avon, and the University of Reading for their invaluable, efficient, and friendly assistance. I am particularly grateful to Sarah Stanton and the readers of Cambridge University Press, to Barbara Matthews of the Cheek by Jowl Theatre Company, and to Liz Curry of the National Theatre, who have all made efforts on my behalf.

My largest debt is to Brian Gibbons, Professor at the Englisches Seminar, the University of Zurich. I have benefited greatly from his perceptive criticism, guidance, encouragement, and friendship throughout all the stages of this work. He supervised three years of initial research at the University of York which led to a D. Phil. in 1983, and from his careful reading of the penultimate draft of this manuscript, offered many valuable suggestions and comments, to which I hope I have done justice.

I am also grateful to Andrew Gurr, Professor of English at the University of Reading who, since we first met in 1980, has always been willing to answer my questions and offer support. He generously read a draft of the manuscript and his careful scrutiny and comments were much appreciated – as were those of the Renaissance Research Seminar at the University of Reading when a version of Chapter 3 was read and discussed.

I would like to thank Michael Hattaway, Professor of English at the University of Sheffield, for first pointing me in this direction many years ago and for encouraging me ever since; the Department of Education and Science, for supporting my first three years of research, and Robin Hood, Senior Lecturer in English at the University of York, for many valuable suggestions and criticisms at that time – as well as much friendship.

If I have inadvertently failed to acknowledge any obligations, I apologise to those to whom they are due.

Reading, 1986

Acknowledgments

I should like to thank the following for permission to reproduce illustrations: Richard Hosley and Methuen and Co. Ltd (Figure 1), the Trustees of the Chatsworth Settlement and the Courtauld Institute of Art for supplying the photograph (Figure 2), Routledge and Kegan Paul P.L.C. and the Philosophical Library Publishers, New York (Figure 3), the Bodleian Library (Douce, C.123 page 14) (Figure 4), Peter Mareš (Figures 5–8), C. Walter Hodges and Cambridge University Press (Figures 9–10), Joe Cocks Studio (Figure 11), the Governors of the Royal Shakespeare Theatre, Stratford-upon-Avon (Figure 12), John Vere Brown (Figure 13).

Introduction

This book explores some of the many traditions behind the staging of adult company drama in the early years of the seventeenth century. The plays studied were chosen to show both historical and contemporary influences: together they offer a combined lateral and chronological approach to dramatic development.

The years 1607–14 are particularly important because they form a transitional era in adult company drama, being the time when the theatrical traditions of the adult and the private boys' companies began to converge with the acquisition of the second Blackfriars theatre by Shakespeare's company, the King's Men. In this period it performed the same plays in both the open air Globe playhouse and the indoor Blackfriars theatre. These years also coincide with the growth in sophistication and popularity of the court masque (associated principally with the partnership of Ben Jonson and Inigo Jones); with the chivalric revival associated with Prince Henry, the Prince of Wales; and with the nostalgic hearkening back to the days of Queen Elizabeth, apparently brought about by disillusionment with James I's court.

A wide range of dramatic entertainment was produced (often simultaneously) at different venues: Thomas Heywood's *Ages* plays at the Red Bull; Shakespeare's last plays at the Globe and Blackfriars; Webster's tragedies – *The White Devil* at the Red Bull and *The Duchess of Malfi* at the Globe and Blackfriars: and at court, the masques. Part of the concern of this work is to explore contemporary performances in relation to the influences they may have exerted on each other, and this involves the ways different dramatists handled inherited traditions, often displaying great innovative flair. As Rosalie Colie remarked:

Certainly for the period in which Shakespeare lived and worked, one *can* have it both ways: just as there was no possibility that any author or artist could 'make it new' by abandoning inherited forms, so also there was an insistence on outdoing and over-doing earlier achievements, each man newly creating out of and against his tradition, in conscious competition with the very best that tradition could offer him.[1]

Much of the book is devoted to the older influences on the drama – mythological, classical, religious, literary, and theatrical. The most effective way of exploring dramatists' individual treatment of these seemed to be through the interactions of dramatic presentation and verbal imagery which they instigated.[2] M. C. Bradbrook calls this identifying 'the scenic proverb'[3] and Michael Hattaway terms such moments 'gests' – from Brecht's 'Gestus': 'a word that means both "gist" and "gesture", moments when the visual elements of the scene combine with the dialogue in a significant form that reveals the condition of life in the play'.[4] Often an allusion to a particular tradition is indicated by a combination of visual and verbal effects which form, in Sidney's words, 'a speaking picture'. The association with emblem books is apparent, although the dramatic, rather than any possible didactic impact, is my main concern. I will endeavour to isolate particular moments in the plays where spectacle and speech create speaking pictures whose meanings can best be appreciated once they are viewed in relation to the traditions on which they are based. This will also help to place them in relation to the design of the whole play.

Since the 1950s, when R. A. Foakes[5] and others saw the need to define and recognise *dramatic* imagery rather than follow the trend of the day which was to treat images solely in relation to verbal poetry,[6] this important aspect of Shakespearean criticism has been considerably developed. In the last decade, many critics have usefully considered dramatic imagery in its theatrical context: the complete list would be too long to cite, but apart from those already mentioned, the works of Craik, Bevington, Dessen, Ewbank, R. M. Frye, Garber, Lyons, Mehl, Ricks, Styan, and Wickham deserve particular attention. The benefits of such ideas for performance have been experienced in the many R.S.C. and B.B.C. productions which have adopted an iconographical approach to differing degrees. As the main focus here is on predominantly symbolic aspects, plays such as Jonson's city comedies, which also appeared during the period, have been omitted: symbolism not being one of their major characteristics. The choice of relevant plays in these years is necessarily selective and differences in depth of treatment are inevitable within the plays which are chosen. In the case of Shakespeare, the earlier and less well-documented tragi-comedies, *Pericles* and *Cymbeline*, are treated in more detail than Shakespeare's other late plays which have, generally, received greater critical attention.

Emrys Jones was right to say that 'Plays are made of scenes before they are made of words':[7] these scenes or dramatic moments are often based on a variety of traditions which can sometimes be expressed simultaneously. Rosalie Colie recognised Shakespeare's 'compressed, allusive, suggestive pluralism' in relation to his characterisation: 'Iago is a masterpiece of mysterious psychological analysis, but he is also a stage machiavel, as such related to another Old Nick, the morality devil, characteristically a presenter of plots and playlets ... Iago is also a parasite, a malcontent, a Brighella, and a braggart soldier as well.'[8] This pluralism pervades his plays and is not only a facet of characterisation. An awareness of the traditions behind the staging often results in a cumulative sense of presence in particular scenes – not only in referring back to previous times and ages in relation to the plays' subjects, but also in relation to theatrical history and the ways in which the subjects have been portrayed on the stage in the distant or even very recent past.

These plays are made up of contrasts and what seems to be deliberate juxtapositioning: the recurrence of certain properties and images is often part of a process of gradually building up a cumulative and complex exploration of a central idea, or, as seems more usually the case, a network of related ideas. With the possible exception of Heywood, the dramatists studied here seem less concerned with the clear portrayal of fixed meaning than with the more exciting challenges of ambiguity and contradictions. A branch of Shakespearean criticism now invites us, more forcibly than ever before, to recognise the creative expression of conflicts within works, instead of crediting them, too readily, with undisputed unity. In many instances, this is as applicable to Webster, Middleton, and Ford as it is to Shakespeare.

Both David Bevington[9] and James Siemon[10] have brought this view to the fore – not in order to imply failure as a craftsman on Shakespeare's part, but rather, it seems, to draw attention to the need his art expresses for 'a rigorous exploration of the ways in which true art complicates and even defies ... a comforting notion of readily perceived meaning'.[11] Bevington notes Shakespeare's 'desire for certitude and skepticism about it'[12] which usually results in worlds of order and meaning being juxtaposed 'with his own vision, in which much is inverted or questioned'.[13] The same might be said of Webster, Middleton, and Ford – with the difference that they do not offer a comprehensive range of comparisons as Shakespeare often does,[14] so that in their case, the audience or reader is more often called upon to supply a vision of normality or alternative meaning to compare with the deviations offered on stage. In writing about the use of traditions by all these dramatists, greater fascination is found in instances where they manipulate, subvert, or distort the norm, than in cases of straightforward observance.

Siemon's study of iconoclasm in Shakespeare's plays relates this to the undermining of 'audience complacence':[15] denying an audience a sense of security would also seem to be a strength of Webster's art, and his manipulation of traditions indicates this very forcibly. Bevington and

Siemon also agree that, within the plays themselves, Shakespeare's methods demonstrate that he frequently challenged the meaning of the ideas and figures he used, to the extent that: 'In the case of Shakespearean drama, the de-constructive enterprise encounters texts that have often already done themselves inside out before the critic arrives to expose them.'[16] He is seen as an artist who 'had faith in his art and scoffed at it too'.[17] Certainly, a not entirely dissimilar questioning approach is shared by most of the dramatists studied here. Perhaps it should be acknowledged, at least in relation to the conventions available to him, that although Shakespeare does, at times, appear to scrutinise and gently mock them, nevertheless he can frequently be seen to counter an exposure of their inadequacies with evidence of effective application elsewhere. A simple example occurs in *As You Like It* where, having held up to gentle ridicule the Petrarchan conceit of a lover being slain by a glance from his true love:

Phebe Now I do frown on thee with all my heart,
      And if mine eyes can wound, now let them kill thee.   III.v.15–16[18]

he then employs it more seriously later in the play in relation to Rosalind and Orlando:

Ros. I thought thy heart had been wounded with the claws of a lion.
Orl. Wounded it is, but with the eyes of a lady.   v.ii.22–4

Here, colloquial prose combines with the hyperbole of a hackneyed poetic conceit to produce a moment which is usually played with strong emotive and dramatic force. As David Bevington shows, gesture has its own language which can question verbal meaning, reinforce, or even surpass it. The exaggerated stare which Phebe usually gives in performance demonstrates an instance where it is absurd to take the metaphor literally: the lingering eye contact between Rosalind and Orlando in the second example, however, may indicate the opposite. This is particularly poignant as the 'lady' here is, at once, the memory he keeps of Rosalind when he first fell in love with her *and* the person with him while he speaks, who is meant to be acknowledged merely as a boy playing the part of his love.

In many ways, *As You Like It* could be said to set the mood for the last plays discussed in this book – and not only in relation to its romance and masque elements. In his essay, 'Deconstructing Shakespeare's comedies', Malcolm Evans refers to Hymen's speech, noticing how his allusion to 'truth' in 'If truth holds true contents' (v.iv.129) gives rise to 'a delirium of wordplays ... which leaves no centre but tautology, endless supplementation, and a textual process whose closure can only be as you like it. The truth about such texts is inevitably conditional, inscribed in contradiction and absence, the work of the poet who affirms "nothing"'.[19] Yet the need for the audience to recognise the conflicts within the drama in a positive way, does seem to be asserted: language and meaning may be undercut, but we are not left with a void. An audience must perceive the world from a variety of angles and expand its range of possibilities: it must question on one hand, but suspend its disbelief on the other. The playwright who gives Orlando a conventionally sounding exit line in 1.ii – 'But heavenly Rosalind!' – also refuses to offer this to the audience as a commonplace declaration. At the close we learn that it was not an idle description for, as the god of marriage bids Duke Senior receive Rosalind as his daughter, he adds:

> Hymen from heaven brought her,
> Yea brought her hither,   v.iv.111–12

Nothing can be taken for granted in this play: Shakespeare seems to scrutinise his language carefully and surprise us with reversals of literal and metaphorical meaning. The imaginative freedom of the play's romance aspect provides the ideal medium for such experiments. All this is also present and is, perhaps, even more daringly explored in his last plays where verbal and visual elements are often juxtaposed in the process.

However, even allowing for wider and less comfortable explorations of meaning than might have previously been considered, we may still be in danger of occasionally crediting these playwrights with unintended ironies and purposes. The problem is E. H. Gombrich's 'the notion of an intended meaning' – and I use the phrase guardedly. After well over three hundred years, how can we be sure what any of these dramatists really intended in every instance? The question may even arise as to whether they were fully aware of all the meanings themselves: today, as then, the unconscious probably plays as important a part in the creative process as does the conscious mind. If challenging juxtapositionings occur – are they necessarily deliberate? In certain instances, a study of the traditions which seem to lie behind these plays may reveal more about the inherent contradictions in the varied dramatic heritage which the dramatists took for granted than it does about their own, individual intentions.

In performance today, usually only one set of ideas is selected to be expressed and developed as there is little time for an audience to appreciate multiple branches of meaning which might have been more obvious in former times. A reader, on the other hand, has the opportunity to consider all the possible ramifications simultaneously in relation to various interlocking traditions and ideas – and if they may no longer be expressed simultaneously on stage, then, at least, there may still be an awareness of the possible complexity of many dramatic moments.

Multiple meanings need to be scrutinised carefully. As Rosalie Colie discovered, there is a danger that an awareness of pluralism can lead to all manner of possibilities being thrust upon the text: 'works so inconclusive *must* be hospitable, the justification seems to run, to *any* interpretation'.[20] This is obviously not the case and in this study I suggest only meanings which seem to me to be both illuminating and plausible in relation to a play's design and major concerns. If, occasionally, I offer what, I hope, are challenging speculations, this is not a perverse attempt to overturn accepted theories: an exploration of the traditions behind the staging of these works is not intended to alter their interpretations drastically. The intention is, rather, to supplement these in new and interesting ways to achieve a greater depth of appreciation.

A careful analysis of a work's genre can provide a good indication of the playwright's concerns. The chapter on *Macbeth* indicates that this play needs to be considered, not just as a tragedy, but also as a topical work. Similarly, the stage spectacle of an eagle descending with a god has a very different significance in Thomas Heywood's *The Golden Age* to that which a, perhaps, identical effect has in Shakespeare's tragi-comic romance, *Cymbeline*. The former is a comedy and the symbolic meaning is limited to that of a stage property traditionally associated with Jupiter. In *Cymbeline* is represents a greater number of possible meanings: as in romance itself, the limits are extended. The appearance of the eagle on the stage is a culmination of the many eagle images and their various significances throughout the play[21] – perhaps going back to the eagle hieroglyphic, Alpha, the origin of life, the beginning. This is particularly fitting in a play which demonstrates tension between its placing at the time of Christ's birth and the knowledge that this is only apparent to the audience who have hindsight. The characters themselves are in the dark; the medium in which they move is timeless – literally before the process of counting time, which we now use, existed.

Their age represents a pagan world stretching back to antiquity: a world which has not yet come to consciousness, not just in the sense of Christianity and our sense of time, but even to the extent that in it, the boundaries between dreaming and waking are blurred. Shakespeare's sense of time is far more complex than that of Heywood: his eagle is not fixed in a particular mythological age; instead it, and its many associates, span the distance between the beginning of time and the present moment.

In Shakespeare's day as in our own, different people would appreciate the plays at a variety of levels. However, there may have been options open to a seventeenth-century audience which are now often closed to us because we do not share the same common experience. Roland Mushat Frye has shown how important this is in relation to *Hamlet*. One of his many examples concerns the 'inky cloak' which Hamlet wears at the beginning of the play. Using enlightening illustrations, he demonstrates that this is of supreme importance because it was the official funeral raiment of the day – usually only worn for the actual ceremony or funeral procession.[22] Hamlet persists in wearing the ceremonial dress of his father's funeral to stress that, for him, the funeral rites are not yet over.

As the rest of the court is dressed brightly in accordance with the recent wedding celebrations, putting Hamlet 'too much in the sun', the two extremes clash on stage. In many productions of the play this contrast is not exploited to the full and because Hamlet is in the minority, we are led to feel that *he* is the odd man out, when perhaps we should feel that he is the only one at the court behaving normally in the circumstances. Mourning for a king, as Frye's book shows, was a lengthy process, if carried out according to protocol. The widow would wear black for some considerable time, as would the whole court. A contemporary audience might have reacted to this anomaly in the play more forcibly than we do now. Hamlet's voluminous, full-length cloak and large hood would have made him a prominent figure from his first entrance. The costume proclaims his role as loyal son and chief (as well as only) mourner, which is crucial in relation to his later response to the nature of his father's death and the Ghost's cry for vengeance. In a sense, the rest of the play can be seen as an attempt to complete these unfinished funeral rites. Peace is achieved for Old Hamlet's Ghost by increasing the death toll until, at the close, by a circuitous and unexpected route, the whole court is, indeed, brought to a state of total mourning.

Frye also, usefully, devotes time to the circumstances of Ophelia's burial.[23] By placing this in its historical context, he shows that it was normal, in such situations, for close relatives to take the body in their arms and place it in the grave. Such knowledge prevents us from interpreting Laertes's behaviour as 'morbid to an unusual degree' and, in other instances, might ensure that we do not lose more by incorporating modern associations which have little in keeping with the essential nature of the plays, than we could ever do merely through our ignorance of the age.

Although I believe a sense of historical perspective is necessary when dealing with Elizabethan and Jacobean drama, it is not inconceivable that occasionally new relevancies which will aid a modern audience's appreciation might be included without destroying the plays' intrinsic qualities.

The Cheek by Jowl Theatre Company achieved this in 1986 with their hilarious and thought-provoking performance of *A Midsummer Night's Dream* at the Donmar Warehouse, Covent Garden, when they found an effective modern equivalent for the rustic Thespians in a church amateur dramatic group. Such characters can still be met in village halls throughout the country and were recognised by the audience with delight. Other plays are more inflexible; for example, *Love's Labour's Lost*, which has been described as being 'plugged into its period as into a life-support system'.[24] Considering the period quality of the play, attempts to counter the Elizabethan debate on conventional beauty ('thy love is black as ebony') by casting a black actress in the role of Rosaline appear risky – even if this could be reconciled with her description elsewhere as 'a whitely wanton'.[25] However, the issue is beyond the scope of this book.

My concern is, primarily, with the original traditions, and it is praiseworthy when theatre companies today portray them effectively, despite the gap in time. Nevertheless, it must be borne in mind that some of the material may be interesting principally from a historical point of view and it may no longer be possible to incorporate all of it into a performance. Madelaine Doran wisely said, 'We cannot turn ourselves into Elizabethans; we should not fool ourselves into thinking we can.'[26] What we can do is attain a better understanding of their dramatic experiences and the workings of their playwrights' minds.

Shakespeare looked back to earlier traditions and, in time, he became himself an 'earlier tradition'. The task of subsequent dramatists was, in a sense, all the more difficult because they followed in his wake. Webster, Middleton, and Ford could not ignore him, but they did not try to compete. Instead, they exploited the memories of his plays which their audiences retained, and used them to achieve their own dramatic effects by allusion and contrast. The process of referring back was obviously a crucial part of Jacobean drama. The medieval aspects of a later play like *The Changeling* bear this out, but it is not just referring to the past which is important, as the many links between contemporary writers and references to social customs and events show.

Ford, a Caroline dramatist, still trying to write within the conventions of the Elizabethan era, demonstrates that these were no longer suited to the age. In *'Tis Pity She's A Whore*, once-popular Petrarchan conceits (although in Shakespeare's day, they were often mocked as well as used) are shown now to be totally inadequate as a viable means of expression. Katherine Duncan-Jones sees Ford's play *The Broken Heart* as an 'elegy on the tainted nobility of the last years of the Elizabethan court',[27] but the links which she makes between the contemporary figures of Penelope Rich and Charles Blount and Ford's two plays attain a further significance in relation to his dramatic technique, which she does not mention. In demonstrating the inadequacy of Petrarchan conceits through the staging of his play, it is clear that the associations go further than character and plot for, as she does point out: 'Charles and Penelope began in the world of Elizabethan love poetry: she as the heroine of the best Petrarchan sonnet sequence of the period, *Astrophil and Stella*; he as a minor poet'[28] – a minor poet who, no doubt, followed Petrarch. They are products of their age in every sense; and that age has declined, taking its traditions with it. The spectacle of a heart on a dagger needs to be viewed in a context where the violent display clearly denies that the 'truth' is 'writ' upon it. Spectacle, and the traditions to which it relates, need to be re-evaluated constantly in relation to the period – and this is where I will begin.

1 · The development and language of spectacle: Thomas Heywood's *Ages* and Shakespeare's last plays

As Bernard Beckerman has estimated,[1] eighty per cent of all Shakespeare's scenes written for the Globe probably could have been performed on a completely bare stage platform and the often itinerant nature of the dramatic companies, combined with the poor accommodation they might find in the provinces, might make such scenes a necessity in certain instances; but this does not mean that the ideal situation was always a bare stage, nor that the inclusion of spectacle in drama is always a defect.

It is an indication of Shakespeare's skill as a practical playwright that his plays were so adaptable but there is a variety of evidence to show that, where facilities and finances permitted, it was unlikely that any contemporary play, even prior to the Jacobean period, would be staged in a deliberately meagre manner. A play previously performed in a public playhouse often obtained new properties or costumes if subsequently taken to court. E. K. Chambers makes it clear that it was 'thought worthwhile to bring in cumberous properties for them and to employ musicians'. He also shows that the Officers of the Revels, 'were concerned with the provision of the fittings of the stage and the properties and apparel necessary to furnish a sumptuous appearance for the players'.[2] A desire for spectacle, therefore, seems to have been an integral part of performance – whenever possible.

Discounting the often lavish costumes, there are many examples of properties and emblematic devices used on the Elizabethan and early Jacobean stage, e.g. throne, crown, hell-mouth, tomb, chariot, arbour. These would hold significant positions in particular scenes and might – like the chariot in *Tamburlaine* or the bower in *The Spanish Tragedy* – be unifying elements in the play as a whole. In proportion to the expanse of a public playhouse stage such properties would occupy a small amount of space, yet their emblematical significance, and therefore their significance as a facet of spectacle, could be great.

My definition of spectacle is very wide, being any form of display, ceremony, show or pageant (however short) used in the course of the drama – encompassing silent, static tableaux as well as singing, dancing, movement, and sound effects. If good playwrights are considered as including little or no spectacle in their work, then a criticism is implied of many of Shakespeare's plays, not to mention the works of Kyd, Marlowe, Webster, and Middleton, or those of private theatre dramatists such as Marston. In such an argument Thomas Heywood's *Ages* plays would be credited with no merit at all. Some degree of spectacle must be acknowledged as part of the life of the drama; it is not merely the inclusion of this element which distinguishes the inferior from the superior playwright, but the relative quality of whatever spectacle exists.

Heywood himself made a distinction in his 1633 Lord Mayor's pageant between meaningful emblematic devices and 'a Modell devised for sport to humour the throng, who come rather to see than to heare', which 'consists onely in motion, agitation and action', and which would not suffer a speaker to accompany it as his words would be 'drown'd in noyse and laughter'. Heywood obviously does not value such an 'interruption' since he fails to leave any description of it, or of any similar instances, yet he justifies its place in the pageant because, 'without some such intruded Anti-maske, many who carry their eares in their eyes, will not sticke to say, I will not give a pinne for the show'.[3] In any consideration of spectacle on the early Jacobean stage this distinction is important: in order to decipher the language of spectacle it must first be ascertained that it has an intelligible voice – only then can the quality of what the voice says be assessed.

In relation to James I's Royal Entry of 1604, Thomas Dekker expressed the necessity to marry the work of the artificer harmoniously with that of the poet in terms of the pageant's 'body' and 'soul':

Many dayes were thriftily consumed, to molde the bodies of these Tryumphes comely, and to the honour of the Place: and at last, the stuffe whereof to frame them, was beaten out. The Soule that should give life, and a tongue to this Entertainment, being to breathe out of Writers Pens. The Limmes of it to lye at the hard-handed mercy of the Mychanitiens.[4]

The word spectacle now has many disreputable connotations, but it could and did excite admiration on the early Jacobean stage and such admiration was well-deserved in those instances when 'body' and 'soul' combined to astonish and stimulate both mind and emotions at a level far deeper than that of the superficial visual catalyst. Whether Heywood achieved this at all in his *Ages* plays will be discussed, but less in dispute is Shakespeare's manipulation of spectacle to intensify dramatic effect in his plays.

The procession was one of the most popular forms of spectacle in Elizabethan drama and, long before the increased popularity of the masque, Shakespeare and others (most notably Marlowe in *Tamburlaine* and *Doctor Faustus*) made dramatic use of such devices which had their roots in civic pageantry – itself akin to medieval drama, with its allegorical and emblematic foundations. Two early Jacobean examples of Shakespeare's adoption of pageantry devices can be found in *Macbeth* and *Coriolanus*. The show of eight kings in *Macbeth* is a procession in which ritual emphasises the supernatural and historical connotations of the event – and the silence enables Macbeth to express his thoughts as it passes. In *Coriolanus*, the procession of Virgilia, Volumnia, Valeria, young Martius and attendants proceeds silently down the stage while Coriolanus (presumably near to the audience) describes it and expresses his conflicting reactions at the same time:

> My wife comes foremost; then the honour'd mould
> Wherein this trunk was fram'd, and in her hand
> The grandchild to her blood. But out, affection!
> All bond and privilege of nature break!
> Let it be virtuous to be obstinate.
> What is that curtsy worth? or those doves' eyes,
> Which can make gods forsworn? I melt, and am not
> Of stronger earth than others. My mother bows,
> As if Olympus to a molehill should
> In supplication nod; and my young boy
> Hath an aspect of intercession which
> Great nature cries, 'Deny not'.   v.iii.22–33

In this scene Shakespeare blends a halted procession into a tableau which culminates in the famous stage direction, '*Holds her by the hand silent*' (v.iii.82). The simplicity and restraint of ceremony and gesture in this scene provide a powerful frame of tension for the contrasting passion and violence in the language. There are no elaborate properties or costumes as there may have been in iv.i.111 of *Macbeth* but this is, nevertheless, a display using pageant techniques and indicates that spectacle could be achieved on many levels.

Spectacle was a common facet of contemporary life and, as well as creating it on stage, the drama could also achieve effects merely by causing the audience to recall its own previous experiences. When Belarius says,

> Stoop, boys: this gate
> Instructs you how t'adore the heavens; and bows you
> To a morning's holy office. The gates of monarchs
> Are arch'd so high that giants may jet through
> And keep their impious turbans on, without
> Good morrow to the sun.   *Cymbeline* iii.iii.2–7

such imagery constitutes more than merely the impression of a romanticising pastoral figure hopping from the concrete to the imaginative and the insubstantial when it is realised that giants were prominent and familiar spectacles in the civic pageants of the time. Just as the pageant giants fused fantasy with reality in the city streets (where the routes of royal processions would be full of gates and arches tall enough to accommodate them without stooping) – so Shakespeare adds yet more layers to the ever dissolving images in *Cymbeline*. The lowly cave is linked with the exotic giants of mythology who, in turn, become representations of the pomp and ceremony of the city life from which Belarius is exiled, and the image can be made to dissolve yet again to return to the concrete reality of crude, man-made effigies which will be removed after the festivities, whereas the cave, though it is also crudely fashioned (yet in an unadorned, humble, and natural way) represents, at this point, permanence and dependability.

It is even more revealing to note that the cave was a popular and recognisable pageant device, dating back to the medieval mysteries, and that the cave property, which may be on view in performance, is itself a paradox – resembling a pageant property, yet representing the opposite in the comparison with the giants. Shakespeare, through a clever combination of property and imagery, has succeeded in juxtaposing two combinations of illusion and reality: the first is achieved by drawing attention to the temporary illusion of concrete reality brought about by an obvious pageant artifice in the world of the drama; and the second is the effect produced in his spectators' minds by making them recall instances in their own lives when similar devices created illusions of fantasy and unreality in the heart of contemporary London. He demonstrates one overlap of drama and life.

This small example does not, in itself, constitute spectacle, but uses connotations of the form to create a striking entrance and, like many scenes in civic pageantry, it also expounds a moral – religious humility versus infidel pride – which is coupled with a topical contrast in favour of the pastoral scene. However, unlike the moralising in Heywood's *Ages* plays, which clearly expresses its author's own views, Belarius's moral is his own rather than that of his creator.

Cymbeline is a good example of Shakespeare's self-conscious awareness of his work as a created art – a characteristic especially prominent in his last plays – and it cannot be denied that the increased popularity of the court masque and the greater concern with elaborate artifice, both in the private and public theatres, may have prompted such a response. This development of spectacle involves cross-currents between the masque and the drama and Shakespeare experimented with this in *The Winter's Tale* to achieve a particular dramatic effect.

Disregarding the songs and the dance of the shepherds and shep-
herdesses (which, M. C. Bradbrook indicates, were imported by the
King's Men from Jonson's masque *Oberon the Fairy Prince*, January
1611)[5] the statue scene is probably the most successful piece of masque-
related stage business in the play. This event does not occur in the source,
Greene's novella, *Pandosto: the Triumph of Time*, and must be regarded
as an invention by Shakespeare to create a dramatic effect using spectacle
as an anticipatory catalyst to provoke thought and feeling. As the many
illustrations of civic pageants and royal progresses show, the idea of
figures standing like statues, and suddenly stepping out of their settings to
address the approaching monarch, would be familiar, even to those of
Shakespeare's audience who had not seen similar sights during the various
court masques with their elaborate 'discoveries'.

Both pageant and masque used actors who were, in effect, also
properties of the scene. In *The Winter's Tale*, after the initial unveiling or
discovery of the statue,[6] Shakespeare does not aim at a reaction of sheer
surprise because, to a contemporary audience, human statues were not
unusual and as the same actors often appeared in pageants, masques, and
the theatre, it would not be difficult to find someone with the necessary
skills. The dramatic policy Shakespeare pursues is one of heightened
anticipation. Paulina's frequent hints that the figure lives and the audience's own previous experience of such effects help to establish this, but
the climax begins at her call for music:

> Music, awake her; strike!
> 'Tis time; descend; be stone no more; approach;
> Strike all that look upon with marvel. Come!
> I'll fill your grave up: stir, nay, come away:
> Bequeath to death your numbness; for from him
> Dear life redeems you. You perceive she stirs: v.iii.98–103

Unlike the usual figures in pageants or in masques, this statue does not
readily come to life but must be coaxed. Thirteen major stops and three
minor pauses in five-and-a-half lines indicate the intensity of Shakespeare's approach. This might make spectators who, in the pageant or the
masque, were used to taking such scenes for granted, think again.
Shakespeare refuses to allow his stagecraft to be treated dismissively. In
the masques musicians would herald the revelation of a scene, yet
Hermione is discovered in silence, and only at the climax of the drama
does the music strike. Shakespeare uses it, not merely for display or
atmosphere, but emblematically, to signify a new awakening to life (as in
Pericles III.ii.90), mystery – perhaps associated with the music of the
spheres – harmony, and a restoration of order. He uses conventions

borrowed from pageantry and masques – and even perhaps from the revelations of the medieval mystery cycles – but invests in them a depth of meaning which can only be appreciated when the object of the spectacle also has a vital place in the outcome of the drama. Pageant and masque figures are shallow in comparison. Their fragmentary performances are usually closely bound to the mythological or historical figures they represent and the moral, instructive, or thinly characterised parts they must play: Shakespeare gives his figure a past in the first sequence of the drama and is therefore able to stimulate a response which other figures of popular spectacle were unlikely to achieve – namely, emotion and a deep, appreciative understanding of the poetic qualities of the play as a whole.

The apparent fulfilment of Leontes's wish and the dream-like quality of Hermione's awakening links it with the masque, yet its magic is juxtaposed with the probability of her preservation by Paulina: dream and real world merge, as they frequently do in the last plays. This scene is a piece of spectacle in which 'body' and 'soul' are admirably allied through using a living property and it demonstrates that spectacle need not be elaborate or complicated to succeed – though it may be complex. The electrifying effect of this scene illustrates Shakespeare's mastery of a technique he also applied in *Pericles*. In contrast, Thaisa's revival was among strangers who did not share her past and it occurred midway through the drama as part of the plot and as a precedent for Marina's recovery, rather than as a climactic resolution in its own right.

The idea of a statue coming to life predates both drama and pageantry, as Leonard Barkan shows in his article, 'Living sculptures: Ovid, Michelangelo, and *The Winter's Tale*', the most famous living statue of all being Pygmalion, whose story appears in Ovid's *Metamorphoses*.[7] An anonymous play of 1605, *The Tryall of Chevalry*, also precedes Shakespeare's use of the technique,[8] yet only Shakespeare appears to be able to combine a striking narrative resolution with the expression of powerful emotion and the wonder of the pageant or masque-like revelation. The tradition also appeared later in Thomas Campion's *The Lords' Masque* (1613) in which Prometheus transformed statues into women, but whether Shakespeare's play influenced this in any way or both works merely shared a popular theme, cannot be ascertained.

In the theatre it had long been the custom to use spectacle to achieve a horrific shock response rather than wonder or delight, as was more common in the pageant or the masque. Marston demonstrated this in *Antonio's Revenge* (1600) when the curtains (either of a bed pulled out onto the stage or of the discovery space itself) were drawn to reveal Feliche's stabbed body – perhaps even hanging above the sleeping

Mellida, as in Peter Barnes's 1979 production at the Nottingham Playhouse, where, if viewed thematically, this foreshadows the confrontation of innocence and treachery in the later killing of Piero's young son. Earlier, Kyd employed a similar device in *The Spanish Tragedy* when Horatio was discovered hanging in the arbour. Marston is clearly indebted to this play, whether or not his own work is seen as a parody of the old plays and their techniques. Later, Webster used yet another variation of this in *The Duchess of Malfi* iv.i.55, although here he deliberately used horrific spectacle to trick the audience. Antonio and the children are not dead at this point, but neither the duchess nor the audience know this. The stage direction reads: '*Here is discovered, behind a traverse, the artificial figures of Antonio and his children, appearing as if they were dead.*'

Shakespeare does employ some sudden revelations in his drama, but these tend to be minor touches and far less controversial. Iachimo's emergence from the trunk in *Cymbeline* ii.ii is such an instance. This occurs once an atmosphere of inexplicable nervousness has been established: 'Who's there? my woman Helen?', coupled with the approach of the witching hour: 'What hour is it?' and the answer, 'Almost midnight, madam.' (ii.ii.1–2). A seemingly inanimate object containing a living creature is closely linked with the conventions of pageantry and the masque where statues are real actors; Time and his daughter issue from a cave (Royal Entry, 1558), and clouds part suddenly to reveal Venus in her swan-drawn chariot (*The Hue and Cry after Cupid*, 1608). The concepts of disguise and unexpected arrival which are at the heart of the masque are also present in the scene in *Cymbeline*. The trunk property with a living man inside it contrasts with the later complications when Imogen finds a different kind of trunk (Cloten's headless body) and, believing it to belong to Posthumus,[9] cannot conceive how life can ever be restored to such an inanimate property – something which appears to have happened when she sees him alive later. In ii.ii the possible similarity between the trunk and a coffin may be a visual aid to the later train of thought – especially if the trunk property was also the coffin used in *Pericles* at earlier performances. This is also described as a chest by the sailors and appears to the servants who find it to resemble a coffin. Here, again, is life concealed in an inanimate object – or so it must seem to the men who find Thaisa's body. Her coffin is, paradoxically, the vessel which preserves her life, so considerable symbolism is present in what need not be a very elaborate stage property.

Details of civic pageantry and court masques have been shown to invade the public stage in many different ways – both major and minor, but such influences were not the only reasons for the development and demand for more elaborate spectacle in the drama at this time. The late sixteenth and early seventeenth centuries also coincided with a revival of tilts and tournaments: according to Glynne Wickham, 'it had all the marks of an archaic revival attached to it, with first a virgin Queen and then a young Prince of Chivalry at its centre'.[10]

An increased interest in chivalric exploits can be linked to the growing popularity of the romance tradition which seems to culminate in Shakespeare's last plays: here the ceremonial spectacle of the joust in *Pericles* also relates to an item of contemporary literature. Rosemary Freeman has shown that three of the knights' devices with their mottoes are depicted in a version of Paradin's *Devises Heroique* by 'P.S.' first printed in 1591.[11] Moreover, the revival of tournaments and jousts indicates a similarity in public and aristocratic interests which is also apparent in the development of the theatres. Glynne Wickham notes that there is surprisingly little difference in the sort of spectacle found in civic pageants (public) and that found in tournaments (predominantly aristocratic).[12] This may be due, in part, to the free migration of both writers and artificers between the playhouse and the tiltyard: Jonson, Inigo Jones and Shakespeare were also involved in tournament entertainments. (In 1613 Shakespeare was paid 43s. for providing the Earl of Rutland with an *impresa*, and Burbage received 43s. for painting it.)[13] However, after Prince Henry's death in 1612, tournaments began to wane in popularity: the influence of the revival was not long-lasting.

The migration of actors and writers between different forms of entertainment, however, went on – accounting for the continuation of crosscurrents between aristocratic and public performances. Just as Jonson wrote masques, private theatre plays and public theatre drama in his lifetime, so public theatre dramatists such as Dekker and Munday also wrote for the civic pageants. As devices grew more elaborate in the Lord Mayor's shows of the seventeenth century, it is clear that rivalry, or at least competitive imitation, existed between such events and the court masques.

The end of the sixteenth century also heralded a revival in the children's theatres (Michael Shapiro dates this 1596/7 and R. A. Foakes, 1599/1600)[14] so rivalry between private and public playhouses is another reasonable supposition – and, again, one which would result in an increase in spectacle in the latter, as the children led the way in introducing machinery, elaborate scene effects, music, and dancing to the stage. As R. A. Foakes points out, the children and their writers, in order to sustain a challenge to the adult companies, instigated experimental aspects into

1   A booth stage set up in an inn yard. Sketch by Richard Southern. The Red Bull
playhouse was a converted inn.

their own work and may have affected the development of the adult
drama more than is usually recognised. The obvious experimentation in
Cymbeline is particularly relevant to this view.

Cymbeline (1609) is probably also the first of Shakespeare's plays to be
performed after the King's Men took over the Blackfriars indoor theatre
from the children's company, so yet another merging of private and public
theatre elements occurred. This is particularly interesting since the lease
for Blackfriars was surrendered in 1608 when Burbage created his King's
Men's syndicate to take it over, but because of plague the theatre was

probably not used by the King's Men until late in 1609 or in 1610; yet there is no evidence of any radical structural changes being made to the theatre during this time[15] which would suggest that the King's Men continued to use the previous facilities and, therefore, became a public company performing under private theatre conditions.[16]

G. E. Bentley's argument[17] that the newly acquired Blackfriars theatre was a prime determinant of the style and form of Shakespeare's later plays ignores the fact that the development they illustrate also applied to the public theatre – *Pericles* (1608) was a Globe play – and was a great success there. Nor were flights and elaborate staging techniques still solely confined to the private theatre, since *Cymbeline*, and later, *The Tempest*, were probably performed both at the Globe and at Blackfriars, while a converted inn such as the Red Bull playhouse could, according to E. K. Chambers,[18] far outdo the most spectacular performance attempted by the King's Men during this period, which was *The Tempest*. The Red Bull plays which Chambers means were Thomas Heywood's *Golden*, *Silver*, and *Brazen Ages* (1611–13) which:

if they were really given just as Heywood printed them must have strained the scenic resources of The Red Bull to an extreme. Here are ascents and descents and entries from every conceivable point of the stage; divinities in fantastic disguise; mythological dumbshows; battles and hunting episodes and revels; ingenious properties, often with a melodramatic thrill; and from beginning to end a succession of atmospheric phenomena which suggest that the Jacobeans had made considerable progress in the art of stage pyrotechnics.

There is no way of discovering how sophisticated the effects, which E. K. Chambers summarises so well, appeared in practice, but even if they fell short of the achievements of Inigo Jones and Ben Jonson at court, it is apparent that the mechanics of spectacle, at least, had taken their place with a vengeance in the public playhouse. The roots of the development of spectacle in the public theatres have been traced to a strange mixture of soils – the medieval mysteries, civic pageantry, aristocratic tournaments, the masque, and the results of private theatre rivalry with eventual partial amalgamation. The influences indicate a combination of old and new traditions and effects which can be traced in the drama. Shakespeare, it has been shown, gives elements from pageantry, masque and tournament a voice in his drama – but how does this differ from the language of spectacle in Thomas Heywood's plays?

If the *Ages* plays are viewed solely in relation to other contemporary public playhouse plays, for example, by Jonson or Shakespeare, they appear tediously narrative, shallow, out-dated in content, and over-dependent on visual effects, noise, and boisterous movement. Yet this does not place them in their rightful context. The course of the public theatre can be said to have moved in a parallel line somewhere between that of the pageant (which remained emblematic until the civil war) and that of the masque (which became increasingly less emblematic). The kinship of Heywood's *Ages* to the pageant seems greater than that to the masque, and even to the techniques of other contemporary drama.

A. S. Venezky points out that the Elizabethan connotation of 'pageant' was synonymous with 'play' – 'designating the imitation of life upon a stage'.[19] By the end of the sixteenth century developments had taken place which are indicated by the way the pageant drama provided for Queen Elizabeth differed in 1591 (Elvetham Progress) from that of 1575 (Kenilworth Progress). D. M. Bergeron notes this important difference as 'a central dramatic action exploring the conflict between the wood gods and the sea gods' which was introduced in the latter pageant. He continues, 'In the sixteen years since Kenilworth the progress pageant form has moved in the direction of dramatic unity, plot, character conflict, and increasing dependence on speech that helps to carry the dramatic burden.'[20] By the time Heywood wrote the *Ages*, civic pageantry and the type of epic public drama he had in mind would seem to be very close in form. Moreover, the views he expressed in his *Apology for Actors* (1612) appear to substantiate this view, even taking into account the fact that he deliberately set out to defend the theatre, and may therefore have stressed its moral value out of proportion. Particularly with his moralistic and nationalistic Lord Mayor's shows of 1630–40 in mind, it is likely that even at this early date he did believe:

Playes are writ with this ayme, and carryed with this methode, to teach the subjects obedience to their king, to shew the people the untimely ends of such as have moved tumults, commotions, and insurrections, to present them with the flourishing estate of such as live in obedience, exhorting them to allegeance, dehorting them from all trayterous and fellonious stratagems.

and that they were concerned with, 'animating men to noble attempts, or attaching the consciences of the spectators, finding themselves toucht in presenting the vices of others'. He added: 'If a morall, it is to perswade men to humanity and good life, to instruct them in civility and good manners, shewing them the fruits of honesty, and the end of villany.'[21] The most comprehensive application of such aims can be seen in the pageant drama of the day rather than in that of the public theatre. Narration above characterisation; didacticism above emotional and intellectual appeal – these sets of criteria appear both in civic pageantry and in Heywood's *Ages*. Accordingly, such considerations provide a definite tone for the aim of the spectacle in the plays, although this (especially in the first three *Ages*) does not preclude an obvious delight in displaying the gods' often *risqué*, and frequently immoral behaviour on stage.

While there are occasional echoes of Shakespeare's works in the *Ages* and, in one instance, a visual duplication from *Cymbeline* (at the end of *The Golden Age*), the two playwrights seem to be at different ends of the dramatic spectrum. It is likely that Gower, the medieval poet in *Pericles*, may have been Heywood's prototype for Homer in the first three plays; however Gower does not take the role of pageant presenter quite as far as does Homer. Gower is an intermediary in one particular tale, but a pageant may have many scenes, linked thematically, yet each representing its own separate story or message, and just as a presenter or character from the pageant may lead the spectators on to the next exhibition, dismissing the last, so Homer quickly ends one story and switches to another:

> Saturne against his sonne his force extended,
> And would have slaine him by his tyrannous hand . . .
> But . . .
> He us'd his force, his father drove from Creet,
> And as the Oracle before had told
> Usurpt the Crowne, the Lords kneele at his feete,
> And Saturne's fortunes are to exile sold.
> But leaving him, of Danae that bright lasse,
> How amorous Jove first wrought her to his power,
> How shee was closed in a fort of brasse,
> Of how he skal'd it in a golden showre,
> Of these we next must speake,   *The Golden Age* IV.i

There is a certain breathless quality underlying Homer's plodding narration: as in the pageant, Heywood's *Ages* are faced with the need for compression, and this seems to be the prime function of the majority of the dumb-shows he employs. Homer's comment towards the end of *The Brazen Age* illustrates this:

> Our last Act comes, which lest it tedious grow,
> What is too long in word, accept in show.[22]

Throughout the first three *Ages*, Homer constantly stresses his blindness – which not only excuses him, as narrator, from any responsibility for the visual elements of the plays, but also enhances the audience's appreciation of the spectacles by emphasising their privileged position.

Homer is also used to link the first three *Ages* together as a sequence; at the end of *The Silver Age* he exclaims:

> Poor Homer's left blinde, and hath lost his way,
> And knowes not if he wander or go right,
> Unlesse your favours their cleare beames display,

> But if you daine to guide me through this night,
> The acts of Hercules I shall pursue,
> And bring him to the thrice-raz'd wals of Troy:
> His labours and his death I'le shew to you.

and a similar link is made at the end of *The Golden Age*.

Just as the spectator is at the mercy of Homer's whim to lead him from one scene to another, so he is also subject to the didactic, often patronising tone of the pageant which creeps into the plays. At the end of *The Brazen Age*, for example, Homer's epilogue is pleasantly insulting:

> He that expects five short Acts can containe
> Each circumstance of these things we present,
> Me thinkes should shew more barrennesse than braine:
> All we have done we aim at your content,
> Striving to illustrate things not knowne to all,
> In which the learnd can onely censure right:
> The rest we crave, whom we unlettered call,
> Rather to attend than judge; for more than sight
> We seeke to please.

An interesting comparison here is Marlowe's approach in *Tamburlaine* – itself a kind of pageant play:

View but his picture in this tragic glass,
And then applaud his fortunes as you please.   *1 Tamburlaine* Prologue 7–8

Marlowe deliberately makes the audience's judgment a difficult task by refusing to moralise in conventional emblematic terms – perhaps patterning his spectacular rise with an equally spectacular fall: he also makes Tamburlaine's rivals far less attractive than himself. Nevertheless, Marlowe does not point his audience in any particular direction, unlike Heywood's approach in *The Silver Age*, where he introduces the action thus:

> The Golden past, the Silver age begins
> In Jupiter, whose sonne of Danae borne,
> We first present, and how Acrisius sinnes
> Were punish't for his cruelty and scorne.

Marlowe expects his audience to judge: Heywood expects the learned to agree with him and the 'unlettered' to learn to agree with him.

However, trial and judgment scenes are often significant highlights in the *Ages*, where spectacle can be used to intensify the dramatic effect; for example, the decision on Proserpine's fate in Act III of *The Silver Age*. After a skirmish in which Hercules: 'fels Pluto, beats off the Divels with all their fire-workes, rescues Proserpine', Rhadamant demands that the gods be called to settle the dispute: the stage direction reads, '*Sownd. Enter Saturne, Jupiter, Juno, Mars, Phoebus, Venus, and Mercury: they take their place as they are in height.*' At this point there are at least twenty-six actors on stage together. Seven of these are, presumably, suspended in the air, contrasting the cool, superior, almost distant attitude of the gods (who are, nevertheless, not above complaining and bickering amongst themselves) with the impassioned chaos of the characters below them. Just preceding the descent of the gods, the three-headed Cerberus slew Perithous and wounded Theseus before Hercules arrived and bound him in chains – all stage action culminating in: '*Hercules sinkes himselfe: Flashes of fire; the Divels appeare at every corner of the stage with severall fire-workes. The Judges of hell, and the three sisters run over the stage, Hercules after them: fire-workes all over the house. Enter Hercules*', closely followed by '*Pluto with a club of fire, a burning crowne, Proserpine, the Judges, the Fates, and a guard of Divels, all with burning weapons.*'

Therefore, before Hercules finally 'fels Pluto', 'rescues Proserpine', and Rhadamant calls on the gods, the stage business has been fast, noisy, and confused – the fireworks adding to the general effect and atmosphere, as well as presumably filling the air with smoke and the smell of gunpowder. A call for order in the midst of such chaos not only helps to resolve the drama, but also has contemporary significance since James I placed great emphasis on peace-making achievements. The judgment aspect of this scene can also be related to the tradition in progress and court entertainments (especially in the days of Elizabeth I) where the monarch was called upon to intervene in the drama and resolve a dispute – as in Sidney's entertainment *The Lady of May*. In Heywood's plays the public stage provides its own monarchial substitute. A compromise is achieved which fulfils the demand for restored harmony and provides a suitable finale. Then, at the very end of the play, Heywood uses the stage emblematically to express the hierarchy of the medieval tradition: '*Exeunt three wayes Ceres, Theseus, Philoctetes, and Hercules dragging Cerberus one way: Pluto, hels Judges, the Fates and Furies downe to hell; Jupiter, the Gods and Planets ascend to heaven.*'

Although the subject is classical, Heywood's treatment of it clearly is not. This scene indicates some of the ways in which he conveys classical material in a manner which blends elements of the mystery plays and earlier contemporary drama with the added sophistication of the masque or the private theatre, where seven actors could be lowered over the stage, kept suspended for the duration of the judgment, and raised again when required. Homer's words, spoken in relation to the variety of the narration, are equally appropriate to Heywood's method of presentation:

> Loath are we (curteous auditors) to cloy
> Your appetites with viands of one tast,[23]

The *Ages* have many weaknesses but, in the first three at least, lack of variety is not one of these.

The judgment scene in *The Silver Age* does not have an obvious moral, other than the restoration of order, but elsewhere in the *Ages*, Heywood uses spectacle as a moral vehicle. The last scene of the second *Iron Age* is such an instance.[24] As the first *Iron Age* play began with Paris taking Helen from Menelaus, so the end of the second *Iron Age* begins with Orestes taking Helen's daughter, Hermione, from Pyrrhus, her betrothed. Heywood seems to be aiming at a symmetry distorted by time to unify both plays. The final scene gains sacrificial symbolism from the altar which is 'set forth' (presumably brought downstage from the discovery space) for the wedding of Hermione and Pyrrhus, and this remains throughout the scene as a background to the slaughter which ensues.

Previously an altar setting was used ironically at the end of *The Brazen Age* when a reformed Hercules made peace before it and accepted the shirt which Deyaneirae (ignorant of its fatal properties) had sent him. Here the shirt became an ironical love-token, taking its place as a symbolic object in the ceremony in front of the altar, before causing Hercules's death. In contrast, the last scene of the second *Iron Age* is played for tragedy rather than irony. The theme of unnecessary sacrifice is still portrayed but here it is the downfall of a people (the Trojans), rather than of one man, which is signified. Human folly rather than inescapable fate is depicted.

The soliloquy by Cethus (who 'riseth up from the dead bodies and speakes'[25]) differs from the lighter tone of the epilogue on the same theme with which Thersites ended part one of *The Iron Age*:

> A sweete exchange of Treasure, term't I may,
> Even earth for ashes, and meere dust for clay:
> Let Ajax kill himselfe, and say 'twas brave
> Hector, a worthy call, yet could not save
> Poore foole his Coxcombe ...
>   all these brave ones dye.
> Ha, ha, judge you; Is it not better farre
> To keepe our selves in breath, and linger warre:
> Had all these fought as I've done...
> These had with thousands more surviv'd: Judge th' hoast,

> I shed no blood, no blood at all have lost:
> They shall not see young Pyrus, nor the Quenne
> Penthiselea, which had they but beene
> As wise as I, they might . . .
> > with many other
> Our second part doth promise:

This is reminiscent of Falstaff at Shrewsbury, but descends from humanist philosophy to light-hearted chiding at the notion of characters being foolish enough to allow themselves to be killed and therefore miss the exciting sequel the theatre promises in part two of the play: the moral is delivered tongue-in-cheek. Near the end of part two, however, Cethus surveys the bodies round him and expresses a more violent reaction:

> What all asleepe? and are these gossiping tongues,
> That boasted nought save warre and victory,
> Now mute and silent? Oh thou ugly rogue,
> Where's now thy rayling? and thou parracide,
> Thy madnesse is now tam'd, thou need'st no chains
> To bring thee to thy wits, darknesse hath don't.[26]

Addressing each dead hero in turn he comes to the traitor, Synon, who let the Greeks into Troy:

> Now is thy blacke soule for thy perjuries
> Swimming in red damnation.

but Synon is not yet dead; he rises up and while Cethus puts forward the Falstaffian suggestion:

> > shall we then
> Divide these dead betwixt us and both live?

Synon refuses and, inevitably, they kill each other – Synon, rhyming out a philosophical moral with his last breath:

> One single fight
> Ends him, who millions ruin'd in one night.

These words recall yet another previous massacre before an altar in III.i (an overworked device). After this particular slaughter Menelaus comments:

> All by Hellen,
> Oh had that tempting beauty ne're beene borne,
> By whom so many worthies now lie dead.[27]

One spectacle relates to another in this play, if a little clumsily, so at the end the result of the Trojan war is represented by a spectacle of approximately fourteen bodies (both Greeks and Trojans) and to complete the picture and the symmetry, Helen, the initial cause of all the trouble, appears with them. As if to stress the circular finality of the episode, she sends for a looking glass and dwells on the comparison between her former beauty and present age. Having already expressed her remorse for being 'the cause of all these Princes deaths', she makes her own sacrifice:

> the world's assured hate
> Is all my dowre, then Hellen yeeld to fate,
> Here's that, my soule and body must divide,
> The guerdon of Adultery, Lust and Pride.

and commits a self-strangling which, if performed today would be dangerously near to producing a comical effect. Such blatant moralising through spectacle implies that, had Heywood tackled the story of Antony and Cleopatra, he would most certainly have followed Plutarch closely in making Cleopatra disfigure herself out of remorse for her wickedness before then killing herself, and would never have been able to approach the achievement of Shakespeare's play where moral considerations are deliberately shelved.

A strong moral tone is more prevalent in the later *Iron Ages* than in the first three plays and, although didacticism itself seems a weakness, Heywood has, nevertheless, developed his art so that the characters themselves now give the moral message – which is one step further from the obvious pageant-like presentation of the earlier plays. In these Homer, as presenter, introduces the dumb-shows with what often sounds remarkably akin to a motto from an emblem book:

> O blind ambition and desire of raine
> What horr'd mischiefe wilt not thou devise?
> The appetite of rule, and thirst of raigne
> Besots the foolish, and corrupts the wise.　　　*The Golden Age* IV.i

In general, the first three *Ages* are of a much lighter nature than the *Iron Ages*, mainly because of the more colourful content of the gods' stories and the opportunities this affords for spectacle, but also because of the often humorous application of a moral combined with this spectacle which is lacking in the later plays. One example can be found in *The Brazen Age* II.ii, where Mars and the adulterous Venus have been caught in a net by the cuckolded Vulcan, who calls on the gods to bear witness: '*All the Gods appeare above, and laugh, Jupiter, Juno, Phoebus, Mercury, Neptune.*' In this instance the judges are not impartial:

> *Nept.* Why should Mars fret? if it so tedious be,
> 　　　Good god of Warre bestow thy place on me.
> *Merc.* By all the Gods, would she do me that grace,
> 　　　I would fall too't even before Vulcan's face.

Vulcan's purpose miscarries as he sought to shame Venus but still keep her, whereas now that her secret is disclosed she need no longer fear its discovery and openly declares her love for Mars. Vulcan's folly is exploited for comic effect. The conclusion Jupiter draws is therefore good-humoured, but not truly moral:

> Vulcan, thy morrall this good use contrives,
> None search too farre th' offences of their wives.

Here the ludicrous spectacle of the two lovers in the net, the angry Vulcan, and the suspended, laughing gods, is carefully constructed for comedy. Unlike the darker *Iron Ages*, the first three plays are a medley of an unusual blend of the classical and tragi-comedy.

The language of spectacle in Heywood's *Ages* speaks in many tongues. There are echoes of Seneca in the first banquet of *The Golden Age*: '*A Banquet brought in, with the limbes of a Man in the Service*' (II.i). This device is also employed in *Titus Andronicus* and in the slightly more recent *Antonio's Revenge* – though not without a hint of parody in the latter. Still in the Senecan tradition, Hector's ghost appears to warn of the fall of Troy (2 *Iron Age* II)[28] and, with echoes of *Hamlet*, the stage direction appears in IV.i of the same play: '*Enter the Ghost of Agamemnon, poynting unto his wounds: and then to Egistus and the Queene, who were his murderers, which done, hee vanisheth.*'[29] (Later, a similar piece of staging was to occur in *The Changeling*.)

In *The Brazen Age*, the nature of Medea's escape seems Senecan in nature, but as such, would probably have been related rather than enacted. When she declares:

> This lad betweene me and all harme shall stand;
> And if the King pursue us with his Fleet,
> His mangled limbs shall (scattered in the way)
> Worke our escape, and the King's speed delay.

it appears to be a metaphor – until Homer reiterates the plan and the subsequent dumb-show apparently illustrates the literal strewing of dismembered bones – perhaps a concession to the supposed Elizabethan preference for actual representation whenever possible.

Mingled with these Senecan facets are aspects preserved from civic pageantry or the earlier mystery plays; properties such as Pluto's chariot or the two dragons, bull's head, boar's head and golden fleece of *The Brazen Age* – not to omit the apparently medieval representation of Hades and the devils. Dragons were particularly popular properties of civic pageants and progress pageantry, perhaps because of the startling fire effects which could be produced. In Elizabeth I's 1572 progress to

Warwick, 'A Dragon flieing casting out huge flames and squibes lighted upon the fort and so set fyere thereon'.[30] Similarly, fire sprouting from Zeal's head set fire to the chariot of Error in Middleton's Lord Mayor's Show of 1613.[31] Heywood employs a sophisticated version of such devices in *The Silver Age* III: '*Thunder, lightnings, Jupiter descends in his majesty, his Thunderbolt burning ... As he toucheth the bed it fires, and all flyes up, Jupiter from thence takes an abortive infant ... Jupiter taking up the infant speakes as he ascends in his cloud.*'[32] This combines familiar old effects of thunder and lightning with timing and newly acquired technical expertise. After the episode Homer humorously brings classical subject and contemporary experimentation together in his comment:

> Let none the secrets of the Gods inquire,
> Lest they (like her) be strooke with heavenly fire.

An awareness and a delight in artifice indicate links with private theatre practice and also show that Heywood has successfully modified a pageant device for the stage.

Heywood's classical choice of subject made inevitable the mythological characters and personifications who would be equally at home in a masque or a pageant display – nymphs, satyrs, Fates, the four winds, Ceres, Proserpine ('attired like the moon'), River Arethusa, and more, including the gods themselves. Many of these characters did appear in contemporary masques and would be recognisable figures – Juno (in *The Vision of the Twelve Goddesses*, 1604, and in *Hymenaei*, 1606), or the Amazon Penthiselea from the second *Iron Age* who also appeared in Jonson's *Masque of Queens* (1609). No single source can be declared for the spectacular elements in the *Ages*: Heywood deliberately juxtaposes a variety of ideas.

Although the civic pageant was greatly influential, certain effects are undoubtedly more closely related to the masque, or to private theatre plays such as Lyly's pastorals, e.g.: '*Enter with musicke (before Diana) sixe Satires, after them all their Nimphs, garlands on their heads, and javelings in their hands, their Bowes and Quivers: the Satyrs sing*', or in *The Silver Age*: '*Enter Ceres and Proserpine attired like the Moone, with a company of Swaines, and country wenches: They sing.*'[33] As in Lyly's work or the masques, the songs are not integrated into the dramatic action as they are, for example, in Shakespeare's later plays. However, the 'lofty dance of sixteene Princes, halfe Trojans halfe Grecians' (*1 Iron Age* III)[34] is not, it can be argued, purely for the audience's light relief (although this may well be needed at this point). The dance is also a device to symbolise the harmony now existing between the two sides and perhaps 'lofty' indicates a ceremonial reserve which will hint to the audience that such harmony is precariously sustained and likely to be shortlived. Elsewhere Heywood is less discriminating in his use of music and spectacle. He frequently uses 'lowd musicke' to herald a spectacle: this is reminiscent of masque practices and, when repeated *ad nauseam*, also bears a similarity to modern-day circus practices. Shakespeare's choice of 'solemn music' etc. seems to be related to the emblematical and atmospheric qualities of the drama, rather than to the nature of the playhouse itself.

Both Heywood and Shakespeare juxtapose old and new traditions. Probably the most striking example of this in the *Ages* plays is the dumb-show with which *The Golden Age* ends. This is the first truly emblematic dumb-show in the play and is narrated throughout by Homer. The stage directions read:

Sound a dumbe shew. Enter the three fatall sisters, with a rocke, a threed, and a paire of sheeres; bringing in a Gloabe, in which they put three lots. Jupiter draws heaven: at which Iris descends and presents him with his Eagle, Crowne, and Scepter, and his thunder-bolt. Jupiter first ascends upon the Eagle, and after him Ganimed ...
Sound. Neptune drawes the Sea, is mounted upon a sea-horse, a Roabe and Trident, with a crowne are given him by the Fates ...
Sound, Thunder and Tempest. Enter at 4 severall corners the 4 winds: Neptune riseth disturb'd: the Fates bring the 4 winds in a chaine, & present them to Aeolus, as their King ...
Sound. Pluto drawes hell: the Fates put upon him a burning Roabe, and present him with a Mace, and burning crowne.

The references to the 'rocke', 'threed', and 'paire of sheeres' refer to the three Fates – Clotho, who carries the distaff; Lachesis, who weaves the web of man's life, and Atropos, whose shears cut the thread when the web is complete. A knowledge of this tradition is necessary, and perhaps this is what Heywood means when he says of the three dominions –

How these are scand
Let none decide but such as understand.

The three Fates would be recognisable by their traditional costume – perhaps a variation of the 'long robes of white taffeta like aged women, with garlands of Narcissus flowers on their heads' used in *La Mascherata della genealogia gegli dei* (Florence, 1565).[35] The globe was a very well-known property: according to Glynne Wickham, 'By far the most popular mechanical device of the pageant stage was the globe which opened or revolved.'[36] Dekker used it in 1603 to welcome James to London and it appeared later in masques such as *Hymenaei*. Heywood, himself, was still using the device in 1637 when he displayed a globe which opened to reveal the four kingdoms united under the Stuarts in his Lord Mayor's show, *Londoni Speculum*. The portrayal of Neptune, Jove, the winds and Pluto is likely to have been a mixture of pageant symbolism and masque-like representation, while the descents and ascents are variations of techniques used in the private theatre, and previously only popular with the light-weight child actors but, at this time, occurring in the masques too. Ceremony, ritual, and attention to emblematic detail are blended with technical expertise to achieve a spectacular rendering of an old form – very different from the unelaborate dumb-shows of *Gorboduc*, for example.

Heywood presents this spectacle as both a culmination of Jupiter's exploits and as a link with the next play in the sequence, since it indicates the kind of episode the audience can expect to see in *The Silver Age* once Jupiter and the gods are deified: in one way it is both *The Golden Age*'s finale and *The Silver Age*'s advertisement trailer. The device is abruptly introduced just before it occurs – probably to intensify the impact on the audience, and although it does relate to the later plays, it seems clumsily welded on to the rest of *The Golden Age*. The spectacle is not a logical consequence of the preceding drama, but seems more of a concession to the audience's demands. Homer has already begun to talk of the future exploits of *The Silver Age* when he remembers this:

> Yet to keepe promise, ere we further wade,
> The ground of ancient Poems you shall see:
> And how these (first borne mortall) Gods were made,
> By vertue of divinest Poesie.

There do not seem to be the same commercial undertones in Shakespeare's work. In contrast, it can be argued that he paves the way to any spectacle he includes at different stages throughout the plays – the vision of Jupiter in v.iv of *Cymbeline*, for example. This belief disputes the view held by some critics, that the scene is a later interpolation. On one level the vision scene is an artistic, literal expression of some of the main imagery in the play. Here, the god who has been constantly referred to and called upon to bear witness to the mortals' acts throughout the play, finally answers an appeal and appears in person upon an eagle which has also figured in the pattern of the play's imagery. It is significant that the appeal is made by the dead, since this is yet another manifestation of an idea elsewhere only expressed in metaphor or through delusion – Imogen's first and second returns to life. Firstly, this takes the form of a metaphor when, having previously considered herself 'dead' if abandoned by her husband, she accepts a new lease of life with Pisanio's disguise plan (III.iv). Secondly, her appearance to Belarius and her brothers after the effects of the sleeping draught have disappeared (v.v), also suggests a return to life.

On this level the vision scene juxtaposes different planes of reality occurring in the play; it also, paradoxically, comes in the form of a dream, yet leaves a token of its reality behind in the tablet which the Leonati leave on Posthumus's chest. Again, the many previous dream-like episodes in the play have prepared for this – Iachimo in Imogen's bedchamber (II.ii); Imogen's journey to Milford Haven (III.vi); and even the unconventional battle scenes in v.ii, which take place in silence with no alarums or usual business of staged battle scenes. J. L. Styan's explanation of this is unsatisfactory:[37] he suggests that by the time Shakespeare wrote *Cymbeline*, the King's Men were so adept at sweeping on and off the stage in imitation of warfare that he left it to them to carry the scene out themselves and saw no need for elaborate instructions. It is far more likely that the simplicity is deliberate, because a dumb-show – which is what the scene resembles – is a silent, dream-like sequence, befitting the spirit of the play as a whole.[38] This old-fashioned device also conveys a sense of reliving history and of looking back into another dimension in time – which is very important in a play with underlying historical significance, such as its setting at the time of Christ's birth and the ancient monarchial links with Milford Haven where the first Tudor, Henry VII, landed in 1485.[39]

L. G. Salingar points out that the vision in *Cymbeline* may be related to Plautus's *Amphitryon*, in which (III.i) Jupiter tells the audience that he has a duty to save Alcmena from her husband's unjust accusation and is described at the climax of the play (v.i), appearing in thunder while Amphitryon lies in a faint.[40] Salingar also draws attention to the archaic verse style (fourteeners) displayed in the vision and suggests that Shakespeare may, in addition to *Amphitryon*, have been remembering plays in the miracle tradition, seen in his youth. This further substantiates the view that Shakespeare's, like Heywood's experimentation, encompassed the old and the new. However, as I have tried to show, Shakespeare produced more complex, dramatically integrated results than did Heywood, for whom the main aim and purpose of spectacle seem to have been to achieve variety and the universal appreciation of display. The latter point is particularly relevant at the end of Act II of *The Silver Age*.

As this episode is the story of Amphitrio it is very likely that a link exists between it and Plautus's *Amphitryon*, yet Heywood's staging differs significantly from that of Shakespeare in *Cymbeline* and from that of Plautus in the parallel episode. In Plautus's play, Amphitryon lies in a faint; in *Cymbeline*, Posthumus is asleep, yet in Heywood's work,

2 Jove on an eagle in 'Tempe Restored' (1632). Drawing by Inigo Jones.

Blepharo, Amphitrio, and Socia, who have been asleep, 'amazedly awake' to view the scene. It is the climax in which the preceding confusion is resolved and Heywood transforms the scene from a personal communication to a public display: '*Thunder and lightning: All the servants run out of the house affrighted, the two Captains and Blepharo, Amphitrio and Socia amazedly awake: Jupiter appeares in his glory under a Raine-bow, to whom they all kneele.*'[41] It seems that it is not sufficient for Heywood to have an audience in the theatre; he must stun everyone on stage too.

Whether the *Ages* plays are, as A. M. Clark believes, dramatisations of Heywood's narrative poem, *Troia Britannica* (1609), or whether they are, as F. G. Fleay supposed, based on the 1595–7 plays, *1 & 2 Hercules*, mentioned by Henslowe, does not seem of much import. It is true that many of the properties for the *Hercules* plays listed in Henslowe's papers also occur in the *Ages* – 'j gowlden flece; j lyone skin; argosse head; Ierosses head & raynbowe; j littell alter; j bores heade & Serberosse iij heades; Mercures wings; j bulles head; Junoes cotte; j great horse with his leagues'.[42] The last item would seem to refute C. Walter Hodges's suggestion that Heywood's Trojan horse was probably a painted cloth[43] (even ignoring the fact that men are directed to issue from it). Neither Clark's nor Fleay's suggestions alter the fact that, whether written in the late 1590s or after 1610, Heywood's plays were concerned with a popular current theme – perhaps out of date in relation to contemporary drama but, if related to the pageant, the tournament, and the masque, it was not only still in fashion, but remained so until a much later date. In 1616, when Prince Charles was made Prince of Wales, the Inns of Court prepared a Barriers and, although stage directions are sparse, there are references to 'A goulden fleece ... Jason ... the character of Jupiter with a thunderbolt'.[44] In Townsend's masque *Tempe Restored* (1632), Jupiter descended on an eagle,[45] and as late as 1660 the device was used in the Turin masque, *L'unione perla Peregrina*.

Heywood's *Ages* cannot be compared with the depth of Shakespeare's later plays, but viewed as a development in popular pageantry, despite the unexciting quality of the poetry and the drawbacks of didacticism, their experimentation, energy, and variety, nevertheless indicate a unique achievement. On a very general level, Shakespeare cannot be compared with Heywood because he attempts to integrate spectacle into the drama, whereas Heywood's concern is to infuse the spectacle with drama. Both playwrights blend old and new traditions, but in Heywood's work the underlying metaphors seem to retain their old emblematic meanings, whereas Shakespeare has the ability to side-step moralising and give a new slant to the familiar. The distinction between their two languages of spectacle is, therefore, between the embalmed and the mutated.

2 · The multiple roots of symbolic staging

The Elizabethans and the Jacobeans could appreciate emblematic or symbolic staging because they, unlike us, were familiar with the concept – not just in relation to drama or masques, but in the emblematical way they viewed the world. Street processions, Lord Mayors' shows, the iconography associated with their monarchy, the rituals of funerals and marriages, all had links with the emblematic tradition. Often small, otherwise insignificant objects can, at vital points in a play, take on an immediate symbolic importance. In a lecture on *Othello* in 1981,[1] M. C. Bradbrook, remarking on the use of the handkerchief in *Othello* and other properties such as the token in *The Spanish Tragedy*, said that violence needed these static objects to act as milestones in the movement of feeling. Such objects are used as a visual means of communication with the audience and as a way of expressing the communication and feeling between characters.

In Shakespeare's later plays, *Pericles* and *Cymbeline*, he is, as Marjorie Garber points out, concerned with making visual, images which might have previously remained in 'the linguistic texture of utterance' rather than the 'dramatic texture of action',[2] and it is partly the repetition and reversal of images (both textual and visual) which is used to gauge the dramatic impact of these plays. Shakespeare seems to have been moving in this direction for some time[3] until, in the final tragi-comedies, he managed to achieve a total fusion of the visualisation of the miracle plays of his youth (where everything possible was represented on stage – down to 'ij wormes of conscience')[4] and the striking textual metaphors of his own tragedies. To achieve this he skilfully combined verbal metaphors with simple stage properties.[5]

The handkerchiefs which M. C. Bradbrook mentioned are part of a common dramatic tradition of blood-stained cloths which appear in Kyd's *The Spanish Tragedy*, and Shakespeare's *Henry VI*, *A Midsummer Night's Dream*, *As You Like It*, *Othello*, and *Cymbeline*. These properties may be traced, in the drama, back to representations of the Holy Shroud or the Veronica napkin in medieval religious plays and in addition to their associations with Christian symbolism they have a place in

34

classical mythology, where the blood-stained cloth is simultaneously a token of both love and grief in Ovid's tale of Pyramus and Thisbe.

It is interesting to trace the use of this motif from early to later plays to see how dramatists – especially Shakespeare – explored various possibilities for the same stage property and often made it an integral part of their plays' designs. In every dramatic instance a blood-stained cloth has the same doubly symbolic connotations that it possesses in its classical or Christian sources – love and grief. In *The Spanish Tragedy*, a play which seems to have influenced most dramatists of the Elizabethan and Jacobean period, the handkerchief smeared with blood which Hieronimo takes from Horatio's dead body with the words:

> Seest thou this handkercher besmear'd with blood?
> It shall not from me till I take revenge: II.v.51–2

is, as Phiip Edwards points out in his note in the Revels edition of the play, probably the source of Shakespeare's use of the blood-stained napkin in *3 Henry VI* (i.iv.79) – especially in view of *The Spanish Tragedy* (III.xiii), in which Hieronimo offers the blood-stained cloth to the old man who, like York in *3 Henry VI*, has also had a son, now murdered:

> Here, take my handkercher and wipe thine eyes,
> Whiles wretched I in thy mishaps may see
> The lively portrait of my dying self.
> > *He draweth out a bloody napkin.*
> O no, not this: Horatio, this was thine,
> And when I dy'd it in thy dearest blood,
> This was a token 'twixt thy soul and me
> That of thy death revenged I should be.   III.xiii.83–9

In *3 Henry VI* the napkin associated with the grief of a father for his murdered son[6] becomes an important focus in the exchanges between Queen Margaret and York – gauging Margaret's hardness against York's grief:

> *York* O tiger's heart wrapp'd in a woman's hide!
> > How could'st thou drain the life-blood of the child,
> > To bid the father wipe his eyes withal,
> > And yet be seen to bear a woman's face?   i.iv.137–40

It is both a token of grief and a challenge:

> See ruthless queen, a hapless father's tears.
> This cloth thou dipp'd'st in blood of my sweet boy,
> And I with tears do wash the blood away.
> Keep thou the napkin, and go boast of this;
> And if thou tell the heavy story right,
> Upon my soul, the hearers will shed tears;   i.iv.156–61

Presumably the bloody cloth is thrust at Margaret or cast off just before his own murder, so that the final impact is of multiple slaughter – both father and son – just as the 'bloody handkercher' is recalled in the penultimate scene of *The Spanish Tragedy* when Hieronimo has revealed Horatio's dead body and given the reason for his revenge.

Between *Henry VI* and *A Midsummer Night's Dream*, however, Shakespeare's use of the blood-stained napkin changed. In the latter play, as in *As You Like It*, the property is used in a situation where mortality is not the issue; and in *A Midsummer Night's Dream*, although the property is similar to that of *Henry VI*, it is not a development of the earlier idea, for a blood-stained mantle existed in Shakespeare's source for the Pyramus and Thisbe story – Arthur Golding's translation of Ovid's *Metamorphoses* (1567). What is interesting here is the way in which a property, used to very different effect in an earlier play, is adapted to a new role.

> And as she fled, her mantle she did fall,
> Which Lion vile with bloody mouth did stain.
> Anon comes Pyramus, sweet youth and tall,
> And finds his trusty Thisbe's mantle slain;

As Quince's words humorously point out, it is the mantle that is slain, not a person – so the undercurrent of successfully diverted violence, which runs throughout the play, at last surfaces in safety in this parodic situation.

Each pair of lovers has avoided actual bloodshed, although hints of this remain strong:

> *Theseus* Hippolyta, I woo'd thee with my sword,
>   And won thy love doing thee injuries;   I.i.16–17
>
> *Hermia* But I beseech your Grace that I may know
>   The worst that may befall me in this case,
>   If I refuse to wed Demetrius.
>
> *Theseus* Either to die the death, or to abjure
>   Forever the society of men.   I.i.62–6
>
> *Demetrius* [to Helena]
>   I'll run from thee and hide me in the brakes,
>   And leave thee to the mercy of wild beasts.   II.i.227–8

and later, Hermia is also threatened with this fate – abandoned and at the mercy of wild beasts, she calls to the absent Lysander, 'Either death or you I'll find immediately' (II.ii.155). The cloth stained with blood in the play-within-a-play is, then, a token for the violence which is not enacted in the play proper. It becomes a cohesive force, drawing various strands of the play's sub-strata together.

When Shakespeare wrote *Othello*, the idea of the blood-stained cloth underwent yet another metamorphosis. As M. C. Bradbrook noted in a Folger lecture,[7] the handkerchief spotted with heart-shaped strawberries is linked to the image of wedding sheets spotted with blood: the former is almost an emblem of the latter, signifying the purity of the marriage which Othello now believes is lost. The idea can be pursued even further if the final scene of the play is recalled, for in this the wedding sheets are put on the bed on which Desdemona dies, but it is Othello's blood, not her own, which finally stains them as he kills himself 'to die upon a kiss' (v.ii.360). The pun on 'die' evokes the passion of a sexual climax and recalls the time at the beginning of their marriage when Othello's passion was not consumed with jealousy, but with love. The contrast between their earlier love and its subsequent tragedy is stressed by the way Othello recalls the handkerchief in the final moments of the play[8] and, once Cassio has made him realise his mistake, moves rapidly to Desdemona on the bed and dies beside her on the wedding sheets. The two properties are, therefore, linked symbolically and, in this final scene, provide a unified double image.

As in the case of *A Midsummer Night's Dream*, the handkerchief in *Othello* also appeared in Shakespeare's source, but Cinthio's narrative merely describes it as: 'a handkerchief which he knew had been given to her by the Moor and which had been worked in a most subtle and Moorish manner'.[9] The strawberry design with its associations of deceit (H. Diehl points out that, though beautiful, traditionally strawberries concealed the serpent) and with its visual similarity to the heart emblem and the spotting of blood, appears to have been Shakespeare's own invention. Moreover, according to Cinthio's story, Desdemona dies after having been beaten to death by a sand-filled stocking and is then left under the rotten timbers of the ceiling which have been made to look as if they accidentally fell on her, whereas in Shakespeare's play her death appears to be a distorted piece of symmetry which underlines the tragedy of their marriage and which is held in a complex design by the juxtaposition of two symbols – the handkerchief and the wedding sheets.

In all these plays religious connotations of sacrifice, love, and grief mingle with the secular expression of the same ideas and, returning to *The Spanish Tragedy*, an uneasy juxtaposition of secular and religious associations is apparent in the staging of Horatio's death because here the symbol of the bloody napkin is reinforced by the image of death on a tree – a combination of symbols which recurs in Shakespeare's *Cymbeline*. The two moments of staging are

Lorenzo Quickly, despatch my masters. *They hang him in the arbour.*
Horatio What, will you murder me?
Lorenzo Ay, thus, and thus, these are the fruits of love. *They stab him.*
Bel-Imperia O save his life and let me die for him!

The Spanish Tragedy II.iv.53–6

and:

Posthumus   Hang there like fruit, my soul,
                    Till the tree die.   Cymbeline v.v.263–4

Both are heightened dramatic moments when ideas of love and death are
juxtaposed – yet in The Spanish Tragedy the climax is provided by the
violent action which tends to overshadow the imagery in the words of the
text, whereas in Cymbeline the completely static quality of the moment
allows the fusion of imagery and symbolic property to frame a brief
tableau effect.

In The Spanish Tragedy, the scene purports to be a love scene and builds
up to an ironical climax:

> Horatio O stay awhile and I will die with thee,
>   So shalt thou yield and yet have conquer'd me.   II.iv.48–9

because at that moment the murderers enter and hang him, turning the
climax of love into one of violent death. It is likely that the arbour may
have resembled the bower shown in the illustration on the 1615 title page,
but the image is one of a tree, and this is recalled by Hieronimo, 'Where
hanging on a tree I found my son' (IV.iv.111), and by Isabella in IV.ii when
she cuts the arbour down before killing herself:

> And as I curse this tree from further fruit,
> So shall my womb be cursed for his sake,   IV.ii.35–6[10]

The inconsistencies in the textual description and stage representation of
the bower are highlighted by her reference to 'this unfortunate and fatal
pine' (IV.ii.7) which, again, does not match the woodcut of the arbour of
the 1615 title page. It is likely that any symbolism intended here (referring
ironically to the pine as a symbol of immortality: pine cones are also
associated with fertility) did not require a corresponding realistic stage
property. In fact, the neutrality of a stage bower would make it possible
for any number of symbolic associations to be imposed upon it at different
points in the play – as indeed they are.

In Isabella's image the tree is cursed for its part in Horatio's murder,
and it even seems that Horatio's dead body is equated with fruit hanging
on a tree. However, in II.iv his body is grotesquely part of the tree and his
wounds are the red fruits, 'Ay, thus, and thus, these are the fruits of love'
(II.iv.55). Lorenzo's words link the visual image of the murdered lover
Horatio with the striking description of the death of the famous classical
lover Pyramus who, when he discovers Thisbe's blood-stained mantle,
kills himself beneath the mulberry tree which was their appointed meeting

place – the equivalent of Horatio's and Bel-Imperia's bower. Ovid tells how he died, 'weeping and kissing the garment he knew so well' and how:

> The leaves that were upon the tree besprincled with his blood
> Were died blacke. The roote also bestained as it stoode,
> A deepe darke purple colour straight upon the Berries cast.[11]

The veil, however, was not stained with Thisbe's blood and when she arrived at the tree and discovered Pyramus's body she, too, killed herself beneath it and the tree became a symbol of their love and their fatal union:

> And thou unhappie tree
> Which shroudest now the corse of one, and shalt anon through mee
> Shroude two, of this same slaughter holde the sicker signes for ay.
> Blacke be the colour of thy fruite and mourning like alway,
> Such as the murder of us twaine may evermore bewray.[12]

In folklore, the mulberry tree is still famed principally for its association with these lovers who sacrificed themselves for each other, but it is not solely a symbol of death. In western parts of England a belief is held in rural communities that there will be no more frost once the mulberry has started to leaf[13] – so in this respect it is linked with spring, new growth, and fertility, and it is probably these associations which lie behind the well-known nursery rhyme, 'Here we go round the mulberry bush ... on a cold and frosty morning.'[14]

Golding's translation of Ovid's *Metamorphoses* was published in 1567 and it is possible that Kyd, like Shakespeare after him, was influenced by the Pyramus and Thisbe story; but the fusion of images which Kyd creates in his visualisation of Horatio's death seems more complex than a mere borrowing from a classical source. In a play where lovers are continually separated by death before they can have their own children, where parents see their children die before themselves, and where sterility, not fertility, is a prominent force, the multiple associations of the mulberry tree – encompassing both the sacrifice for love and the promise of fertility and new life – are ironically apt.

On one level, Lorenzo's words, 'Ay, thus, and thus, these are the fruits of love' could be a reference to the love rites of the May tree festival which was very popular in the reign of Elizabeth I. As the puritanical Philip Stubbes wrote in his *Anatomie of Abuses* in 1583:

Against May, Whitsonday, or other time, all the yung men and maides, olde men and wives, run gadding over night to the woods, groves, hils, and mountains, where they spend all the night in pleasant pastimes; and in the morning they return, bringing w^t them birch and branches of trees, to deck their assemblies withall. And no mervaile, for there is a great Lord present amongst them, as superintendent and Lord over their pastimes and sportes, namely, Sathan, prince of hel: But the cheifest jewel they bring from thence is their May-pole ... this May-pole (this stinkyng ydol, rather), which is covered all over with floures and hearbs, bound round about with strings ... And thus beeing reared up, with handkercheefs and flags hovering on the top, they straw the ground rounde about, binde green boughes about it, set up ... bowers and arbors hard by it. And then fall they to daunce about it like as the heathen people did at the dedication of the Idols, wherof this is a perfect pattern, or rather the thing itself. I have heard it credibly reported ... by men of great gravitie and reputation, that of fortie, threescore, or a hundred maides going to the wood over night, there have scaresly the third part of them returned home againe undefiled.

These be the frutes which these cursed pastimes bring forth.[15]

Horatio and Bel-Imperia go to a bower (similar to the ones described by Stubbes) for their own love games, but Horatio becomes a parody of the decked tree – with the blood-stained scarf which was previously Bel-Imperia's love token to Andrea taking the place of the 'handkercheefs and flags hovering on the top' of which Stubbes writes. Similarly, the carefree dancing at the foot of the May tree is substituted by Bel-Imperia's frantic movements from Lorenzo to Balthazar, pleading for Horatio's life, and their equally vigorous violent movements as they stab Horatio. The line, 'Ay, thus, and thus, these are the fruits of love' suggests a horrible distortion of the light-hearted May-rites or other joyful pastimes associated with the old fertility festival. It is possible that Kyd superimposed a contemporary custom on to a popular classical myth to create an ironical and extremely powerful piece of dramatic spectacle. In addition, and juxtaposed with this secular pattern of associations, is the idea of Christ's death upon a tree.

In the illustrated edition of J. G. Frazer's *The golden bough*, there is a plate entitled, 'The tree of Life' from St Clemente, Rome, which depicts Christ on a cross which is worked into a pattern of vine scrolls, and accompanying it is an extract from the sixth-century poet, Venantius Fortunatus:

> Faithful cross among all others
> one and only holy tree;
> none in foliage, none in blossom,
> none in fruit thy peer may be.[16]

According to legend, the cross, 'was made out of the wood of the "dry tree", the tree of knowledge of good and evil which had lost its verdancy because it was the occasion for original sin'.[17] Unlike the tree of Life in Paradise which never lost its verdancy or fruit, the tree of good and evil had to wait for Christ's redemption before it could flower again. The visual image of Horatio's murder has a sacrificial quality which associates it with Fortunatus's words – and also with an engraving of the fecundity

3　Symbol of the fecundity of sacrifice: the cross bears fruit.

of sacrifice, dating from 1512, in which the cross is portrayed bearing fruit.[18] Both the secular and religious ideas seem simultaneously present in this piece of staging, and in both, the blood-stained handkerchief and the tree are complementary properties which culminate in a complex range of symbolic associations – all expressing the violent severance of Horatio and Bel-Imperia's union.

The moment in the final scene of *Cymbeline* where Imogen is reunited

4   Emblem of marriage.

with her husband also expresses a paradox of sacrifice and fecundity.
Posthumus, like the less fortunate Pyramus, has believed his wife to be
dead and is still, presumably, wearing the cloth, supposedly dipped in her
blood, as a token of his grief, when she is unexpectedly restored to him
and he utters these words as he embraces her:

> Hang there like fruit, my soul,
> Till the tree die.

There is no bower or tree property here: Posthumus himself is the representation of the image and Imogen, clasping his neck, is new fruit to replace the token of death and sacrifice (the blood-stained cloth) which may still be hanging round his neck, beneath her arms. On one level this could be seen as a version of the sacrificial tree finally bearing fruit. On another level it expresses the neo-Platonic idea of the androgynous union of man and woman as depicted in an emblem of marriage (see Figure 4). Together they form a tree which is also a genealogical tree and will bring forth a different kind of fruit in the offspring of the marriage. Perhaps the Gordian knot which binds the man and the woman together in the illustration is linked to the vine which entwines round a tree in another emblem for steadfast friendship and marriage – to which Philip Edwards refers when he notes, 'the point is usually that the vine held up the elm in its embraces even after the elm was dead'[19] – which links with Posthumus's words, 'Till the tree die'.

However, the effect in *Cymbeline* is one of cementing the union between Posthumus and Imogen, whereas in *The Spanish Tragedy* Horatio uses the emblem in a way which hints at the eventual hopelessness of his union with Bel-Imperia, by suggesting that the tree will fall despite the vine – or perhaps even that it will be pulled down by it:

> Nay then, my arms are large and strong withal:
> Thus elms by vines are compass'd till they fall.   II.iv.44–5

Here the vine also has sacrificial overtones as its appearance in the illustration from St Clemente, Rome, suggests. The fertility symbolism inherent in the visualised image in *Cymbeline* is, therefore, expressed positively, whereas in *The Spanish Tragedy* it is distorted – yet it is possible that the earlier play may have provided some stimulus for the latter. Even if this is not the case, it is clear that between these two dramatic moments the property of the blood-stained cloth, as a symbolic device in the drama, underwent a vigorous exploration.

Deliberate allusions to earlier dramatic incidents were often exploited. In I.iv of *The Spanish Tragedy*[20] Bel-Imperia 'lets fall her glove' in the company of her future lover, Horatio and her would-be lover, Balthazar:

She, in going in, lets fall her glove, which HORATIO, *coming out, takes up.*
> *Hor.* Madam, your glove.
> *Bel.* Thanks good Horatio, take it for thy pains.
> *Bal.* Signior Horatio stoop'd in happy time.
> *Hor.* I reap'd more grace than I deserv'd or hop'd.   I.iv.100–3

Here the glove is related to the scarf which she first gave to Andrea, and which Horatio, having taken it from Andrea's dead body as a memory of his friend, has just shown her. Both the scarf and the glove are love tokens – but also have other, darker connotations. The scarf is a memory of a man whose death is to be revenged and is now worn by the man who Bel-Imperia believes will revenge it:

> Yes, second love shall further my revenge.
> I'll love Horatio, my Andrea's friend,
> The more to spite the prince that wrought his end.
> And where Don Balthazar, that slew my love,
> Himself now pleads for favour at my hands,
> He shall in rigour of my just disdain
> Reap long repentance for his murd'rous deed:
> For what was't else but cowardice,
> So many to oppress one valiant knight,
> Without respect of honour in the fight?
> And here he comes that murder'd my delight.   I.iv.66–76

The glove is dropped, presumably as an encouragement to Horatio, but also as a taunt and a challenge to Balthazar – and in being given to Horatio, it is also a symbolic acceptance of the, yet unspoken, challenge which Bel-Imperia has decided upon – that Andrea's death be revenged. Horatio is blind to the significance of accepting the glove at this point. It is only a favour or love token to him: he has no idea of the consequences which will ensue from his liaison with Bel-Imperia – no idea that accepting the challenge to make love to her will also make him the victim of Balthazar's murderous plans which stem from the challenge which *he* saw in the dropping of the glove and Horatio's 'happy chance'. This paves the way for the bower scene with its dramatic switch from the playful war of love to actual bloodshed – by a skilful combination of stage properties and symbolic associations.

In I.i of *The Changeling*, the following contrasting incident occurs:

> Als. [aside] How shall I dare to venture in his castle,
>   When he discharges murderers at the gate?
>   But I must on, for back I cannot go.
> Bea. [aside] Not this serpent gone yet? [Drops a glove]
> Ver.   Look, girl, thy glove's fall'n;
>   Stay, stay – De Flores, help a little.
> [Exeunt VERMANDERO, ALSEMERO, JASPERINO, and
>   servants]
> De F. Here, lady. [Offers the glove]
> Bea. Mischief on your officious forwardness!
>   Who badc you stoop? They touch my hand no more:
>   There, for t'other's sake I part with this,
>   [Takes off the other glove and throws it down]

> Take 'em and draw thine own skin off with 'em.
> *Exeunt* [BEATRICE *and* DIAPHANTA.]
> *De F.* Here's a favour come, with a mischief! Now I know
> 　　She had rather wear my pelt tann'd in a pair
> 　　Of dancing pumps, than I should thrust my fingers
> 　　Into her sockets here, I know she hates me,
> 　　Yet cannot choose but love her:
> 　　No matter, if but to vex her, I'll haunt her still;
> 　　Though I get nothing else, I'll have my will.　　I.i.222–37

N. W. Bawcutt, the editor of the Revels edition, notes here, 'The audience is probably intended to regard the dropping of the glove as an accident, though Beatrice may have dropped it deliberately for Alsemero to pick up and return to her. There is nothing to correspond to this striking incident in Reynolds.'[21] If, as Bawcutt says, this incident did not originate in Middleton and Rowley's source material, it may be an original innovation – or, what seems more probable, in view of Middleton's familiarity with *The Spanish Tragedy* in his reworking of the masque at the end of *Women Beware Women*, it could be an adaptation of Bel-Imperia's action cited above.

In both cases the desired lover and the undesired lover are present together and the heroine drops her glove – a property commonly accepted as a love token (as De Flores's comment 'Here's a favour' seems to imply). Whether Beatrice-Joanna does this accidentally in her distraction at seeing the detested De Flores still by her, or whether it is a deliberate ploy to attract Alsemero (in which case her words concerning De Flores – 'Not this serpent gone yet?' would merely express irritation that her scheme is being overlooked) seems unimportant. What is significant is that she drops her glove and, unlike Bel-Imperia's experience, the wrong suitor picks it up and claims it. Beatrice-Joanna may have thrown it down as a challenge to Alsemero, but De Flores is the better opportunist and it is he who takes up the invitation. The element of challenge is no longer linked to a harmless flirtation, but to the chivalric associations of a challenge between two rivals for one woman – a woman who is, herself, ultimately a symbolic property as well as a character: 'a woman dipped in blood'. This was expressed visually in a past Birmingham Rep. production of the play in which her dress became increasingly stained with blood from the hem upwards until, in the final act, it was completely red. This scene in the first act of *The Changeling* shows what happens when *The Spanish Tragedy* prototype does not go according to plan. Beatrice-Joanna is not glad that De Flores has her favour – she is filled with loathing, and her act of throwing down her other glove too, not only shows her displeasure, but

also provides another challenge to De Flores: he has both gloves now –
what can he hope to obtain next?

As in the case of *The Spanish Tragedy*, the incident is a forerunner of a
later event. Here, Beatrice-Joanna has unwittingly given De Flores the
chance to take something he desires: his violation of her glove with his
hand:

> Now I know
> She had rather wear my pelt tann'd in a pair
> Of dancing pumps, than I should thrust my fingers
> Into her sockets here,

is a precedent for his later violation of her body; for, just as her
single-minded expectation that Alsemero should be the one to take her
token may have led her to cast it down without heeding that the gesture
could be abused and subverted by De Flores, so her single-minded design
to have Alonso murdered causes her to cast herself – as carelessly as she
cast her gloves – into De Flores's hands. In *The Spanish Tragedy*, the
dropping of Bel-Imperia's glove fuels Balthazar's jealousy and leads to
the downfall of the man who picks it up: in *The Changeling* the situation
is reversed – the wrong man picks up the glove and the result is the
downfall of its owner. In both the early play and the later, the use of a
glove property depends on a shared tradition of associations – the love
token worn by the knight for his Lady and the challenge to do battle,
thrown down by the challenger (who is, in both cases, also the Lady).
However, the effect in *The Changeling* may rely partly on a comparison
with the earlier incident in *The Spanish Tragedy* which has been grossly
distorted, and promises a very different set of dramatic possibilities in the
subsequent action of the play.

Dramatists can invest simple stage properties with great symbolic
significance, but a more complex piece of stagecraft, which can be traced
through a variety of plays, is the association, on the stage, of a property
with Pandora's box. Frank Ardolino draws attention to the fact that the
gallows scenes of Pedringano's execution in *The Spanish Tragedy* are a
distortion of a famous *commedia dell' arte* piece in which, 'the common
trickster commits a number of murders and is condemned to be hanged.
However, on the scaffold the wily trickster pretends not to know how to
put his head into the noose and convinces the executioner to demonstrate,
whereupon he tightens the knot and thus "hangs the hangman"'.[22] In
Kyd's version Pedringano does not escape the noose, but does have a
'posthumous last laugh' when the letter found by the hangman which
implicates Lorenzo is passed directly into Hieronimo's hands (III.vii.19).
This piece of staging is, quite rightly, considered by Ardolino to be part of

a pattern of ironic reversals which relate to Kyd's use of dramatic irony in the play as a whole; and the pattern of the gallows episode is completed by another ironic motif – that of the empty box, with its associations with the mythological story of Pandora.

Ardolino's detailed and slightly complicated analysis of Kyd's treatment of the myth could be considered too complex for an audience's immediate appreciation and it seems sufficient to point out that the main thrust of the ironic reversal in this staging is the fact that the box is totally empty and, unlike the original, does not contain hope in any shape or form. That the box is related to the Pandora myth is apparent from the page's words:

> My master hath forbidden me to look in this box, and by my troth 'tis likely, if he had not warned me, I should not have had so much idle time: for we men's-kind in our minority are like women in their uncertainty: that they are most forbidden, they will soonest attempt: so I now.　　　　　　　　　　　　　　　　III.v.1–5

Ardolino seems to be giving a great deal of weight to such a simple property, but his summary is relevant:

> The interpretive importance of Kyd's adaptation of the Pandora myth is the strong moral and emblematic quality it adds to Pedringano's execution and the manner in which its symbolism combines with the play's overall dark and tragic mood to create the Neoplatonic theme that all earthly action is, in many respects, as delusory and doomed as Pedringano's hope for a pardon.[23]

Both moral and emblematical qualities are also present – in a very different way – in Shakespeare's apparent allusion to the myth of Pandora's box in the casket scene of *The Merchant of Venice*. Again, the technique is one of ironic reversal, but here the caskets are not empty: the irony is in the deceit of their appearances and the discovery that the most beautiful caskets contain the most unpleasant truths. When the Prince of Morocco opens the gold casket he reads the moral:

> All that glisters is not gold,
> Often have you heard that told, –
> Many a man his life hath sold
> But my outside to behold, –
> Gilded tombs do worms infold:
> Had you been as wise as bold,
> Young in limbs, in judgment old,
> Your answer had not been inscroll'd –
> Fare you well, your suit is cold.　　　　　　　　　　　　II.vii.65–73

The silver casket holds equally disappointing contents for the Prince of Arragon (II.ix.63–72). As in *Pericles*, it is the plainest casket which contains the likeness of a beautiful woman – entombed here in lead for her safety, just as Thaisa's adorned dead body (which is in a sense a representation or likeness of the living Thaisa) is sealed into a 'caulked and bitumed' chest for protection.

In *The Merchant of Venice* it appears that Shakespeare is employing two facets of the Pandora myth – the first is that, like the seemingly harmless and insignificant jar or box which Pandora opened, the external appearance of a casket bears no relation to the gravity or worth of its contents – and secondly, he creates a Russian dolls' effect in that each time a casket is opened and the bad tidings released for that particular suitor, hope of winning Portia still remains in the casket for the one who follows, until eventually it is solely this hope for a happy union which is left – and which can only belong to Bassanio because he has first obeyed the command, 'Who chooseth me must give and hazard all he hath.' (II.vii.16). Such a command would be equally appropriate in *Pericles*, where Pericles, in choosing to be devoted to the memory of the wife he was forced to cast adrift in a common ship's chest, can only see the fruition of his hope for being reunited with her once he has given and hazarded all he has – including his daughter, Marina.

In *Pericles*, the Pandora myth becomes an integral part of the play's pattern of unexpected reversals. The birth of Antiochus's daughter is related to the creation of Pandora, who was an image animated by Athena or Prometheus, 'and perfected by all the other gods, each of whom contributed an appropriate gift (hence the name "Pandora") and since the gifts of Aphrodite and Hermes were harmful rather than beneficial, the final product turned out to be a καλὸυ κακου, a "beautiful evil"'.[24] Antiochus's daughter also represents an accumulation of gifts:

> to glad her presence,
> The senate-house of planets all did sit
> To knit in her their best perfections.   I.i.10–12

In likening her to the 'beautiful evil' of Pandora she is also associated with Pandora's box, and Pericles's description of her as 'this glorious casket stor'd with ill' also recalls the message of the golden casket in *The Merchant of Venice*. If Pericles had opened the casket, i.e. had made her his wife and Queen of Tyre, then the implication is that her evil past would have introduced disease and impurity into the future line of kings: as in the case of Pandora – opening the box would have loosed a great many ills.

Pericles, however, does not succumb to temptation and this particular version of Pandora's box remains tightly closed and is ultimately destroyed. Yet even this box of evils is not without the traditional ingredient of hope which was left in the box when the evils had been discovered:

> Ant.   Young prince of Tyre,
>   Though by the tenour of our strict edict,

Your exposition misinterpreting,
We might proceed to cancel of your days,
Yet hope, succeeding from so fair a tree
As your fair self, doth tune us otherwise: I.i.III–16

It is soon clear that the hope Antiochus offers is merely a ploy: his only intention is to kill Pericles before the secret can be revealed and so a reversal occurs because his hesitation under the pretext of salvaging the union of his daughter with Pericles, ironically gives Pericles the opportunity to flee – taking the hope 'succeeding from so fair a tree as [his] fair self' with him (115–16). When he makes his second wooing attempt in II.ii this is represented visually in his motto and device:

A wither'd branch, that's only green at top;
The motto, *In hac spe vivo.*

'In this hope I live' has other, added connotations if his earlier encounter with Antiochus is borne in mind: it is not only that the hope of a union with Thaisa gives him the will to live, or that he has taken the new shoots of a withered branch (traditionally a symbol of resurrection) as an encouragement for hope of recovery from his rundown state – but it is also an expression of the way he still clings to the original fragment or branch of hope which Antiochus unwittingly offered him in I.i, and takes it with him on his quest – much as Aeneas carried the golden bough into the underworld, or Dante, the rush, when he journeyed into purgatory: in a sense Pericles is part of the same tradition. It is this hope which brings him to Thaisa and the second evocation of the myth of Pandora's box in the play – an evocation which is also a reversal of the first allusion.

The movement of *Pericles* seems to be akin to the movement of the sea which is so influential in its action. The play moves in waves which roll forward, then recede. Each forward movement is countered by a return movement which washes up a previous parallel or image – sometimes in a new or unexpected form. The tournament scene of II.ii recalls the wooing of Antiochus's daughter in I.i and is itself recalled later in the brothel scenes of Mytilene (IV.ii): the death's net of I.i is recalled in the actual net in II.i which sustains Pericles with new hope – and the Pandora myth is one part of this pattern.

When Thaisa dies on board ship giving birth to Marina she is placed in a chest and cast overboard so that when Cerimon and the others find her they discover a mysterious box and they open it not knowing what they might find:

Cer. What's that?
I. *Serv.*   Sir, even now

> Did the sea toss up upon our shore this chest;
> 'Tis of some wreck.
> *Cer.*   Set't down; let's look upon't.
> *2. Gent.* 'Tis like a coffin, sir.
> *Cer.*   Whate'er it be,
> 'Tis wondrous heavy. Wrench it open straight.
> If the sea's stomach be o'ercharg'd with gold,
> 'Tis a good constraint of fortune
> It belches upon us.
> *2. Gent.*   'Tis so, my Lord.
> *Cer.* How close 'tis caulked and bitumed! Did the sea cast it up?
> *1. Serv.* I never saw so huge a billow, sir, as tossed it upon shore.
> *Cer.* Wrench it open: soft! it smells most sweetly in my sense.
> *2. Gent.* A delicate odour.
> *Cer.* As ever hit my nostril. So, up with it.
> O you most potent gods! what's here? a corse!
> *1. Gent.* Most strange.   III.ii.49–66

The link with the Pandora myth is substantiated by the Panofsky description of the original jar which was later transformed in the stories, into a box: 'this vessel is invariably designated as a πίθοδ (*dolium* in Latin), a huge earthenware storage jar used for the preservation of wine, oil, and other provisions, and often large enough to serve as a receptacle for the dead or, later on, a shelter for the living'.[25]

Thaisa, in her plain coffin, becomes a reversal of Antiochus's daughter – 'this glorious casket stor'd with ill' – for Thaisa's casket is not glorious, yet, like the lead casket in *The Merchant of Venice*, it contains beauty, goodness, and hope. Thaisa appears like a jewelled icon at the point when she is restored to life – contrasting death and life by juxtaposing the statue image with the newly breathing woman:

> *Cer.*   She is alive!
> Behold, her eyelids, cases to those
> Heavenly jewels which Pericles hath lost,
> Begin to part their fringes of bright gold.
> The diamonds of a most praised water
> Doth appear to make the world twice rich. Live,
> And make us weep to hear your fate, fair creature,
> Rare as you seem to be.   *She moves.*
>   III.ii.99–106

The hope which was buried deep in this version of Pandora's box is the hope of resurrection which is realised here. In *Pericles* Shakespeare not only evokes an image of the original Pandora's box in relation to Antiochus's daughter, but he also transforms this and offers his own, non-evil alternative.

Unlike her mother, Marina is not actually placed in a coffin, but her captivity in the brothel at Mytilene is a metaphorical burial in that her true identity is now dead and she is entombed or trapped in a decaying world of moral and physical corruption, presided over by Boult, a man related to the porter at the gates of hell, whom Lysimachus calls, 'thou damned door-keeper' (IV.vi.118). That Marina is the 'virgin' who props up Boult's house, i.e. hell, from sinking and overwhelming him, using her virtue as a force, is significant in relation to the similarity of her situation with that of a famous virgin of Antioch (martyred in *c*.278)[26] who was also known as Marina. F. D. Hoeniger, in his notes to the *Dramatis Personae* in the play's Arden edition, remarks on the similarity of the name and adds, 'But it seems improbable that Shakespeare had heard of her.' He gives no details of her legend and fails to mention that at one time she was the most popular English female saint and that depictions of her story existed in Europe in the early sixteenth century.[27]

Marina, or Margaret, of Antioch refused to marry the Governor of Antioch and was thrown into a dungeon where the devil, in the form of a fire-breathing dragon, tried to terrify her. She was swallowed by the dragon and made the sign of the cross which grew and split its body so that she emerged unharmed. She rose out of the dragon as Jonah was belched out of the whale, and there are obvious links with the way Marina in *Pericles* refuses to prostitute herself to the Governor of Mytilene and is imprisoned in a brothel resembling hell – to burst out of her captivity because her great virtue and her faith in Diana preserve her from harm. It is also interesting to note that, according to Butler's *Lives of the Saints*, Marina of Antioch is also directly linked with the myth of Pandora's box for, after combating the devil:

she had conflict with another demon, whom she overcame, and they talked together, and he told her how he had been with others like him enclosed in a brazen vessel by Soloman, and how the vessel had been found in Babylon and broken open by people who thought it to contain treasure, so that the demons were released to plague the world.[28]

This could be related to Marina's victory over Boult and seen as a symbolic description of the reality of the brothel world.

The Pandora myth is only one part of a multiple design which brings legend and religious associations together. Another part of this pattern emerges in the parallel ordeals which Marina and her mother undergo. Unlike Marina, Thaisa is literally coffined and revived. When the coffin is brought to him, Cerimon gives commands to open it:

> If the sea's stomach be o'ercharg'd with gold,
> 'Tis a good constraint of fortune
> It belches upon us.   III.ii.54–6

A whale who swallows men has already been evoked in the scene with the fishermen and Thaisa's delivery from the sea is also linked with Jonah's ordeal inside the whale – from whence he was eventually belched forth onto dry land. A woman rising from the sea – apart from the connection with Venus (discussed later) also has a religious counterpart, as Mark Frank noted in one of his sermons: 'Maria is *maris stella*, says St. Bede: "the star of the sea", a fit name for the mother of the bright Morning Star that rises out of the vast sea of God's infinite and endless love.'[29] Throughout *Pericles*, the classical myth of Pandora has been allied and adapted to merge with Christian tradition so that lurking behind the symbolism of the whole play is the most potent image of all – that of Christ rising from the confines of the Holy Sepulchre. The effect is cumulative and multi-layered.

The image of the sepulchre is also present in *Cymbeline* – again in the sub-structure of the symbolism. In *Pericles* and in *Cymbeline*, Shakespeare uses the Pandora myth in a more complex way than his use of the tradition in *The Merchant of Venice*. In '*Cymbeline* and the languages of myth', Marjorie Garber links the Freudian associations of the box or trunk in which Iachimo hides in II.ii with an additional mythological reading. The chest can, as she suggests, be read as a symbol of the honour and chastity which are violated by Iachimo, but it is also a 'box, which is supposed to contain precious things, like gold and plate, but which in fact contains Iachimo – that is, guile and lust'.[30] Similarly, she draws attention to the Queen's box or casket which Pisanio gives to Imogen:

> My noble mistress,
> Here is a box, I had it from the queen
> What's in't is precious: III.iv.189–91

Again, appearances deceive: the contents of this box are harmful and cause Imogen to fall into a death-like state in the cave of Belarius. The structure of *Cymbeline* appears to work in a similar way to that of *Pericles* – through repetitions and reversals. As Marjorie Garber indicates, in *Cymbeline* it is Belarius's cave which provides the reversal of the myth of a harmful Pandora's box:

In the two court boxes, then, we have objects which promise the opposite of what they perform – the boxes, like Pandora's, which set loose upon an unsuspecting and to some extent Edenic populace a world of sin and experience, and almost of death. On the other hand, in the cave we have a box-like structure which contains more than its exterior promises ... Out of the humble cave, the humble box, or mythic container, or womb, comes real value, real wealth, real royalty.[31]

The cave, therefore, can be equated with Thaisa's coffin in the sense that both are life-giving reversals of a destructive, or death-associated idea –

and in both cases, this reversal moves outside the range of one classical myth and is allied to wider religious and symbolic associations. Thaisa's coffin is a kind of ark which preserves and ensures rebirth; like the cave, it is a symbol of the human heart as the spiritual centre – and both are symbols of the womb. In Christian tradition the ark symbolises Mary as the mother of Jesus, and Thaisa in her coffin can, therefore, be associated with Stella Maris – rising from the sea – whose pagan counterpart in the play is obviously the image of Venus rising from 'simple shells'. All these associations may be present simultaneously: just as the cave of Belarius is not only a lowly opposite to Cymbeline's court and a reversal of the Pandora's box images earlier in the play – but is also linked to the resurrection of Christ in the sepulchre and, through Imogen's confused state of mind:

> *Imo.*   I hope I dream:
> For so I thought I was a cave-keeper,
> And cook to honest creatures. But 'tis not so:
> 'Twas but a bolt of nothing, shot at nothing,
> Which the brain makes of fumes. Our very eyes
> Are sometimes like our judgments, blind.   IV.ii.297–302

to Plato's cave in Book VII of *The Republic*, where reality is confused with shadows.

In *The Spanish Tragedy*, Kyd juxtaposed the myth of Pandora's box with a deviation of a popular *commedia dell' arte* routine, to considerable effect. By the time Shakespeare began writing his last plays, he was using the same myth in a much more complicated design and the comparison with *The Spanish Tragedy* should show the multi-layered, multi-associational quality which Shakespeare was developing in his later plays. He was not using very different basic materials to other dramatists of his time, but he combined these with a wealth of symbolic associations. It is unsatisfactory to adopt the attitude which E. E. Stoll displayed in relation to *Macbeth* and say dismissively of a play, 'How the multiple meanings confuse and obscure it.'[32] Rather, an awareness of multiple meanings should provide a greater understanding of the play's hidden depths; even if these are only partly evoked consciously by the dramatist to stir the minds of those in his audience, and also partly exist (despite no deliberate attempt of his own to display them) as the inevitable result of the mixed dramatic heritage which is his medium of expression.

To us, the interest is both artistic and historical. After 1559[33] it was wiser for playwrights to eliminate religious issues or allusions from their works, but as many later plays show, such things were not entirely abandoned. As is sometimes the case where censorship or suppression exists, mutations occur and elements of the forbidden or the suppressed emerge in a new, often oblique form – as in the religious undertones in the works of the Russian film director, Tarkovsky. In the case of Tarkovsky, this sublimation of meaning can make the works seem additionally complicated to outsiders, and the same is probably true of Elizabethan and Jacobean drama. We may find it difficult to grasp the simultaneous connections between Diana, Venus, Elizabeth I, and the Virgin Mary – but to Elizabethans, they were part of a popular cult. This does not suggest that every Elizabethan or Jacobean play is a distortion of suppressed religious drama – only that this element is sometimes present amongst a large variety of other shared traditions and myths which these magpie dramatists exploited time and time again – blending them as they blended many other seemingly incongruous aspects, such as symbolism and realism, or apparently believable acting and postured, rhetorical delivery.

This chapter shows that even the most simple stage property could have far-reaching roots, and demonstrates the blend and scope of the traditions with which these dramatists worked – each developing them to suit their own dramatic demands. As Sidney said, the drama was 'mungrel'; it is characterised by its lively and individual use of material common to all, and by the way dramatists used each others' achievements to set off their own – by the cross-currents which occurred between them. M. C. Bradbrook's summary of the general situation also includes a good description of the background to this book:

There is no longer a single central classical tradition for the presentation of plays; but when the Jacobean theatre was at its greatest, there was no single tradition either.

Players had used to be scornfully termed chameleons rather than comedians; but the Protean art sustained its integrity by tension between manifold styles: between Shakespeare and Jonson, and Jonson and Middleton, between the Red Bull and the Inns of Court, between all of these playwrights and the theatres and the Court rituals, or the civic triumphs.[34]

3 · The masque and the drama: *Macbeth* and *Lord Hay's Masque*

The way in which dramatists could draw from a common pool of ideas and traditions, yet preserve their individuality by manipulating their materials to achieve very different effects, also applied to more topical themes. In the years 1606–7, James I's interest in a total Anglo-Scottish union was a dominant political and social concern. An exploration of Thomas Campion's *Lord Hay's Masque* (which celebrates an Anglo-Scottish marriage) in relation to Shakespeare's *Macbeth* may illuminate the relationship between the court entertainments and popular drama – both in relation to their treatment of this topical issue and the traditions they exploited. When Campion's masque began, the knights of Phoebus (Apollo) had been turned into trees by the goddess of chastity for trying to seduce her nymphs, and preparations for the marriage celebrations of one of them were interrupted until news arrived that Phoebus had pacified Cynthia (Diana) and that the trees were to be set free. After a dance, and at a sign from Night, they became men again, whereupon they offered their green robes to the tree of Diana to appease the goddess, and were subsequently revealed in their true splendour so that the festivities could continue. On the surface this would seem to have little to do with *Macbeth*, but differences are more important than similarities here.

Chronologically the two works are very close. Campion's masque was performed on Twelfth Night, 6 January 1607 and although the date of *Macbeth* is uncertain, it can be placed between the summer of 1606 and the early part of 1607: their performances can be calculated to be, at most, six months apart – possibly much less. We do not know which work has chronological precedence and the orthodox view would be to assume this as *Macbeth*'s – but, to some extent, the order is still open to question. Until now, the most popular date for a first performance of *Macbeth* has been the summer of 1606, to coincide with a number of topical references,[1] but I have found no evidence which totally refutes the idea that *Macbeth* may have been performed after, rather than before, *Lord Hay's Masque*. The topical references would still be effective as the aftermath of the Gunpowder Plot was presumably felt for some time and the Tyger, a ship which had been voyaging for over a year and a half, would not be forgotten in a matter of months. Nor do possible links between *Macbeth* and other contemporary works rule out a slightly later date—early in 1607.[2]

Both *Macbeth* and *Lord Hay's Masque* occurred at a time when any allusions to the union of Scotland and England necessitated careful handling: in 1606 'sundry were committed to Bridewell' for their part in Day's *Isle of Gulls* in which, as E. K. Chambers points out, 'evidently the Arcadians and Lacedaemonians stand for the two 'nations' of English and Scotch'.[3] In his article, 'Campion's *Lord Hay's Masque* and Anglo-Scottish union'[4] David Lindley draws attention to the way James forced his Parliament to devote time to the issue and encouraged propaganda which supported his aim. Both works, in the loosest sense, can be considered part of that propaganda: it was much safer to be viewed in this way than to risk being seen as implied criticism. However, both deal with the topic very differently.

M. C. Bradbrook's view: '*Macbeth* is the sublimation of spectacle into poetry, but it does not directly reflect masquing, rather contrasts with it', is revealing. She continues, 'If later, he was able to use and adapt the material of the masque for his theatre, it was as one who had recognised the gulf between these two forms, who was seeking a new way to reconcile popular and courtly audiences.'[5] It could be argued that when he wrote *Macbeth*, Shakespeare was not yet totally committed to reconciling popular and courtly drama: he seems much more interested in exploring the gulf between the two forms at this stage. There is even a possibility that he may have been trying to demonstrate the superiority of the popular drama by juxtaposing it with various characteristics of the court masque, so that *Macbeth* can be seen in terms of distortions of commonplace masque techniques and ideas.[6] It is interesting that Shakespeare, although presumably as capable as Ben Jonson, never produced (or perhaps was not asked to produce) masques as well as plays.

Certain critics, particularly Northrop Frye and M. C. Bradbrook, have linked *Macbeth* with the masque in general terms,[7] but the fullest treatment the play has received in this respect is probably Alexander Leggatt's essay, '*Macbeth* and the last plays',[8] and there is still scope for further exploration. Ben Jonson obviously saw a connection when he produced an anti-masque of fantastic hags in his *Masque of Queens* (1609), which was probably inspired by Shakespeare's witches, and there are many other masque-like features in the play. The witches are at the centre of a series of distortions and imitations, while the spectacle of the show of kings and the revelation of the three apparitions both suggest links with pageantry and masques. *Macbeth* employs numerous choruses and chanted dialogue in the witch scenes. The witches speak in the rhyming couplets commonly used in masques – as does Macbeth when he is concerned with his dark intentions: he is, significantly, the only other character who consistently slips into their rhyme.[9]

Ideas related to the masque seem to creep into the drama. At II.iii.110, Macbeth offers a strange description of the murdered Duncan: 'His silver skin lac'd with his golden blood'. Attempts have been made to explain this, for example, that of W. A. Murray, which likens Duncan's blood to an alchemical tincture with religious significance.[10] On a mystical level this works very well, but it does not fully exploit the striking visual qualities here. An alternative, or supplementary view is to liken the image to rich court dress, particularly masque finery. In Jonson's masque, *Hymenaei*, the lords were described in these terms:

Their bodies were of carnation cloth of silver, richly wrought, and cut to express the naked, in manner of the Greek thorax,   559–61[11]

and in Campion's *Lord Hay's Masque*, the costumes of the knights are even more closely linked to the image in *Macbeth* as these were 'of Carnation satten layed thicke with broad silver lace'. It is as if Macbeth's imagination has transformed Duncan's mutilated, naked body into an elaborately embroidered masque or court costume.

Duncan is a saintly king, likened to the sun (I.v.61), so it is fitting that Shakespeare should describe his blood as golden – a term sometimes used for red,[12] but the flesh-coloured satin of fine masque costumes, such as those of Campion's knights is, on Duncan (who resembles their leader, Apollo, the sun god) changed to actual flesh drained of blood, and therefore silver, the grey of a corpse. In this way Shakespeare may be using a purely verbal image to stimulate a visual mental picture by pitting the masque, so obviously a product of comfortable luxury and elegant fantasy, against the equally fictitious but, in comparison, far more realistic demonstration of events on the public stage, which would seem to indicate his manipulation and understanding of the different natures of the two theatrical experiences and his skill in using the former to strengthen the impact of the latter.

Macbeth and *Lord Hay's Masque* contain similar elements: one could almost be a reworking of certain characteristics of the other. In both works, in accordance with popular tradition, nine, the number of the muses, is symbolically significant. In the masque there are nine trees and nine hours and the number is important because it is the self-multiple of three and is especially potent in the use of magic:

> *Night* Thus can celestials work in human fate,
>   Transform and form as they do love or hate,
>   Like touch, and change receive: the gods agree
>   The best of numbers is contained in three.   358–61

In *Macbeth* the magic is of a much darker nature and is controlled or expressed by the three witches who themselves become the powerful self-multiple through their movements on the stage:

> The Weird Sisters, hand in hand,
> Posters of the sea and land,
> Thus do go about, about:
> Thrice to thine, and thrice to mine,
> And thrice again, to make up nine.
> Peace! – the charm's wound up.   I.iii.32–7

It is a charm to ensnare human life, not to set it free, as is the case in Campion's masque when, three by three, the trees are released from their captivity to become men. In the masque the number nine is associated with white magic whereas in the play it is part of the black magic rituals. However, even here, a fortunate nine eventually points to an optimistic future and the hint that the pious Malcolm and his force from England will counter the evil; for the apparitions, brought about by adding the blood of a sow who had eaten her nine farrow, end in a show of nine – the eight kings and Banquo.

There is further significance attached to the number three as W. R. Davis notes: 'it figures marriage, as combining the female or even 2 with the male odd 1.'[13] *Lord Hay's Masque* was written and performed in honour of a marriage which James had arranged to strengthen the union of England and Scotland: it was a gesture of peace. *Macbeth* is also concerned with the eventual union of England and Scotland, but Macbeth himself is identified, very early in the play, with a different sort of marriage. He is described as Bellona's bridegroom (I.ii.55), and as the play progresses it becomes clear that this marriage only celebrates the fruitless union of Macbeth with bloodshed. There are other kinds of marriages which can be made – with war and ambition. The most striking union of male and female in Shakespeare's play is not associated with a marriage couple, but with the witches, whose number could be said to combine 'the female or even 2 with the male odd 1'. They incorporate both female and male characteristics. Banquo addresses them:

> You should be women,
> And yet your beards forbid me to interpret
> That you are so.   I.iii.45–7

In *Macbeth*, three, signifying the union of male and female, is portrayed grotesquely by the witches in a theatre where women were represented on stage by men. It is not the symbol of beauty, harmony, and fertility which Campion's masque expresses.[14] The masque-like characteristics of the

witches are stressed when Banquo addresses them in I.iii, for his words do
not seem as applicable to characters on the public stage as they might have
been to creatures of the masque – he hints at metamorphosis:

> What are these,
> So wither'd and so wild in their attire,
> That look not like th'inhabitants o'th'earth,
> And yet are on't? Live you? or are you aught
> That man may question?   I.iii.39–43

They are of the earth rather than inhabitants of it: as if they were part of
the heath, the stones, and the scrub land – an impression which is later
intensified in the way they seem to vanish into the air – much as characters
in masques could be concealed by their surroundings. When Macbeth
addresses them: 'Speak, if you can: – what are you?' (47), he also betrays
the suspicion that a metamorphosis of some kind has taken place and talks
as if he were demanding speech of inanimate objects which, as the
masques (Campion's in particular) frequently demonstrated, were really
transformed beings. In a masque, as in the world of Ovidian mythology on
which many of them were based, it was possible to address a tree or a rock
and receive an answer. Up to this point, Banquo and Macbeth's attitudes
may have been light-hearted, treating the witches as fantastical beings: but
when the witches speak the joke seems to rebound, for it is not the
language which the two men would expect to hear from old women on a
heath – however strange they may have looked. The Weird Sisters who
'have more in /them than mortal knowledge' (I.v.2–3) are indeed 'imperfect speakers' as Macbeth calls them (I.iii.70): they are imperfect in
appearance, but they declare their parts as if they were speakers in a
dramatic entertainment.

It is almost as if the tired soldiers inadvertently took a wrong turn on
their way home from battle, passed through a time warp, and found
themselves in the middle of a performance in the Banqueting House at
Whitehall. Even Banquo seems to imply that he wonders if they have
indeed wandered into the imaginary world of which the masque was part:

> I' th' name of truth
> Are ye fantastical, or that indeed
> Which outwardly ye show?   I.iii.52–4

Later, in IV.i, the witches may be associated with a parody of the
transformation scenes found in masques, for when Macbeth demands an
answer of them, his words not only bid them risk the total anarchy and
destruction of the world, but also involve connotations of the destruction
of the masque fabrication – waves, trees, castles, palaces, pyramids –
collapsing like toppled scenery:

> though the yesty waves
> Confound and swallow navigation up;
> Though bladed corn be lodg'd, and trees blown down;
> Though castles topple on their warders' heads;
> Though palaces and pyramids, do slope
> Their heads to their foundations;   IV.i.53–8

Macbeth and Campion's masque involve similar transformations; the most striking contrasts are those of night and day – a common device, but one which plays an important part in both works. The setting of darkness and confusion in *Macbeth* is eventually purged by Malcom and transformed. In Campion's masque a more picturesque version of night and day is portrayed, and again, the former dissolves into the latter.

The setting of the masque involved a high stage: all enclosed with a double veil, so artificially painted that it seemed as if dark clouds had hung before it; within that shroud was concealed a green valley with green trees round about it, and in the midst of them nine golden trees of fifteen foot high.   16–20

The Bower of Flora stood at one side of this screen, and at the other was the House of Night: between them lay a hill with the tree of Diana. The House of Night was stately with black pillars and high turrets from which 'were placed on wire artificial bats and owls, continually moving' (39–40). This, with the Bower of Flora (full of flowers and lights), represented the extremes of day and night. Night and darkness pervade *Macbeth* just as the veil, painted with dark clouds, obscured the scenery behind it in Campion's masque – and in both cases the darkness is parted for the entrance of trees who become men.

In *Lord Hay's Masque* Night freed the trees from their fifteen foot high gold casings and they became men clothed in green leafy costumes. At the House of Night they discarded these too, and were revealed as knights of Apollo – the sun. They climbed the hill to offer their discarded robes to the tree of Diana and moved on to the Bower of Flora, a symbol of the day. In *Macbeth* the trees march up the hill to Dunsinane and also discard their leafy disguises – this time to reveal an army of men who will kill Macbeth and, like the knights of Apollo, bring the promise of a new dawn to Scotland.

These transformation scenes show how both works exploit similar ideas in different ways: the celebration of Campion's masque is dependent on the trees opening to reveal the men beneath, and in *Macbeth* the final liberation of Scotland is only achieved through the turning of trees into men. Even the terminology is the same: in v.v.38, the messenger refers to the sight as a 'moving grove'; not a wood or a forest, but the very word used in Campion's masque. Malcolm's men carry branches before them in

Holinshed's account, but Holinshed passes quickly over the incident with few details. It is striking that such similar ideas were staged in different works within such a short period of time, although this may only demonstrate the popularity of this particular tradition of metamorphosis. However, *Lord Hay's Masque* was presented on Twelfth Night and was, therefore, the most important masque of the year and likely to be much discussed.[15] Shakespeare's company, the King's Men, provided the speaking parts, so Shakespeare was probably familiar with it early in its preparation and may have been intrigued at the way the world of a contemporary masque merged with the material from Holinshed's *Chronicles* with which he was concerned. Campion's masque recalls the mythological transformations of both stones and trees:

> *Night* Seems that so full of strangeness to you now?
>   Did not the Thracian harp long since the same?
>   And (if we rip the old records of fame)
>   Did not Amphion's lyre the deaf stones call,
>   When they came dancing to the Theban wall?
>   Can music then joy? Joy mountains moves,
>   And why not trees? Joy's powerful when it loves.
>   Could the religious oak spread oracle
>   Like to the gods? and the tree wounded tell
>   T'Aeneas his sad story? Have trees therefore
>   The instruments of speech and hearing more
>   Than they've of pacing?   274–85

In III.iv when Macbeth says, 'Stones have been known to move and trees to speak' (122), he is referring to this mythological phenomenon which is also recalled and, in part, re-enacted in *Lord Hay's Masque*. Night's speech continues:

>   and to whom but Night
>   Belong enchantments? Who can more affright
>   The eye with magic wonders? Night alone
>   Is fit for miracles, and this shall be one
>   Apt for this nuptial dancing jollity.   285–9

In *Macbeth* night's powers 'affright/The eye with magic wonders' which are not in keeping with 'nuptial dancing jollity': night is not 'fit' for miracles, but for horrors – the true miracle is not brought about by magic as we may have been led to expect – but by men, and it occurs by day. When Macbeth, in reply to the third apparition's prophecy, exclaims:

>   That will never be:
>   Who can impress the forest; bid the tree
>   Unfix his earth-bound root?   IV.i.94–6

the play's audience may not have been aware of the explanation in
Holinshed's *Chronicles* and could have been expecting a much more
fantastic occurrence than Shakespeare eventually gave them, especially if
they had a knowledge of masques – because there, such wonders were
magically possible. Campion's masque contained one who could, indeed,
'bid the tree/Unfix his earth-bound root':

> *Night* Earth then be soft and passable to free
> These fettered roots! Joy, trees! the time draws near
> When in your better forms you shall appear.
> Dancing and music must prepare the way;
> There's little tedious time in such delay.   290–4

Although it could happen in a contemporary masque, other twists and
distortions have already appeared in the play, so a recognition of links
between the staging of a masque and *Macbeth* would probably only
heighten an audience's anticipation of some, as yet unperceived, final
dénouement. This is similar to Shakespeare's manipulation of his audience's expectations in the statue scene of *The Winter's Tale*.[16]

Music was an important component in any masque. In *Lord Hay's
Masque* harmonious music changed discord to concord and the transformation song began:

> Move now with measured sound,
> You charmed grove   303–4

The trees presumably moved in time to the music. *Macbeth* is not a play
associated with music, but the trees of Birnam Wood also move in time –
to the harsh sounds of drumming associated with battle: '*Enter, with
drum and colours*, MALCOLM, *old* SIWARD, MACDUFF, *etc., and
their army, with boughs*' (v.vi). As Night's earlier speech and the song
indicate, the masque trees moved through joy and love:

> Much joy must needs the place betide where trees for gladness move:
> A fairer sight was ne'er beheld, or more expressing love.   311–12

In contrast, Shakespeare's trees move in war – the joy is to come later, and
should not be prematurely celebrated. In the masque, the trees became
knights and led out the audience to dance: in *Macbeth* the trees become
soldiers and lead out Macbeth to fight with Macduff.

The public playhouse equivalent of the harmonious music of masques
is, here, provided by well-known, unsophisticated sound effects. In the
Prologue to *Every Man in His Humour* Jonson wrote:

> Nor nimble squibbe is seene, to make afear'd
> The gentlewoman; nor roul'd bullet heard
> To say it thunders; nor tempestuous drumme
> Rumbles, to tell you when the storme doth come.

The sound of thunder was apparently produced by rolling a bullet (a ball) down a channel, or – more popularly – by banging a drum. Music, in *Lord Hay's Masque*, as in many others, was light and pleasant, expressing joy, harmony, and magical miracles. In Shakespeare's play the most prominent sound effect is the threatening or sinister drum – either signifying thunder and heralding the entrance of the witches, or beaten at a different pace to signify battle and stress Macbeth's affinity to the witches, as a drum is also used to announce his appearance:

> A drum! A drum!
> Macbeth doth come.   I.iii.30–1

Finally, the measured drum beat of Malcom's army leads up to the play's parallel to Campion's miraculous, musical transformation:

> Now, near enough: your leafy screens throw down,
> And show like those you are.   v.vi.1–2

and suddenly this analogy with a masque-like transformation recalls Banquo's words in I.iii:

> I' th' name of truth,
> Are ye fantastical, or that indeed
> Which outwardly ye show?   I.iii.52–4

Yet the transformation of trees into men not only provides verbal echoes from an earlier part of the play – perhaps it even brings about a visual manifestation of an earlier image. In II.ii of *Macbeth*, the lines 59–62 have posed interpretative problems for many editors, but there could be an additional meaning which can be more easily revealed by linking them with the trees which turn into men in *Lord Hay's Masque*:

> Will all great Neptune's ocean wash this blood
> Clean from my hand? No, this my hand will rather
> The multitudinous seas incarnadine,
> Making the green one red.

The image has roots in the Book of Revelation 16.3 and was not new to the drama: it appeared in works by Chettle and Munday and Barnabe Riche.[17] Superficially it is quite acceptable to explain this as a contradiction of Lady Macbeth's later words, 'A little water clears us of this deed' – expressing the impossibility (in Macbeth's view) of the water mass of the planet being able to cleanse his murderous hand of its guilt.

However, the lines also have a hallucinatory, visual quality which suggests that they may be prophetic. Macbeth could be describing a symbolic vision which he sees in his mind, yet cannot interpret correctly – not unlike the plight of the soothsayer in *Cymbeline*. Whether this is the case, or whether Macbeth is deliberately made to say the words unknow-ingly, there is a visual link between a mass of men marching beneath green branches and a huge green tidal wave or sea. On stage, with the advent of Malcolm's army, Macbeth's mistake – or Shakespeare's touch of irony – will become clear. Perhaps this is behind Macbeth's final ironic words:

> Blow wind! come wrack!
> At least we'll die with harness on our back.   v.v.51–2

He rushes off the stage with these words at the end of v.v just as the mass of men, disguised beneath green boughs, sweep on and transform them-selves into a human army ready for 'blood and death' (v.vi.10). It is significant that his cry before he goes to meet them suggests that he feels he is fighting a tempest and recalls his earlier image of a vast sea. Macbeth's affinity with the witches has already been shown by his lapses into rhyming couplets at significant times, but now it seems that he may, unwittingly, pronounce his own doom. It is possible to offer another, not alternative, but supplementary reading of the lines ii.ii.59–62.

In his note on this speech, Kenneth Muir says of Shakespeare's use of 'incarnadine', 'Properly it would mean "make flesh-coloured", but Shake-speare obviously means "turn blood-red". He may have been thinking of a crimson blush.' I suggest that Shakespeare *was* using the word 'properly', and that as well as the superficial image of blood, he was supplying a further meaning – 'to make flesh-coloured'. The sea is not only the image of the vast oceans of the globe juxtaposed against one man's hand – it is also a moving green mass, brought into existence by the need to stop the exploits of 'a hand accurs'd' (Lenox's description of Macbeth, iii.vi.49, when plans are afoot to form an army under Malcolm and march against him). Once the army has reached its destination, the green does indeed turn flesh-coloured – into living men who will destroy Macbeth. Shakespeare does not describe multitudes of seas, but calls the seas 'multitudinous' in ii.ii.61, which, combined with the connotations of 'incarnadine' – his other unique addition to the old image – suggests a multitude of inhabitants made flesh. In v.v the green tide becomes a flesh and blood army and the 'hand accurs'd' goes out to meet it, as if abandoning himself to the perils of the sea. In this, an earlier verbal image finally finds visual expression.

'Making the green one red' was also the concern of the trees who became men in *Lord Hay's Masque*. Whether by coincidence or design, both works stage a similar effect. In the masque the men discarded their green leaves for the costumes of the Knights of Apollo – the sun, whose dawning indicates the break of day; accordingly, their garments symbo-lised this. As Campion stated, 'the stuffe was of Carnation satten'. While it may occasionally mean a deeper crimson, the first two definitions of carnation in *The Oxford English dictionary* are: 'the colour of human flesh or skin [and] a light rosy pink'. It is both the colour of human skin and of the dawn. The men in *Macbeth* may only be flesh-coloured because they are living men and not because of their costumes, but the allusion to green transforming into red still works symbolically in both the masque and the play.

At the end of the play when Macduff exclaims, 'the time is free' (v.ix.21), it is an indication that day and light have at last triumphed over the night and darkness which held them enthralled. Metaphorically, Malcolm's army is seen as heralding the dawn of a new day and a new era of hope in the history of Scotland. If the transformation on stage were visual as well as verbal, it would enact the metaphor of exchanging darkness for the rosy hue of dawn and would replace 'black Macbeth' (iv.iii.52) and the deep crimson of spilt blood, with the warm human flesh of men whose aim is to provide blood for new life. This would also support the association of the green branches with fertility and spring rituals which has been noted by John Holloway and others.[18]

In *Lord Hay's Masque* James is, unquestionably, the Phoebus who is commander of the knights, just as Malcolm, at the end of *Macbeth*, brings about the dawn of a new day and leaves the way open for James's rule of peace. Both works, to differing degrees, compliment the King. The first dedication to Campion's masque is:

> To the most puisant and
> Gratious James King of great
> Britaine.

The disunited Scithians, when they sought
To gather strength by parties, and combine
That perfect league of freends which, once beeing wrought,
No turne of time or fortune could untwine,
This rite they held: a massie bowle was brought,
And ev'ry right arme shot his severall blood
Into the mazar [bowl] till 'twas fully fraught.
Then having stird it to an equall floud
They quaft to th' union, which till death should last,
In spite of private foe, or forraine feare;
And this blood sacrament being knowne t'have past,
Their names grew dreadfull to all far and neere.
O then, great Monarch, with how wise a care
Do you these bloods devided mixe in one,
And with like consanguinities prepare
The high, and everliving Union
Tweene Scots and English: who can wonder then
If he that marries kingdomes, marries men?

The description of the bloody ceremony seems a strange opening to a marriage masque until it becomes clear that Campion employed it as a metaphor for the more civilised mixing of bloods which James decreed through arranging a marriage union between Scotland and England. *Macbeth* is also concerned with the mixing of blood, but not always in such a civilised fashion. The same traditions appear in both works, but they are expressed in very different ways.

The sign for Macbeth to go and spill Duncan's blood is the bell – supposedly rung to tell him that his drink is ready. Juxtaposed in this way, it implies that he is really attempting to grow by drinking Duncan's blood; thereby developing the ironic insinuation found in Duncan's earlier words to him:

> I have begun to plant thee, and will labour
> To make thee full of growing.   I.iv.28–9

The tree which Malcolm declares 'is ripe for shaking' (IV.iii.237–8), was earlier fertilised by a dead king's blood, unlike Malcolm, who can be associated with the metaphor in Campion's dedication – being a king fertilised by the blood of a living king. Malcolm has Duncan's blood naturally in his veins, but Macbeth unnaturally consumed it, as the juxtapositioning of his call to enact the murder with his call to his bed-time drink infers. This positioning is recalled at his remark at the discovery of the deed:

> The wine of life is drawn, and the mere lees
> Is left this vault to brag of.   II.iii.93–4

Later in the play the staging again juxtaposes Macbeth's action of drinking wine with the shedding of blood: in III.iv he is presumably drinking at the banquet when Banquo's ghost reappears:

> *Macb.*   Give me some wine: fill full:-
> I drink to th' general joy o' th' whole table,
> And to our dear friend Banquo, whom we miss;
> Would he were here!
> > *Re-enter Ghost*
> > To all, and him, we thirst,
> And all to all.   III.iv.87–91

Whether or not the appearance of Banquo's ghost is regarded as a figment of Macbeth's imagination or as a genuine supernatural occurrence (whatever that might be), the sight of a bloody man whose death he decreed might well make him equate the wine which has passed his lips with the blood he sees before him. If this is the case, when he shouts 'thy blood is cold' at Banquo's ghost (93), he does so, not only to convince himself that the figure cannot harm him because it is dead, but also because Banquo is the toast – not merely the subject to whom the drink is dedicated, but also the object – the drink itself. 'thy blood is cold' invokes a horrible distortion of transubstantiation: Macbeth knows that Banquo's blood is cold because he has just tasted it.

The most grotesque enactment which equates the spilling of blood with a banquet occurs in iv.i, the witches' cauldron scene. This is a parody or parallel of the earlier banquet and the juxtaposition of bloodshed and preparing a brew is pointedly made when the witches actually cool the concoction (as if to make it ready for drinking) with 'a baboon's blood' (36) and, as a parallel to Macbeth summoning (inadvertently) Banquo's ghost – they summon (deliberately) the three apparitions by pouring in sow's blood (64–5).

It seems that good blood is mixed with good to achieve a good cause, and vice versa. The sow who has mixed the blood of her offspring with her own by murdering and consuming them – thereby ensuring the end of her strain – is countered by the future mixing of blood suggested by Banquo, who follows the eight kings of Scotland with a prophesying glass in his hand to imply that his blood was sacrificed so that, through his son, it would produce a future line of kings. On another level, Old Siward, the general of the English forces, accepts the sacrifice of his son's blood because he fought bravely in the joint cause of England and Scotland.

It is not merely the act of spilling blood which is important in the play – as in the dedication to Campion's masque – it is the mixing of this blood which is significant. Both Lady Macbeth and Macbeth dip their hands in Duncan's blood: 'My hands are of your colour' (ii.ii.63), but the act is not a true mixing and only brings about their destruction: they die without heirs. Macbeth's words are prophetic when he says that the witches placed 'a fruitless crown' on his head and 'a barren sceptre' in his 'gripe' (iii.i.60–1).

In both the dedication to Campion's masque and the play, the mixing of blood is equated with a very potent drink, so the porter was right in quite another way from the usual sense when he said of drink, 'it provokes the desire, but it takes away the performance' (ii.iii.28–9). Macbeth's desire to shed more blood grows as he desperately tries to safeguard his right to the throne, but conversely, he becomes less and less fit to perform the role of king. His deranged behaviour at the banquet seems to illustrate his earlier comment that murdering Duncan has 'Put rancours in the vessel of my peace' (iii.i.66) – an image (according to the Arden editor's citation of Grierson) drawn from the sacramental cup: the vessel in which body and soul are supposed to unite to achieve peace.

In Campion's masque Diana allowed the trees to be freed by Night because James (Phoebus) decreed that a marriage to achieve peace must take place. As Night said, 'Night must needs yield when Phoebus gets the day' (257). This idea is also present in the promise of a new line of Scottish kings in *Macbeth* – of which James is the latest example. Furthermore, in the process of the trees' transformation, Night instructed them to:

> Frolic, graced captives, we present you here
> This glass, wherein your liberties appear: 262–3

The 'glass' is glossed in Davis's edition of the masque as 'apparently Diana's gem is meant', but this situation is not unlike the procession of kings in *Macbeth* which, according to the 1623 Folio, Banquo follows 'with a glasse in his hand'. Here the glass is also associated with an act of liberation – the freeing of the Scottish line of kings from Macbeth's tyranny. No description has been found of the property used in *Macbeth*: it could have been a crystal glass, a prospective glass, or some kind of mirror (perhaps convex, as was usual then – which would reflect in miniature and would enable the entire circle of kings to be continuously portrayed). In *Measure for Measure* Angelo likens the law to a prophet who 'Looks in a glass' to forestall 'future evils' (II.ii.95–100) and Scot writes of 'strange conclusions in glasses' in *The Discoverie of Witchcraft* (Book XIII, chapter xix). Whichever sort of glass was used in both *Macbeth* and *Lord Hay's Masque*, there would seem to be links with a tradition of prospective glasses used for divination, which was well-known in the drama. Once again, the masque and the play included a similar piece of staging.

Just as the unsophisticated drum effects of *Macbeth* can be seen as a parallel to the music of a masque; so what might have been a very simple dramatic action of throwing down a rough disguise of leafy branches can be contrasted with the sophisticated machinery of Campion's transformation scene:

Presently the sylvans with their four instruments and five voices began to play and sing together the song following, at the beginning whereof that part of the stage whereon the first trees stood began to yield, and the three foremost trees gently to sink, and this was effected by an engine placed under the stage. When the trees had sunk a yard they cleft in three parts, and the masquers appeared out of the tops of them; the trees were suddenly conveyed away, and the first three masquers were raised again by the engine.   331–8

Shakespeare's transformation is less elaborate, but was probably more successful at the time because at the performance on Twelfth Night, the machinery of the masque failed to work as planned. This would not have passed unnoticed and must have been an embarrassment to Campion, who remarked: 'Either by the simplicity, negligence, or conspiracy of the painter, the passing away of the trees was somewhat hazarded the patterne of them the same day having been showne with much admiration, and the nine trees beeing left unsett together even to the same night.'[19] If Shakespeare's play definitely preceded Campion's masque, then this might be seen as an attempt to transform a stage effect from the public stage (which was probably also performed at court) into a piece of grand masque spectacle – an attempt which, ironically, failed. If, however, *Macbeth* came after *Lord Hay's Masque* then there could well be a hint of parody – and Shakespeare's successful, easily obtained effect might remind the courtly elements of his audience of Campion's embarrassment not long before.

Both *Lord Hay's Masque* and *Macbeth* contain political undertones concerning the Anglo-Scottish union,[20] but Shakespeare's tactics seem more forceful and less coyly decorative. The show of kings, for example, has a dual function. In accordance with masque tradition, a compliment to King James is implicit in the procession of his ancestors; yet, to Macbeth, this will seem to be linked to the three apparitions which D. J. Palmer described as 'a diabolical parody of the emblematic pageants and allegorical masques with which royalty was greeted ... often at a banquet', remarking that, as in court entertainments, the principal guest is directly addressed and counsel and flattering assurance offered.[21] Masque-like flattery is not allowed to stand alone in *Macbeth*: the genuine compliment to the real-life king is countered by a sinister parody.

As well as writing a powerful psychological tragedy, a disturbing play of the supernatural, and an imaginative, dramatic excursion into Scottish history which would please his monarch, Shakespeare may also provide a witty commentary on the cross-currents which could occur between the public stage and the court masque. Even if all the links shown here are purely coincidental – and there are a great many to dismiss – then, as the works appeared within months of each other and probably involved some of the same actors from the King's Men, they would still demonstrate, very forcibly, the way writers of the period could start from a pool of shared sources and traditions and transform these into independent, yet associated, topical works of art.

4 · *Pericles*: the old and the new

Pericles is, in many ways, nearer to the pageant than the masque. Like Heywood's *Ages* plays, it is based on an old tale, but its dramatisation was a new departure for Shakespeare: it is the first of what have become known as his last plays. Like *Macbeth*, *Pericles* draws on new as well as old traditions and, in order to understand the play more fully, it is important to view it not only in relation to the older traditions of miracle play and chivalric romance, but also in relation to contemporary influences and popular traditions; for it may be in a fusion of the two that some explanation of *Pericles*'s peculiarly experimental nature lies.

Pericles was entered on the Stationers' Register on 20 May 1608, although the quarto, from which all existing versions sprang, was not published until the following year. The play was, presumably, performed early in 1608, or even late 1607, which would make it contemporary with John Day's collaborative play, *The Travailes of the Three English Brothers* (Stationers' Register June 1607), and with Beaumont's *The Knight of the Burning Pestle*, which followed and satirised the former. Whether or not Day was also involved in the writing of *Pericles*, there is evidence to suggest that this play was influenced to some extent by *The Travailes*,[1] and there may have been a family link if, as has been suggested, Shakespeare's brother Edmund (who died in December 1607) acted in Day's play at the Curtain earlier in that year.[2]

Apart from general similarities – the use of a chorus technique, the episodic nature of the chivalric adventures, and the call to the audience's imagination to make the rapid stage transitions from one country to another – there are specific scenes in the play which suggest links with *Pericles*. In *The Travailes*, two of Sir Thomas Shirley's sons journey to Persia and an exchange between the Sophy's niece and her companion, Dalibra, seems pertinent:

Neece   what dost thou thinke of the two English brothers?
Dal.   I thinke, Madam, if they be as pleasant in tast as they are fayre to the eye, they are a dish worth eating.
Neece   A Caniball, Dalibra? Wouldst eate men?
Dal.   Why not, Madam? fine men cannot choose but bee fine meate.
Neece   I, but they are a filling meat.

Dal.	Why, so are most of your sweet meats; but if a woman have a true appetite to them they'le venter that.
Neece	Ide not be free of that company of Venturers.
Dal.	What, tho their voyages bee somewhat dangerous? they are but short: thei'le finish one of their voyages in forty weekes, and within a month after hoist saile and too't againe for another.
Neece	You sayle cleane from the Compasse, Dalibra: I onely questiond you about the Christians habites and behaviors.[3]

This passage, full of sexual innuendoes is, paradoxically, associated with the Sophy's chaste niece, future wife to the virtuous knight, Robert Shirley. The references to virility and producing children are important because the play ends with their child – the new heir to the Sophy's empire – being christened, and supposedly heralding an empire of Christian offspring which they will produce.[4] Virility is a good subject for comic *risqué* word play, but it is also a serious consideration on which hope for the future depends in the play.

Both of these aspects seem apparent in the banquet in *Pericles* at which the courtship of Thaisa occurs. When Thaisa declares:

> By Juno, that is queen of marriage,
> All viands that I eat do seem unsavoury,
> Wishing him my meat.   II.iii.30–2

her words are part of the same tradition as those of the Sophy's niece. Such word play was especially common in comedies (*Comedy of Errors* II.ii.116–17). In *Pericles*, this comment of Thaisa's is only the first of many highly charged exchanges between father and daughter which parallel the niece's exchanges with Dalibra – Simonides quickly retorts:

> He's but a country gentleman;
> Has done no more than other knights have done;

with its echoes of Hamlet's 'country matters'. Later Simonides prompts Thaisa to approach the stranger and, 'say we drink this standing-bowl of wine to him' (II.iii.65) which, in turn, evokes *Macbeth* and the porter's, 'makes him stand to, and not stand to' (II.iii.33–4).

The word play continues as Simonides requests all the knights to dance:

> I will not have excuse with saying this:
> Loud music is too harsh for ladies' heads,
> Since they love men in arms as well as beds.   II.iii.96–8

After the dance he declares:

> So this was well ask'd, 'twas so well perform'd.
> Come, sir, here's a lady that wants breathing too;
> And I have heard, you knights of Tyre
> Are excellent in making ladies trip,
> And that their measures are as excellent.   II.iii.99–103

An undercurrent of double meanings abounds in relation to the talk of performance, the lady that needs exercise, the knights 'excellent in making ladies trip' and the pun on 'measures'. The word play finally culminates in stage action and a dance between Thaisa and Pericles which suggests a wordless expression of their courtship – carried out before the eyes of all present – in the chaste context of a chivalric setting. As William A. McIntosh infers, it is no accident that Shakespeare makes Simonides end the dance with the words 'Unclasp, unclasp', which deliberately recall the incestuous Antiochus and Pericles's words to him: 'your uncomely claspings with your child' (I.i.29).[5]

This technique would appear to be one of exaggerating the contrast between the two scenes. Here, 'clasp' does not mean the sexual act but, as the staging has made obvious, only the clasping of hands, and by inference, of hearts. Shakespeare borrowed much from Gower's original account of the tale, but departed from his text in this episode – perhaps because a recent contemporary work suggested more interesting possibilities. By demonstrating that a particular set of sexual innuendoes could be successfully associated with a virtuous hero and heroine who were not the subject of humour, Day's play may have paved the way for a development of scenic contrasts in the staging of *Pericles*; for there is a possible parallel to II.iii later in the play in the brothel scene (IV.ii) and, furthermore, both these scenes can, by sexual insinuation, be linked to the earlier episode of Antiochus's daughter.

Like Antiochus's court, the brothel at Mytilene also harbours a woman who is, literally, the death of knights –

Pand. Thou sayest true; there's two unwholesome, a' conscience. The poor Transylvanian is dead, that lay with the little baggage.
Boult Ay, she quickly poop'd him; she made him roast-meat for worms. But I'll go search the market.   IV.ii.19–23

Verbal links with the banquet scene are plentiful: Boult's 'Performance shall follow'; and even the Bawd's words to Marina are associated with her mother's earlier wish:

Yes, indeed shall you, and taste gentlemen of all fashions.   IV.ii.74–5

She goes on:

If it please the gods to defend you by men, then men must comfort you, men must feed you, men stir you up.   IV.ii.87–9

Visually, IV.v and IV.vi contrast with Thaisa's wooing episodes in which many knights vied for one lady. Here the 'cavalleria' of Mytilene also vie for one virgin and are rejected – except one – but the wooing takes a very different form. This complex interplay of scenes may owe some small initial inspiration to *The Travailes*, and as there is another episode in Day's play which appears to be linked to the stagecraft of *Pericles*, the argument is strengthened.

At a time when the younger brother, Robert Shirley, has fallen from favour with the Sophy, the ruler accuses him of being a traitor and attempting an unlawful contract with his niece – to which Shirley replies:

> Yon fire
> That lightens all the world knows my desire
> Durst never look so high.[6]

On being accused once more, he denies it more forcibly:

> Never; for had I harbord such intent
> Nothing cold make me basely to repent:
> But I had never: Any life nor death
> Can make a Christian falsefie his breath.[7]

The Sophy's opinion of him is probably beginning to change at this point but, unlike the corresponding scene in *Pericles* (III.v), the audience does not benefit from the equivalent of Simonides's asides. Moreover, Day's play is much less subtle and the effect he attempts is deliberately more sensational. Shirley is dismissed and the niece is summoned to confront her uncle and a 'counterfeit head like Sherley's'. Even when threatened with death she insists on his virtue:

> his worth recorded stands
> Upon yon file of stars: he has the hands
> Of all the holly Angels to approve
> What bloud ha's spent in quest of Christian love.
> I speake not like a strumpet, that being fild
> With spirit of lust, her owne abuse to gild,
> Slanders her friend: till now I never lov'd him,
> And now by yonder Sunne I dote on him.
> I never heard him vowe, protest or speake
> Word that might his approov'd alleageance breake.
> Oh you have done a deed blacker than night,
> A murther that would murthers foule affright:
> Your very foes will say, when this is knowne,
> In cutting off his head you have scard your owne.
> Were I his brother, country-man, or slave
> Ide kill his murtherer, or digge my grave
> Under the *Sophies* feete: oh you have wone
> The Ire of heaven and hate of Christendome.[8]

The Sophy's mind is, at last, seen to be changed, and the lovers are united – more sensationally, but just as abruptly as Simonides unites Thaisa and Pericles, whom he too had accused of being a traitor:

> Therefore hear you, mistress: either frame
> Your will to mine; and you, sir, hear you:
> Either be rul'd by me, or I'll make you –
> Man and wife.
> Nay, come, your hands and lips must seal it too;
> And being join'd, I'll thus your hopes destroy,
> And for further grief, – God give you joy!   II.v.80–6

In contrast, Day's earlier counterpart concluded:

> Sop.   Then we confesse our spleene ha's done amisse.
> Neece   Redeeme it then, and in his winding sheete
>   Let his dissevered head and body meete:
>   Returne them me, let me the credit have,
>   And lay his mangled body in a grave.
> Sop.   Take it with our best love and furtherance,
>   And having joynde his body to the head
>   His winding sheete be thy chast mariage bed.
>   *Enter Sherley*
> Neece   Then lives young Sherley.
> Sop.   Yea, and still shall stand
>   Lov'd of the Sophy, honor'd in his land:
>   All stiles and offices we late took off
>   We back restore.[9]

The text is similar in both instances and the abrupt reversals indicate a possible link between the plays which were so close chronologically. Again, no such situation exists in Gower's tale – *Pericles*'s main source – so it seems likely that, once more, a fusion of the old tale with a piece of contemporary staging occurred.

Despite the current satires of knights and their adventures in *The Knight of the Burning Pestle* and the associated *Don Quixote* (1605), whose earliest English version probably dates from 1607, Shakespeare chose to write a chivalric romance which proved to be extremely popular – probably both with public and private playhouse audiences. The initial unfavourable response to *The Knight of the Burning Pestle* at Blackfriars may, as Walter Burre, the publisher of the 1613 quarto wrote to his friend, Robert Keysar, have been due to the audience who lacked 'judgement' or did not understand 'the privy mark of irony about it'; but it is also possible that it occurred because there was an unforeseen number of the citizen class whose tastes were being satirised, present in the audience – or even that members of the upper classes were displaying an unaccountable (in his view) liking for the popular chivalric drama and disliked such ridicule, however Quixotic and entertaining.[10] It has to be noted that chivalric subjects were also popular in the court masques of the time – the early Ben Jonson and Inigo Jones masques and others like Campion's *Lord Hay's Masque*.

By choosing to dramatise the tale of *Pericles*, Shakespeare adopted a hero who, at an important point in the play, shared a striking visual resemblance to the satirical figure of Don Quixote. Pericles arrives at the court of King Simonides to take part in the tournament for his daughter's hand wearing the armour bequeathed him by his father, now rusty through its misfortunes at sea. Don Quixote, as many would know, started on his adventures by causing, 'certaine old rusty armes to be scoured, that belonged to his great Grand-father, and lay many ages neglected and forgotten in a by-corner of his house'.[11] Perhaps Cervantes deliberately created an opposite to the knight in shining armour of romantic legend; or perhaps his comment was more specific – being an imitation of romance figures like the 'ill furnisht knight' in Chapter 17 of Sidney's new *Arcadia* who defeats Philantus and is described as having, 'neither picture, nor device, his armour of as old a fashion (besides the rustie poornesse) that it might better seeme a monument of his grand-father's courage'. However, despite possible associations with satirised contemporary plays such as *The Travailes*, *Pericles* defies ridicule and appears to support the current chivalric revival associated with James I's eldest son, Prince Henry. No-one could have envisaged that the young Prince of Wales would die tragically in 1612, and when *Pericles* was written he was still the person in whom rested the best hope for the future of the realm.

Although a number of contemporary plays such as Day's *The Travailes* were nationalistic, and although Gower's original tale in Book VIII of the *Confessio Amantis* also included comments on the duty of a king and prayers for the state and for Richard II, the king of the time – it would be too conjectural to assume that, in *Pericles*, Shakespeare was attempting to supply a lesson for the young future king in the guise of a fairy-tale romance. Even if Prince Henry attended a performance of the play, he would probably have been too young to appreciate the point. Moreover, didacticism is one dramatic flaw of which Shakespeare, unlike some of his contemporaries, cannot be accused. However, it is impossible to ignore the fact that while *Pericles* is not obviously a religious or nationalistic morality play, it does contain certain traces of these elements, subtly integrated into the dramatisation of a quest for perfection and ultimate harmony.

G. Wilson Knight suggested that *Pericles* 'might be called a Shakespearian morality play',[12] and in his Arden edition of the play, F. D. Hoeniger comments on the similarity between the plot of *Pericles* and that of the old play of Mary Magdalen, in particular.[13] *Pericles* is not as didactic as Gower's original tale which is told in the context of showing 'what is to

love in good manere' and moves cyclically from the heavenly love present
at the Creation, man's fall and gradual salvation through earthly love to
the final attainment of redemptive heavenly love at the end of Book VIII.
Yet, in one respect, *Pericles* is also the story of a progression from earthly
perfection to heavenly perfection in the lives of its main characters (a
theme which Shakespeare continues in *Cymbeline*), and in dramatising
this aspect of Gower's material, Shakespeare employs a wide variety of
traditions, including the biblical and the classical.

God's desire to create a perfect world introduces Book VIII of the
Confessio Amantis of which the tale of *Pericles* is a central part. God's
purpose was to replace the angels who had fallen from bliss and the vision
of a Paradise peopled by humans who are fit to replace angels is, therefore, at the heart of Gower's work. As *Pericles* progresses it becomes clear
that the central figures also possess certain saintly characteristics and are
striving towards a similar ideal vision. Gower makes the point quite
obvious when he writes of Apollonius:

> He taketh the Harpe and in his wise
> He tempreth, and of such assise
> Singende he harpeth forth withal,
> That as a vois celestial
> Hem thoghte it souneth in here Ere
> As thogh that he an Angel were.   Book VIII, lines 777–82[14]

In *Pericles* the association is primarily an undercurrent and the transition from earthly to heavenly bliss is largely expressed through the
play's use of music and Pericles's final perception of the music of the
spheres. In relation to the link made (in Chapter 2) between Thaisa,
Venus and Stella Maris, or Mary, who all rose from the sea, it is not
irrelevant to note here that, as Anna B. Jameson shows, the Virgin was
also the 'especial patroness of music and minstrelsy': Saint Cecilia patron-
ised sacred music, but all music and musicians were under the protection
of Mary.[15]

The stress on 'cresce and multiplie' at the beginning of Gower's tale
occurs in the context of increasing the company of angels – of remaking
the Paradisal society – and in *Pericles*, this idea seems to be channelled
into the driving force of survival which runs throughout the play in the
lives of the virtuous characters. In this respect *Pericles* appears to dramatise a process of divine selection. The principal reason which Pericles gives
for his journey to Antioch is to:

> purchase . . . a glorious beauty,
> From whence an issue I might propagate,
> Are arms to princes and bring joys to subjects.   I.ii.72–4

Like the aim of the Creator in the *Confessio Amantis*, his purpose is to secure the future of a good society.

As the visual impact of the first scene stresses, Antiochus's daughter is not the woman to be the mother of a thriving state. As she enters, 'apparell'd like the spring', her background is provided by the heads of dead men – displayed like hunters' trophies. As McIntosh indicates, Pericles's words relating her to the distortion of heavenly music imply that Antiochus and his daughter, 'are engaged not only in the "olde daunce" of lust but also in the dance of death'.[16] Pericles calls her 'a fine viol':

> and your sense the strings,
> Who, finger'd to make man his lawful music,
> Would draw heaven down and all the gods to hearken;
> But being play'd upon before your time,
> Hell only danceth at so harsh a chime.
>   [*Turning towards the princess*]
> Good sooth, I care not for you.   1.i.82–7

Visually the heads reinforce his words. They represent all her previous would-be partners, now removed from the dance, and as she moves down the long stage to the accompaniment of music, it must seem to the audience that she is coming to claim Pericles as her next partner in the fatal dance. This scene, apart from being a powerful emblem of the dance of death, and a striking dramatisation of Gower's narrative, also provides a contrast with II.iii when Pericles accepts Simonides's invitation to dance with Thaisa, his future wife, at the climax of a scene which has dispelled all notions of death and destruction by its concentration on life and fertility. As Sir Thomas Elyot wrote in *The Boke Named the Governour* (1531), 'And for as moche as by the association of a man and a woman in daunsinge may be signified matrimonie, I coulde in declarynge the dignitie and commodite of that sacrament make intiere volumes, if it were nat so communely knowen to all men'.[17] The contrast between the two scenes is further stressed when the banquet scene is immediately followed by Gower's account of the destruction of Antiochus and his daughter: it is almost as if a curse has been lifted.

The contrast between Antiochus's daughter and Thaisa can also be related to the Renaissance adoption of Plato's idea that there were two Aphrodite or Venus figures and that the love which emanated from the common Aphrodite was apt to move men more likely to love the body than the soul, whereas the love of the heavenly Aphrodite was faithful and not wanton – expressing a life-long devotion of a higher nature. Two Renaissance paintings which show these figures are Botticelli's *Primavera* and his *Birth of Venus*. The heavenly Venus is born from the sea – as is

Thaisa, whereas the Venus of the *Primavera* represents the earthly goddess. The transition between the two is made by the change in settings – Edgar Wind elucidates:

The transition from the elemental to the pastoral setting is defined by the flowered mantle of Spring which is spread over Venus as she approaches the earth. In the Platonic scale of things this is a descent, a vulgarisation; for the wealth of colours and variety of shapes that delight the eye when it perceives beauty on earth are but a veil behind which the splendour of the pure celestial beauty is concealed.[18]

Antiochus's daughter, like the Venus of the *Primavera*, is 'apparell'd like the spring', and she is associated with Venus by Pericles when he says, 'See, where she comes ... Graces her subjects' (I.i.13–14), for the Graces did traditionally accompany Venus. However, unlike the goddess in the painting, she does not have a background of trees hung with golden fruit like the fruit of the Hesperides, to which both her father and Pericles liken her. Instead, she stands in front of a cluster of heads, 'Yon sometimes famous princes ... with speechless tongues and semblance pale ... martyrs slain in Cupid's wars' (I.i.35–9): neither Cupid nor the Graces are present here, yet they are evoked in the imagery. A distortion of the earthly Venus figure is apparent in this scene through various explicit associations.

Shakespeare probably never saw Botticelli's paintings, but Venus and the Graces are mentioned in Spenser's *Faerie Queene* (VI.x) and such references are common in Renaissance literature.[19] Thaisa's rebirth could be linked to the birth of Venus from the sea even if Botticelli's painting did not exist, for both the Greeks and the Romans depicted Venus rising from a shell and the myth was well-known.[20] Not only does the combination of fire and sea water used in effecting Thaisa's rebirth provide the warm and moist characteristics commonly associated with Venus, but it is also significant that Pericles stresses that his dead queen will rest with 'simple shells'.

Peter and Linda Murray argue: 'Italian art of the fifteenth and sixteenth centuries, even when treating a "classical" subject, is entirely Christian in its roots and in its meaning.'[21] It is possible that, in *Pericles*, Shakespeare was attempting a similar blend of traditions. Pericles's meeting with Thaisa heralds the unification of two well-governed, godly states, whereas the heads of the first scene provide a visual statement that Antiochus's daughter deprives states of their heirs, rather than provides them. The guilty secret of incest is shown to signify a perverted unhealthy family structure which might, directly or indirectly, risk the future of a whole people. In Gower's original work, man's expulsion from Paradise is followed by an account of the history of mankind on earth, involving the Flood and God's covenant and forgiveness. One of the ways in which

God's laws were broken after this time was by the continued practice of incest – allowable only in the former age because of practical necessity, but since abandoned in the new age of Abraham and his descendants. Gower's story of Apollonius begins as a lesson against incest, so Pericles, who condemns Antiochus's guilt, is upholding the laws of Abraham and the new age, while Antiochus and his daughter are representatives of a bygone era which must not be allowed to threaten a world which has renewed its covenant with its creator and is striving once again towards the perfection of his original intention.

Shakespeare's treatment of the Antiochus episode differs from that of Gower, and it is clear that Shakespeare's interest did not lie in looking back to the old ways, either in relation to the biblical incest subject on which Gower dwells, or in relation to the old theatrical devices which could be used to dramatise its elimination. If he had wished, Shakespeare's theatre could have presented the deaths of Antiochus and his daughter as a gripping piece of spectacle. As Philip Brockbank noticed,[22] Greene and Lodge's *A Looking-Glass for London and England* staged a similar effect in the early 1590s. In this play Rasni, King of Nineveh, plans to marry his sister Remilia, but just before the ceremony she is killed on the stage with the direction: '*Lightning and thunder wherewith Remilia is strooken*' (Sc.v.529).[23] Even in the 1590s this morality play technique may have appeared unsophisticated: '*He drawes the Curtaines and finds her stroken with Thunder, blacke*' (Sc.v.551). Later in the same play another purge occurs when the disowned mother of the court favourite prays for vengeance on her ungrateful son:

> *Samia.* Oh all you heavens, and you eternall powers . . .
> Poure downe the tempest of your direful plagues
> Upon the head of cursed Radagon.
> *Upon this praier she departeth, and a flame of fire appeareth from beneath, and Radagon is swallowed.*   Sc.ix.1224–31

Such old-fashioned sensational effects were rejected by Shakespeare in dramatising *Pericles*, although they were still being practised as late as 1611–12 in Thomas Heywood's *Ages* plays. Shakespeare's intention was obviously not to achieve purely sensational effect by dramatising an old idea using a dated technique: his aim seems instead, to be concerned with moving forward with those in the play who are looking towards a more ideal vision, and to dramatise their struggles in overcoming various ordeals along the way. Antiochus and his daughter are, literally, written off: it is with Pericles and his line that undistracted dramatic interest must lie.

In the *Confessio Amantis*, once the tale of Apollonius has been told, the

Confessor seems to indicate that part of the tale – Pericles's shipwreck – is
an important metaphor:

> For conseil passeth alle thing
> To him which thenkth to ben a king;
> And every man for his partie
> A kingdom hath to justefie,
> That is to sein his oghne dom.
> If he misreule that kingdom,
> He lest himself, and that is more
> Than if he loste Schip and Ore
> And al the worldes good withal:
> For what man that in special
> Hath noght himself, he hath noght elles,
> Nomor the perles than the schelles;
> Al is to him of o value:
> Thogh he hadde at his retenue
> The wyde world riht as he wolde,
> Whan he his herte hath noght withholde
> Toward himself, al is in vein.
>
> Book VIII, lines 2109–25[24]

By increasing the number of fishermen and introducing lively metaphorical dialogue, Shakespeare adds to the impact of this episode in the
play; and by putting philosophy into the mouths of humble fishermen, he
supplies an emblematic undercurrent to their comic, low-life roles which
is similar to his treatment of the gardeners in *Richard II*.[25] The storm itself
is not dramatised – perhaps because Shakespeare's skill in this direction
was yet to develop and attain its height at the opening of *The Tempest*; or
perhaps because, like the deaths of Antiochus and his daughter, it would
have involved unnecessary sensationalism. As the metaphor (to which
Gower draws attention) indicates, it is not the storm itself which is
important, but its results – Pericles washed ashore destitute, without
'Schip and Ore' and lacking 'al the worldes good', yet still able, with the
fishermen's help, to summon his spirits, rescue his father's armour, and
have enough faith in himself to continue his quest. Like John Levay, I do
not think it 'too far-fetched' to suggest 'that in this scene, so full of Biblical
echoes, the incident of Pericles' armour, which he inherited from his
father, echoes the "armour of the Lord" in the New Testament – e.g.
Ephesians, vi.1off'.[26]

Gower stresses the significance of this episode only indirectly, by
relating it to the metaphor in the lines quoted earlier: Shakespeare
manages to dramatise it in deliberately metaphorical terms. Not only does
he put the most striking dialogue on the dangers of humanity preying on
itself into the mouths of the fishermen – thereby making this scene the

centre of an ongoing theme in the play, but he also accumulates a wealth
of biblical connotations in bringing fishermen onto the stage who are,
almost literally, 'fishers of men' – except that their net contains, not an
actual man, but his shell or armour. Above all, these men serve a king
called Simonides, whom Gower named Artestrates and Twine, Alti-
strates: only Wilkins's novel, believed to be based on Shakespeare's
play, uses the former name, and perhaps Shakespeare's reason for
deliberately deviating from the names in his sources was because 'Simonides' is easily associated with Simon Peter, the fisherman leader of the
disciples and the gate-keeper of Paradise. In this last respect the undercurrent provides an obvious additional reason for contrasting the scenes
at his court with the brothel scenes where Boult is twice accused of
being a 'damned door-keeper' (IV.vi.118; 164), with implications of
Hell.

The scene of the fishermen is full of biblical associations. The image of
the whale which swallows men suggests Jonah's adventure, and this
biblical agent is recalled at Thaisa's sea-burial with the reference to the
'belching whale'. Jonah was a popular dramatic character and played a
prominent part in Greene and Lodge's *A Looking-Glass*, in which a ship
was also caught in a storm: '*Enter the merchants of Tharsus, the M[aster]
of the ship, and some sailers, wet from the sea; with them the Governour
of Joppa.*' Although Shakespeare apparently rejected this play's sensational staging of an incest purge, he did adopt a similar, more simple old
stage technique to express the aftermath of his tempest through the stage
direction: '*Enter Pericles, wet.*' In the old play, Jonas is cast into the sea to
save the ship from wrecking in the storm, in accordance with the sailors'
superstition, and in this respect the incident parallels that of casting
Thaisa overboard in the storm in *Pericles* and may have suggested the
image of the 'belching whale' in the latter episode.

Unlike the allusions in the *Confessio Amantis*, the biblical connotations
in *Pericles* take the form of a symbolic undercurrent. God is not an
obvious presence, as in the former work. Shakespeare deliberately secula-
rised the tale through his substitution of the goddess Diana for God, and
his refusal to indulge in the didactic moralising which Gower enjoyed and
which is also present in other sixteenth and early seventeenth-century
drama – including *A Looking-Glass*. *Pericles* is concerned with the victory
of good over evil, but it is not a hell-fire sermon: it differs considerably
from Greene and Lodge's play, as Jonas's last speech demonstrates:

> London, awake, for feare the Lord do frowne.
> I set a looking Glasse before thine eyes,
> O turne, o turne, with weeping to the Lord,

And thinke the praiers and vertues of thy Queene,
Defers the plague which otherwise would fall.
Repent O London, least for thine offence,
Thy shepheard faile, whom mightie God preserve;
That she may bide the pillar of his Church
Against the stormes of Romish Anti Christ;
The hand of mercy overshead her head,
And let all faithful subjects, say Amen.   Sc. xx.2399–409

This moralising tradition is not blatantly present in *Pericles*, although it was still being pursued by Thomas Heywood in the *Ages* plays as late as 1613.

The secularisation which occurs in *Pericles* is an important adaptation of Gower's source. In a note on Diana in the *Dramatis Personae*, F. D. Hoeniger remarks: 'The goddess is referred to only twice in Gower and in Twine, but about a dozen times in the play, which may be significant.'[27] This would seem to be an enormous understatement. In the *Confessio Amantis*, Thaisa's equivalent had a mother, but when he dramatised the tale Shakespeare omitted her character. It could be argued that he was merely attempting to achieve dramatic symmetry in providing yet another father and daughter relationship for comparison with that of Antiochus and his fated offspring, foreshadowing Pericles's own role with Marina; and it is true that fathers and daughters had an important place in Shakespeare's dramatic development: such relationships occur frequently from *Titus Andronicus* in the early 1590s, evolving through various stages in *A Midsummer Night's Dream*, *The Merchant of Venice*, *As You Like It*, *Hamlet*, *Othello*, *King Lear* and *The Winter's Tale*, to culminate in the dramatisation of Prospero and Miranda in *The Tempest*; and the idea is also present in *Henry VIII*. However, apart from these considerations, it seems that Shakespeare carefully deprived the play of an active mother-figure. Until the end, none of the characters have such a guardian – the role is supplied by Diana, who plays a central part throughout.

Only Lychorida, in her role as Thaisa's midwife and Marina's nurse, comes close to providing an earthly mother substitute and, as Pericles's words in iii.i indicate, Lychorida, the earthly midwife, is clearly linked to Lucina, the goddess of childbirth – which is also another name for Diana, at whose temple Thaisa eventually takes sanctuary. When Thaisa is in labour during the tempest, Pericles calls for Lychorida who does not, at first, respond. In the same breath he calls to Lucina, who apparently does hear him, for when Lychorida enters at last, she carries his child:

Lychorida! – Lucina, O
Divinest patroness, and midwife gentle
To those that cry by night, convey thy deity

> Aboard our dancing boat; make swift the pangs
> Of my queen's travails! Now, Lychorida!
> *Enter* LYCHORIDA [*with an infant*].   III.i.10–14

The tiny child which Lychorida holds is a visual dramatisation of the fragmentation which has occurred in his family. Instead of a healthy wife and child, all Lychorida offers him is:

> this piece
> Of your dead queen.   III.i.17–18

The cost of 'making swift the pangs' of Thaisa's travails has been her life. Pericles called on Lucina to 'convey thy deity aboard our dancing boat', and it seems that her influential presence is implied, since not only does the child arrive immediately after Pericles's invocation, but later the coffin in which Thaisa is put to sea, as if by divine intervention, finds its way to Ephesus, the home of Diana, goddess of growth; the great fertility mother who is, by tradition, worshipped by magical rites – of which Cerimon seems to have some knowledge. It is no coincidence that Thaisa's first words on reviving are, 'O dear Diana' (III.ii.106). These words do not appear in Gower's tale. The miracle is not, as Gower suggests, that Thaisa is fortunate to be found by a clever physician, but rather that, having died, Diana in her role as Lucina the midwife, causes her to be returned to a surrogate womb, to be buried in a casket and, after a sea journey, be born again – once the right conditions are created.

This event is staged symbolically, and Jonson's masque *Hymenaei* (1606) helps to illuminate Cerimon's use of fire in the rebirth. As Reason indicates, fire and water together are potent in any rebirth process:

> *Reason* The tede of white and blooming thorn
> In token of increase is borne,
> As also with the ominous light
> To fright all malice from the night.
> Like are the fire and water set,
> That, even as moisture mixed with heat
> Helps every natural birth to life,
> So, for their race, join man and wife.   158–65[28]

This belief is also found in Ovid's *Metamorphoses*:

> For when that moysture with the heat is tempred equally,
> They doe conceyve, and of them twaine engender by and by
> All kinde of things. For though that fire with water aye debateth
> Yet moysture mixt with equall heate all living things createth.[29]

In the marriage procession in *Hymenaei* there are two singers – one of whom carries fire, the other, water. Thaisa has been surrounded by water and, by ordering fire to be brought, Cerimon completes the rite. He also, rather mysteriously, asks for cloths. In Gower's tale, these were heated and laid on the body to warm it, and it seems significant that Cerimon talks of an Egyptian who was revived in this way, since in the Egyptian system of hieroglyphics, bandages or cloths possess a double symbolism – 'embracing both the swaddling-clothes of a new born babe and the winding-sheet of the corpse in the tomb'.[30] This episode abounds in symbolism, both ancient and biblical: the casket is associated with the ark, with rebirth, sanctuary and survival. It is linked to the legends of Adonis, Moses, Perseus and Tammuz. Above all, it seems to be a female symbol, signifying not only the womb, but also the Christian Church and Mary, the mother of Jesus.[31] By stressing the significance of Diana's role in the play, Shakespeare allows this episode and the female symbolism to suggest a demonstration of the powers of the many-sided goddess.

Diana, in one respect, is not merely a surrogate mother, but actually causes Thaisa's rebirth – if insinuations are to be followed. The coffin or ark as a symbol in relation to a church or sanctuary is also present in Thaisa's voluntary 'burial' from the world in the Temple of Diana, and it is interesting to note that Diana's Temple at Ephesus was considered one of the seven wonders of the ancient world – a fitting setting for Shakespeare's own miraculous revelation. Thaisa only emerges from the temple when Diana has reunited her with Pericles, and in one sense Pericles was inaccurate when he declared, upon finding her:

> o come, be buried
> A second time within these arms.   v.iii.43–4

for this last, most pleasant 'burial' was, in some ways, her third; and as it also symbolised a return to her old life and the life of the outside world, the dual symbolism in the burial metaphor – embracing both life and death – becomes clear in a fusion of verbal and visual expression.

Diana is far more important in Shakespeare's play than in Gower's original, where Thaisa's counterpart merely requests to retire to:

> some temple of the Cite,
> To kepe and holde hir chastete,   Book VIII, lines 1243–4[32]

and it is later reported that she has gone to Diana's Temple – although, unlike Shakespeare's dramatisation, the goddess never becomes a character in the narrative.

In *Pericles* Diana seems to be important for more than her associations with birth – she is a complete goddess of Lucina, Diana, and the Greek Artemis of Ephesus. Most of the vows in the play, which in Gower's tale were made to God, are here made to Diana. In II.v Simonides tells the knights that Thaisa has vowed that, 'One twelve moons more she'll wear Diana's livery', and whether this is meant to be Thaisa's own invention or is merely spoken by Simonides without her knowledge, to disperse her suitors, is not clear. It does not occur in Gower's tale. In *Pericles* the vow is not talked of lightly:

> This by the eye of Cynthia hath she vow'd,
> And on her virgin honour will not break it.   II.v.10–11

and yet it is broken in Simonides's next speech:

> She tells me here, she'll wed the stranger knight,
> Or never more to view nor day nor light.   II.v.16–17

The vow to Diana was Shakespeare's invention and it seems more than coincidence that when Diana is later invoked, as Lucina in III.i, the payment she seems to exact for the swift deliverance of the child is the fulfilment of the vow – that Thaisa will indeed wear Diana's livery and serve in her temple.[33] When she revives, it is, again, not by chance that Thaisa immediately calls to Diana. She is obviously the mysterious force behind much of the play's unexplained action. In III.iii Pericles vows, 'By bright Diana, whom we honour' that his hair shall not be cut until Marina's wedding day – and unlike Thaisa's vow, this is not broken. In Gower's narrative a similar vow was made to God, but here, his wild appearance on stage is not only an indication of his disturbed emotional state, but is also a constant reminder of his faithfulness to the goddess. The couple are closely linked to the deity and she appears to exert a powerful influence on their child, Marina, who successfully appeals to her in IV.iii with 'Diana, aid my purpose'.

When the goddess eventually appears to Pericles in person, in a vision, it is, therefore, not an example of *Deus ex machina* staging, for an awareness of the importance of her presence has been growing steadily throughout the play. The unification of the family takes place with thanks to Diana, and only after a reassertion of Pericles's loyalty to her does he terminate his vow – the conditions having been fulfilled:

> Pure Dian,
> I bless thee for thy vision, and will offer
> Night-oblations to thee. Thaisa,
> This prince, the fair betrothed of your daughter,
> Shall marry her at Pentapolis. And now
> [   ] this ornament
> Makes me look dismal will I clip to form;
> And what this fourteen years no razor touch'd
> To grace thy marriage-day I'll beautify.   v.iii.68–76

5   The Cheek by Jowl Theatre Company in *Pericles* (1984), directed by Declan Donnellan and Nick Ormerod. Sadie Shimmin (Diana) and Andrew Collins (Pericles): Diana appears beneath her image which has been on stage throughout the play. Photo: Peter Mareš.

Diana appears as a guardian to the whole family – her influence being particularly associated with birth and marriage. Her good influence is set against the false care of Marina by Dionyza and the Bawd, who are both defeated by the purity and strength of a girl who is described by Gower's chorus in terms which link her to 'immortal Dian':

> She sings like one immortal, and she dances
> As goddess-like to their admired lays.   v.3–4

These lines suggest the concealed guardianship, especially as Marina is saved from death at Leonine's hands by pirates whose surprise entrance might seem merely another coincidence (as indeed it is in Gower's work), if it is not noted that their landing by chance was probably dictated by sea conditions and that Diana, in her role as Cynthia, goddess of chastity – in which she was protecting Marina – was represented by the moon, the controller of tides. In 1984, the touring company, Cheek by Jowl,[34] gave an excellent performance of the play with a minimum of properties and only very basic distinguishing costumes: Thaisa and Dionyza were played by the same actress, Sadie Shimmin, contrasting real mother and evil guardian. The concealed guardianship of Diana (played by Dierdrie Edwards, who also played the Bawd) was dramatised at the end of iv.ii in a particularly imaginative way when Marina, in a desperate attempt to save her virginity, cried, 'Diana aid my purpose' as she sprang on to the multi-purpose platform, then representing a bed in the brothel – her hands clasped in prayer. Suddenly she became a statue as the Bawd's words faded into those of Dionyza, talking to Cleon at the foot of Marina's monument in Tharsus.

Through the central use of the Diana image, Shakespeare has provided the play with a complex symbolic structure which adds a new dimension to Gower's narrative events. Diana is, therefore, associated with the otherwise apparently ambivalent role of the sea. It could be argued that Diana, as Artemis, goddess of growth, took Pericles to Tharsus to save the starving population; as goddess of fertility, she shipwrecked him on the shore of Pentapolis, which led him to his future wife; as goddess of childbirth, she delivered his child and caused his wife to be reborn; and as goddess of chastity, she protected his child until she could be married. Hoeniger's earlier comment illustrates that Diana's symbolic significance in this play is usually underestimated. The entrance of the goddess on stage in v.i has been prepared throughout the course of the play and the final vision is a way, at last, of revealing to the audience the figure behind the miraculous events of the story.

In *A Midsummer Night's Dream*, Diana's many-sided character was

6 The Cheek by Jowl Theatre Company in *Pericles* (1984). Amanda Harris (Marina), Sadie Shimmin (Dionyza) and Duncan Bell (Cleon): the statue of Marina at Tharsus. Photo: Peter Mareš.

explored through Shakespeare's different treatment of the moon image which encompassed chastity, fertility, and childbirth: in *Pericles* he seems to have developed what, in the earlier play, was only one of several themes, until it became an underlying unifying factor of both poetry and staging. The importance of Diana in *Pericles* also reveals Shakespeare's fascination with the composite Venus/Diana symbol which he later developed in *Cymbeline*. Diana's many-sided character and her role as unifier of lovers links her with this popular Renaissance dual personification; and the link is made even more specific in her association with the sea and with Thaisa's rebirth.

When Pericles's last speech to his dead queen is examined it appears to contain more than one hint as to the play's later developments. Not only does he talk of the 'belching whale' who threw Jonah safe ashore in an earlier tale (and 'belched' is the term Cerimon uses when the chest is washed ashore), but there is also the implication that Pericles is mistaken to relinquish all hope for Thaisa since, from a simple shell, and out of the sea, the goddess of love was born. If Shakespeare's adoption of Diana instead of the Christian God of Gower's tale seems a strange development, it may appear less unusual if it is remembered that secularisation of religious romances was common and that religious material in the drama had been subject to certain constraints since the days of Elizabeth I, and was often avoided in case misunderstandings arose concerning dogma. More importantly, at this particular time in James I's reign, there is evidence to suggest a nostalgic hearkening back to the days of the old queen, and a corresponding disillusionment with James's court. This is apparent in plays such as Thomas Heywood's *If You Know Not Me* (1605), Dekker's *Whore of Babylon* (1607), and Day's *The Travailes* (1607).[35]

The revival of interest in Elizabeth I, the chaste figure who had also long been associated with Diana, and with the composite Venus/Diana character, seems particularly significant in relation to *Pericles*, for this hint of disillusionment with James might well be one of the reasons why an apparently old-style play which glorified a goddess associated with the old queen, and dealt with a world in which states were finally brought to live in harmony and prosperity under her guardianship, was so popular. Diana, therefore, is, in more ways than one, a prominent symbolic force; drawing together a wealth of traditions – both ancient and contemporary.

In Gower's narrative, *Pericles* was a tale which involved certain uncomplicated metaphors: in Shakespeare's dramatisation, the poetic substance of the work is increased by an intensification of its metaphorical quality – often culminating in the surprising visual reversal of an image on the stage. In this technique reversals are often used to point to contrasts: in the first scene Antiochus warns Pericles that he is driving headlong into 'death's net' (1.i.41). At this point in the play this is a threatening image, but at the beginning of the second act, the image is reversed and Pericles is not caught in a symbolic death's net; instead, an actual fishermen's net enables him to salvage a remnant of his inheritance. It is not a destructive trap, but a means to salvation:

> Thanks, Fortune, yet, that after all thy crosses
> Thou giv'st me somewhat to repair myself;   II.i.120–1

Similarly, in 1.i.78, Pericles describes Antiochus's daughter as 'this glorious casket stor'd with ill', which recalls Pandora's box and the evils that

could be released into the world;[36] then in III.ii the image is reversed and
visualised when Cerimon discovers the perfumed body of virtuous Thaisa,
richly clothed and lying with jewels inside a common chest. The impression given is that characters are helpless to control these reversals, yet
although they never know what might confront them next, there is an
underlying sense of purpose. Fate or the presiding goddess allocates to
each according to their needs or deserts in a particular situation. The
world of the play seems unpredictable, but not without a pattern. This
involves a symbolic structure and the visualisation of images found in the
text, suggesting a controlling hand outside the immediate action of the
play.

   Moreover, Diana was also goddess of woods and forests, so yet another
string of references can be integrated. In I.i Pericles ironically associates
Antiochus's daughter with the tree in the garden of Paradise, or in Venus's
garden – for even if he had been allowed to 'taste the fruit of yon celestial
tree' (I.i.22) he would unknowingly have introduced the taint of evil into
his, otherwise uncorrupted, state. The image also invokes the tree of the
Hesperides which, appropriately, was guarded by a dragon. This image is
countered in the same scene by Antiochus's reference to Pericles as a 'fair
tree' (I.i.114) and the insinuation is of a long genealogical heritage as well
as Pericles's own attributes. This idea is later developed in I.ii.31 when the
whole of Pericles's state is seen as a forest, threatened by Antiochus's
wrath –

> Our men be vanquish'd ere they do resist,
> And subjects punish'd that ne'er thought offence:
> Which care of them, not pity of myself, –
> Who am no more but as the tops of trees
> Which fence the roots they grow by and defend them –   I.ii.28–32

Helicanus echoes this view when he compares Pericles's subjects looking
up to him with the plants who

> look up to heaven, from whence
> They have their nourishment.   I.ii.56–7

All these images are finally recalled on stage in the motto which Pericles
takes to present to Thaisa at the tournament –

> A wither'd branch, that's only green at top;
> The motto, *In hac spe vivo*.   II.ii.42–3

'In this hope I live' is a fitting motto for the ruler in search of a wife who
will provide children and give the withered branch of state new life and
roots. It is also an appropriate symbol for the man whose hopes of

happiness ultimately depend on the goddess of the forest. Viewed in relation to the accumulation of other details, its significance goes far beyond the superficial references to his present state which Simonides mentions:

> A pretty moral;
> From the dejected state wherein he is
> He hopes by you his fortunes yet may flourish   II.ii.44–6

Not only Pericles's own personal hopes, but those of his country are involved here, for Marina, the issue of the marriage (described as 'a sapling', IV.ii.85) is eventually to rule the country of Tyre (V.iii.82). This unsophisticated dramatic property of a withered branch – green at the top – is one of the play's most poignant symbols of survival.

This play dramatises many aspects of survival – the survival of Pericles, the king, from a treacherous plot; the survival of Pericles, the man, in the shipwreck; the survival of Thaisa after death; the physical survival of Marina against threat of murder; her moral survival in the brothel; the collective survival of the family, finally reunited, and the survival of the state – kept together in Pericles's absence by Helicanus. All these struggles for survival are placed in the wider context of the universe by Shakespeare's use of the familiar image of the tempest in the play's imagery and staging.

As a metaphor, the ideas has a long tradition in literature, but in *Pericles* it is more than an isolated piece of allegory. As in *King Lear* and *Macbeth*, the tempest is an integral part of the play's structure. At the beginning of the play it is merely an image as Pericles considers how he might save his country from becoming a victim of Antiochus's wrath, in terms of stopping 'this tempest ere it came' (I.ii.98). In a different context Pericles appears on stage as the victim of an actual storm which has deprived him of all his men, ships, and possessions, and provides a metaphor associated with that of Gower's narrative: as Shakespeare's Gower says,

> I'll show you those in trouble's reign,
> Losing a mite, a mountain gain.   II.7–8

Pericles loses all worldly goods, but salvages his integrity and wins Thaisa. The insinuation that Neptune and Diana, the moon, control the tempests which, in turn, direct the main actions of the play, is at the heart of *Pericles*. The tempest at the time of Marina's birth appears to have moulded her personality, for her entrance to the world was not peaceful – unlike the birth of Antiochus's daughter, of whom it is said:

> to glad her presence,
> The senate-house of planets all did sit
> To knit in her their best perfections.   I.i.10–12

However, this 'conception' was beautiful but evil. Marina, on the other hand, was born when the north wind blew and the waves and wind were 'never ... more violent' (IV.i.59). Accordingly, her greatest characteristic, greater even than her beauty, is her strength of character. As the Bawd's words imply in IV.ii, the women of the brothel are both morally and physically weak:

> The stuff we have, a strong wind will blow it to pieces.   IV.ii.17–18

Marina, however, is able to withstand such tempests, being a product of them. The tempest as an underlying image and as a development in the plot is associated with both suffering and redemption, and its supernatural aspect – strikingly present in *Macbeth*, a play quite near *Pericles* chronologically – is also an important undercurrent. As in *Macbeth* and in *King Lear*, the tempest image has a wide scope: in its broadest sense it evokes an expression of the whole universe; in its narrowest, it focuses on the internal turmoils of one man. As Gower says of Pericles in the episode at Marina's tomb:

> He bears
> A tempest, which his mortal vessel tears,
> And yet he rides it out.   IV.iv.29–31

Pericles has, like Macbeth, become a vessel in a storm; and although both try to ride out the storm, only Pericles succeeds because the gods are on his side and, being virtuous, he has proved himself worthy of being saved. Despite his final courageous stand, Macbeth has lost his integrity: he and Pericles are at opposite ends of the metaphor cited in Gower's narrative:

> And every man for his partie
> A kingdom hath to justefie,
> That is to sein his oghne dom.
> If he misreule that kingdom,
> He lest himself, and that is more
> Than if he loste Schip and Ore
> And al the worldes good withal:
> For what man that in special
> Hath noght himself, he hath noght elles, ...
> Al is to him of o value: Book VIII, lines 2111–21[37]

The climax of the use of the tempest image in *Pericles* occurs in v.i – the meeting of Marina and her father. It is an important piece of staging not only in this respect, but also because it brings about the first, and probably most moving part of the uniting of the family, and also because, visually, it recalls a previous moving scene in the play – the death of Thaisa, the missing figure in the reunion. The Cheek by Jowl production was

7 The Cheek by Jowl Theatre Company in *Pericles* (1984). Amanda Harris (Marina) and Andrew Collins (Pericles): Marina singing to a shrouded Pericles. Photo: Peter Mareš.

particularly fine: portraying strong mutual suffering, it forced the audience to experience every gradation in the painful struggle of reliving loss and, finally, recognising joy. Andrew Collins's Pericles emerged from shroud-like wrappings to reject and mentally torture the daughter he later gratefully acknowledged. The original staging of v.i is unclear as the stage directions are sparse, but it seems possible that Pericles may have lain on stage in the discovery space, almost as if he were dead:

> A man who for this three months hath not spoken
> To any one, nor taken sustenance
> But to prorogue his grief. v.i.24–6

He would give the impression of an emaciated man in a coma of grief and, lying as if lifeless in the curtained off area at the back of the stage, the scene might well recall Thaisa's sojourn in the coffin. She was cast adrift in a vessel which acted as an ark and took her to safety: Pericles's vessel or ark is his own body, framed in the confined stage recess. Like Thaisa, he is floating in a storm and will be rescued – in his case, by Marina, the daughter he supposes returned from the dead:

> O Helicanus, strike me, honour'd sir!
> Give me a gash, put me to present pain,
> Lest this great sea of joys rushing upon me
> O'erbear the shores of my mortality,
> And drown me with their sweetness.   v.i.190–4

As Pericles is revived from his death-like state in a tempest metaphor caused by Marina, the recollection of Thaisa's burial is a powerful image; for, to Pericles, Marina, at first, seems to be a reincarnation of his dead wife, and the terms in which he describes Marina hint at his last sight of her mother in the coffin:

> Her stature to an inch; as wand-like straight;
> As silver-voic'd; her eyes as jewel-like
> And cas'd as richly;   v.i.109–11

Thaisa, richly clothed and surrounded by jewels, resembled an icon – yet another of the statues in the play which represent living people – like that of Pericles at Tharsus, and that of Marina. When Cerimon saw that Thaisa lived, he too used the imagery of the jewel or loved beautiful object which had been lost and was now restored:

> She is alive!
> Behold, her eyelids, cases to those
> Heavenly jewels which Pericles hath lost,
> Begin to part their fringes of bright gold.
> The diamonds of a most praised water
> Doth appear to make the world twice rich.   iii.ii.99–104

Act v.i contains references to all the burials in the play – Pericles's own, enforced burial in grief, Marina's supposed burial in the tomb at Tharsus, and the sea burial of Thaisa. It also contains all the seeds of their reunion, for after Pericles and Marina are united, the music of the spheres heralds the vision of Diana telling Pericles to go to Ephesus. The staging at the beginning of the scene, of Pericles in his death-like state, is important because only by visually reinforcing the image of 'burial' and verbally recalling the image of the tempest, can the full dramatic power of rebirth be realised – and, like Thaisa, Pericles does undergo a new birth, as he shows when he addresses Marina: 'Thou that beget'st him that did thee beget' (v.i.195).

The transition from earthly to heavenly happiness, on the other hand, is

8 The Cheek by Jowl Theatre Company in *Pericles* (1984): Diana's temple. The doors of the earlier image of Diana have opened to show the goddess with outstretched arms. Photo: Peter Mareš.

made particularly through the play's use of music. This culminates in the heavenly music of the spheres in v.i – perhaps heard by Pericles, Marina, and the audience, but not by the other characters on stage.[38] Like the tempest image, this progression builds up throughout the play: it begins with the music associated with the dance of death which announced the arrival of Antiochus's daughter. At Simonides's court, the knights' dance (which John P. Cutts believes to have been a mock combat and fertility rite 'matachine' dance)[39] and the dance of Pericles and Thaisa signify life's triumphs over the death associations of the earlier scene; and the life-giving qualities of music are also apparent in its use to revive the dead queen. Finally it is the music of the spheres which not only announces the vision of Diana (as Jupiter's vision is announced in *Cymbeline*), but also indicates Pericles's elevated state and prefigures the restoration of order in the unification of the whole family and the end of their tempestuous trials.

Shakespeare's use of music is a prominent feature of the last plays. Apart from its symbolic associations it seems to be part of an attempt to find a way of expressing ideas and emotions beyond the confines of words – and in this respect it is linked, in *Pericles*, with his use of the archaic dumb-show technique. In earlier plays, Shakespeare had already discovered the dramatic potency of wordless expression – in the powerful scene between Coriolanus and his mother, with the stage direction, '*Holds her by the hand, silent*'; in Cordelia's silence, and in the dramatic pause which invariably occurs when Mariana begs Isabella to plead for Angelo's life. In *Pericles*, actions without words have an important place. Thaisa and Pericles do not have a conventional courtship – very little is said as a preliminary, and the culmination of their attraction becomes apparent largely through their dance. As it ends, Simonides indicates that they have made their emotions clear without needing words:

> Thanks, gentlemen, to all; all have done well,
> [*To Pericles*] But you the best.   II.iii.107–8

The dumb-show of their departure from Pentapolis is probably the exception to this view as it seems partly a telescoping of events, and partly an effective way of distancing the audience and reminding them that they are watching an old tale from another age; yet the second dumb-show which takes place at Marina's tomb seems to be a clear example of an attempt to indicate a grief beyond the expression of words. It is also an effective way of demonstrating the cause of Pericles's later speechless state, since – from his first view of the tomb – Pericles does not speak a word on stage until Marina breaks through to him with the aid of her song. Music is the obvious way of attempting to express the unexpressible in this play since, as Gower declares in its first words, the whole of *Pericles* is a song:

> To sing a song that old was sung,
> From ashes ancient Gower is come,   I.1–2

T. R. Waldo summarises the effect, 'Although Pericles returns to this world in response to Marina's song, he has been near enough to death to identify the music of the spheres and to hear the voice of the goddess Diana ... Through his submission to divine will, Pericles has regained his temporal position and at the same time obtained an insight into eternity. Silence and music have made both possible.'[40] An increased use of music in the drama indicates an added sophistication in the public playhouse which now appears to have adopted a tradition from the private theatres; but the use of a chorus figure seems, at first sight, to counter this sophistication.

Gower in *Pericles* is part of an old tradition, recently revived in plays like Barnabe Barnes's *Devil's Charter* or Day's *The Travailes*, but it seems that Shakespeare had his own experimental reasons for employing the technique. Some of these obviously relate to the quaint, archaic style in which Gower speaks, which evokes a sense of another age long past, and provides a background atmosphere for the tale: some reasons are probably linked, as Philip Brockbank suggests, to the need for a mediator between 'the sophistication of the audience and the naivety of the tale'[41] – but most importantly, it is appropriate that the basic structure of the play should be provided by a dead man who has been reborn, like the phoenix from the ashes, specifically to people a stage with ghosts who will enact their story of life conquering death in an attempt to ennoble and enrichen the lives of those watching. In this respect, the more sophisticated use of music and the old Chorus technique, with its accompanying dumb-shows, work well together, for the combination of silence and music is particularly effective in reminding the audience of the dream-like world of ghosts who live only as long as the play lasts; and it also emphasises or frames the various tableaux effects mentioned throughout this chapter. These are not necessarily always static tableaux; as in the dumb-shows, they may be moving pictures – the entrance of Antiochus's daughter or the dance at Thaisa's banquet.

Pericles is an experimental play and its blend of old and contemporary elements may be one reason why its authorship is suspect – apart from the question of an irregular text. However, G. Wilson Knight made an important point when he wrote, 'whatever we think of certain parts, the whole, as we have it, is unquestionably dominated by a single mind; that mind is very clearly Shakespeare's'.[42] The patterns of imagery and staging based on the various themes in the play and their firm adhesion to the traditions on which they were based, seem to substantiate this view. In addition, it can be shown that the symbolic subtext in *Pericles* may have a precedent in *King Lear*. Leo Salingar points out that in the reconciliation between Lear and Cordelia is 'the tone and central theme of Shakespeare's last plays'[43] and there is a religious undercurrent which links the play with the morality tradition, in much the same way as *Pericles* is allied to this.

Edgar's role in his father's mock suicide in IV.vi resembles the battle between the good and the evil angel for power over a man's soul – and Edgar skilfully plays both parts. Later, Lear's crown of weeds is visually reminiscent of the crown of thorns (a fact which was apparent in the B.B.C. television performance, directed by Jonathan Miller); this is further supported by Edgar's cry when he sees Lear, 'O thou side-piercing sight' with its obvious associations with the crucified Christ. All of these associations culminate in Lear's final entrance, which M. C. Bradbrook calls, 'The icon of Lear entering with the dead Cordelia in his arms':[44] a reversal of a *pietà* – not Christ in his mother's arms, but Cordelia in her father's. Although an audience cannot be sure, at this point, that Cordelia really is dead, the reversals in *King Lear* constantly deny the respite from tragedy which has previously been promised, and the religious subtext intensifies the sense of suffering. In both *King Lear* and *Pericles* the pagan and the Christian traditions are fused; M. C. Bradbrook states, 'Shakespeare gave a new mythology to the world',[45] but in *Pericles*, that world was romance, founded on suffering and hope rather than suffering and despair.

5 · 'Beyond beyond': the multi-layered quality of *Cymbeline*

In her article, '*The Second Maiden's Tragedy*: a Jacobean saint's life',[1] Anne Lancashire persuasively argues that 'what have heretofore been considered by scholars merely to be marks of the play's sensationalism and lack of realism' are, in fact, the key to its dramatic structure, once the tradition behind them is recognised – the depiction of a Christian martyr's life. This insight throws a new light on the play and again raises the query – how many other nuances of meaning are now lost in twentieth-century appreciations of plays of this period because we fail to see them in their original contexts? Aspects of *Cymbeline*'s performance will be considered here, especially in relation to popular traditions and contemporary theatre practice.

The play seems to consist of infinite layers, ranging from actual representation on stage (Jupiter's eagle), to the expression of metaphysical ideas in the play's imagery (the eagle vanishing in the sun's beams – associated with spiritual rebirth). This chapter will attempt to penetrate some of these layers and demonstrate possible relationships between them.

Shakespeare, when writing *Cymbeline*, obviously made certain assumptions based on his audience's knowledge of contemporary culture. Anne Lancashire has pointed out similar assumptions in *The Second Maiden's Tragedy*,[2] but *Cymbeline* is a very different play; however, considering it, too, in relation to a Jacobean saint's life, is not totally inappropriate, for Imogen's purity is her most recognisable characteristic – although any consideration of her as a possible saintly figure must take Shakespeare's unconventional application of the saint tradition into account.

One aspect of her portrayal which is linked to the saintly heroine tradition is the idea of death as a preserver of chastity: this was a common theme in sixteenth and early seventeenth-century drama – *The Atheist's Tragedy* (1609), Marston's *Sophonisba* (1605), and Munday and Chettle's *Death of Robert Earl of Huntingdon* (1598) – the story of Matilda 'martyrde for her chastitie'. The tradition was popular both before and after the writing of *Cymbeline*, and it may well be linked to the chivalric revival which took place in the latter part of Elizabeth's reign and lasted until the death of Prince Henry.

In *The Second Maiden's Tragedy* (1611), the virtuous Lady kills herself rather than become the tyrant's mistress and Giovanus appeals to the audience, 'Help me to mourn, all that love chastity.'[3] Her spirit later appears 'all in white' with a 'great light' and a 'great crucifix on her breast'[4] in a ghostly resurrection scene where Giovanus discovers that the tomb is empty and her body missing: according to Lancashire, saints' lives often contained parallels with the life of Christ. The suffering of Amoret in III.xii of Spenser's *Faerie Queene* is probably allied to the same tradition.

Imogen, like these women, refuses to be corrupted, and there are hints of the Virgin Mary in her association with the divine and the fact that, like Mary, although married, she is also considered to be sexually pure: Posthumus says,

> Me of my lawful pleasure she restrain'd,
> And pray'd me oft forbearance ...
>   that I thought her
> As chaste as unsunn'd snow.   II.iv.161–5

Imogen is willing to die for the sake of pure love, but she is more interesting than the conventional saintly heroine of *The Second Maiden's Tragedy* because she inhabits two worlds – the sensual as well as the saintly.

In II.ii of *Cymbeline*, Shakespeare seems to evoke the traditional idea of death as a preserver of chastity by atmosphere, spectacle, and insinuation alone. Iachimo's attempted rape is only conjectural, therefore Imogen's seeming-death must exist on the same plane. The tradition is evoked but not enacted. In relation to the saintly-sensual paradox, echoes of Christian theology blend with the pagan setting throughout the play and are particularly noticeable here. In Imogen's prayer, the words, 'To your protection I commend me, gods' recall Jesus's last words at the crucifixion (Luke 23.46). An undercurrent of death runs through the scene and visually it has a precedent in early Shakespeare. The link between Imogen's death-like sleep – to which Iachimo draws attention – and Juliet's sleep which resembles death, is striking. Iachimo recalls v.ii of *Romeo and Juliet* with his words:

> O sleep, thou ape of death, lie dull upon her,
> And be her sense but as a monument,
> Thus in a chapel lying.   II.ii.31–3

At line 15 he addresses Imogen as 'fresh lily': the lily is an emblem of chastity, but is also a flower associated with death. The adjective 'fresh'

9 Romeo with Juliet's body. This is not meant to represent a particular public playhouse stage, although the pillars (to support the heavens) may be similar to those in some open-air playhouses. See the New Cambridge Shakespeare series for reconstructions of contemporary staging conditions. Sketch by C. Walter Hodges.

expresses the paradox of life and death existing simultaneously. In the earlier play Romeo views Juliet by the light of a torch; here, Iachimo views Imogen beneath the taper she requested to be left burning. In the public playhouse, both scenes would have been performed in daylight, and even at Blackfriars, it is unlikely that all the candles would be extinguished during a performance of *Cymbeline* for such a short scene – after which, they would all need to be re-lit. The torch and taper are, therefore, necessary properties to signify night and darkness. Both scenes suggest a funereal atmosphere where a body lies in state and a candle or light burns beside it as part of the ritual.

Apart from signifying night, the taper has other emblematic properties. Like Lady Macbeth, Imogen constantly has light by her to dispel her fears, but unlike Lady Macbeth's, Imogen's light symbolises her purity of conscience. Imogen specifically asks for it to be left burning which is the opposite practice to scenes of illicit love. In *The White Devil* light is removed so that sin can go unnoticed in darkness:

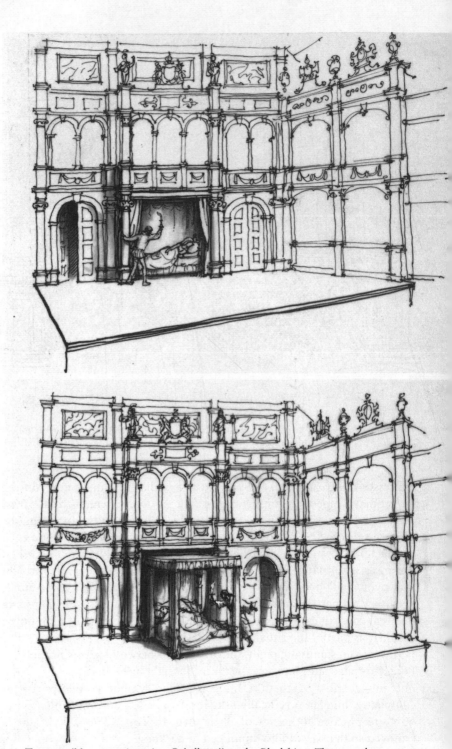

10 Two possible ways of staging *Othello* v.ii at the Blackfriars Theatre, where
Cymbeline was probably performed. Methods adapted from (a) Ross and (b) Hosley.
See *Othello*, ed. Norman Sanders (Cambridge, 1984), p. 191. Sketches by C. Walter
Hodges.

'tis his pleasure
You put out all your torches and depart.   I.ii.8–9

Even Iachimo does not put out Imogen's taper, implying that his actions will not destroy her: his deed is not so terrible that it merits darkness – unlike Othello's 'Put out the light, and then put out the light' (v.ii.7) – on the contrary, Iachimo comes primarily to view Imogen and the room where, unlike the scenes in *Romeo and Juliet* or *Othello*, a light is already burning. His presence has no effect on the visual aspect: Imogen is always illuminated.

The simultaneous presence of life and death in Imogen's person is also evoked by Iachimo's description of the perfume in the chamber. This suggests the incense and spices used to camouflage the odours of death and preserve the body, as is shown in the opening of Thaisa's coffin in *Pericles*: but here, the perfume is produced by Imogen's breath and is a sign of life. Whether or not incense would actually be used is not known. There would seem little point in an outdoor public playhouse, but at court, or at Blackfriars, it is a possibility as it could be a valuable atmospheric agent for the tomb-like quality of the scene.

Imogen's body becomes an object of worship for Iachimo in this scene where religious and sensual elements are inextricably entangled. Presumably Iachimo approaches her with the awe and reverence associated with a sacred object, yet not without the longing to get as close to it as he can – 'That I might touch' (II.ii.16). He takes the bracelet from her arm after he imagines her as a monument in a chapel, so this action has the double connotations of robbing the dead (linked to his bird of prey associations) and of robbing a religious image – either taking a relic or behaving sacrilegiously.

Iachimo's action is almost an enactment of the excuse Romeo gives Balthesar:

> Why I descend into this bed of death
> Is partly to behold my lady's face
> But chiefly to take thence from her dead finger
> A precious ring, a ring that I must use
> In dear employment.   v.iii.28–32

Unlike Romeo, he actually takes a jewel from the body. Both men undergo a type of ritual with the supposedly dead bodies, describing their beauty and kissing them. Romeo's 'Thus with a kiss I die' (v.iii.120) involves both physical death and the dying associated with sexual passion (as is the case with Othello). Both senses of dying would be known to contemporary audiences and II.ii of *Cymbeline* also contains them by implication – in

Iachimo's passion for the unconscious figure: if he does not actually kiss Imogen at 'But kiss, one kiss!' (II.ii.17) then the desire is there.

Clifford Leech comments on the 'strong sense of illicit intimacy'[5] in this scene, and if it ends with a curtain or door enclosing the occupants within the discovery space – as would probably happen, even if the bed had been drawn out earlier onto the main stage – then Iachimo and Imogen are ultimately shut in together. In this respect Leech is right in saying that, innocent as Imogen is, the two of them do, after a fashion, spend the night together.[6] This visual impression of intimacy has a parallel in IV.ii when Imogen and Cloten's headless body lie side by side, alone on the stage, and this is mentioned in the second part of this chapter.

In II.ii Shakespeare relates the undercurrent of sexual passion associated with Iachimo to religious fervour, an undercurrent associated with Imogen. In Imogen's portrayal, sexual love is always submerged in purity, which has religious connotations:

> or have charg'd him,
> At the sixth hour of morn, at noon, at midnight,
> T'encounter me with orisons, for then
> I am in heaven for him;   I.iv.30–3

She does not ask for love poetry, but prayers, and she does not see their love in earthly terms, but in terms of the divine. Similarly, in III.ii Pisanio describes her as 'more goddess-like than wife-like'. As suggested earlier, Imogen is an object of worship for Iachimo and is associated with a religious image. She does not have 'crimson' lips like Juliet, but 'Rubies unparagon'd': it is as if she has become a jewelled religious statue – an icon. It seems significant that, at II.ii.32 Iachimo refers to her, not as an actual body lying in death, but as the 'monument' or effigy on the tomb. However, at one point she is the image of an object inside the church and at another, she becomes the building itself. At IV.ii.55 Imogen is called 'divine temple' and earlier her eyes are:

> th'enclosed lights, now canopied
> Under these windows, white and azure lac'd
> With blue of heaven's own tint.   II.ii.21–3

This description, although associated with wooden shutters by Kathleen Tillotson,[7] is also reminiscent of the stained glass in church windows, which seems a more appropriate image in the context. The changing perspectives in *Cymbeline* suggest that it is experienced through a continually flexing lens, switching from microcosm to macrocosm without warning. Not only is Imogen both an image in the temple and the temple itself, but she is both living and an unbreathing work of art – the staging of II.ii suggests a monument in a tomb, but the audience also have the memory of the living girl glimpsed at the beginning of the scene – no goddess or icon, but a girl with childish fears. Imogen is a composite character; sometimes alarmingly human, yet at others, a detached ideal – while on stage she would have been represented by a boy actor. It is the imagery of the play, above all, which must blend these elements together.

In the imagery Imogen always seems to have a brightness about her associated with light: in the staging this relates to the taper burning beside her even in sleep. According to Plato, light and beauty are reflections of the divine, so it seems appropriate that 'divine Imogen' be likened to the sun (I.iii.30 and I.vii.86): this achieves added significance in one of the play's final images – the eagle vanishing in the sun's beams (v.v.471–3), but more of this later. In II.ii the illumination of the taper, the lustre of rubies and the image of light through coloured glass, link her with religious iconology, and also with the detail that Anne Lancashire mentions,[8] that saints, in life and death (like ghosts), were sometimes accompanied by light. The Renaissance belief that eyes were the windows of the soul is also relevant here, for although Iachimo tries to see them they are safely guarded by sleep.

In *Cymbeline*, elements of a saint tradition are not part of the surface layer of the play as they apparently are in *The Second Maiden's Tragedy*, therefore it would be inappropriate to make a blatant parallel between Imogen and a saint – although the white garments, great light, and huge crucifix of the latter play obviously do this for that particular heroine. In *Cymbeline*, insinuation, rather than representation, conveys aspects of the tradition.

As Imogen has the potential of belonging to either the saintly or the sensual world, this affects Shakespeare's treatment of the tradition of death as a preserver of chastity. Her dual characteristics allow the possibility that the sensual woman might overthrow the saint, given the opportunity,[9] and the death-like sleep in II.ii is necessary to protect her from the possible corruption of Iachimo's attentions. If he does kiss her she is unaware of it and therefore there is no danger of her succumbing to the man sent to test her virtue, as does occur with Anselmus's wife and her husband's friend in *The Second Maiden's Tragedy*. At the same time, the saintly Imogen's shape, 'a heavenly angel', restrains any plan of actual rape which Iachimo may have been entertaining.

Cymbeline is packed with parallel scenes taking place on different levels. II.ii has a counterpart in III.iv where Imogen offers to die since Posthumus no longer loves her, but because she is wrongly accused she undergoes a metaphorical, rather than a real death and changes her identity by donning the clothes Pisanio provides. Again, this is linked with the preservation of chastity as, unknowingly, she is shielded by her disguise from Cloten and his projected rape. It is also the method she chooses to symbolise being 'dead' to her husband (III.iv.132), yet is still able to be a devoted wife and remain near him.

Another such devoted wife is found in Tourneur's *The Revenger's Tragedy* (1607) in Lady Antonio who, having been raped, kills herself and dies with a prayer book open in her hand:

> with a leaf tucked up,
> Pointing to these words:
> *Melius virtute mori, quam per dedecus vivere.*
> [Better die virtuous than live dishonoured]   I.iv.16–18[10]

David Bevington deals with Shakespeare's use of books of devotion and mentions that, 'in traditional medieval and Renaissance iconography they are attributes of the Virgin Mary, various saints, and pious patrons'.[11] In *Richard III*, 'a book of prayers' is said, by their murderer, to have lain on the pillow of the two innocent princes: in *Cymbeline*, such a tradition is subverted by the nature of Imogen's book. This puts a disturbing slant on her death-like sleep in II.ii in which she has the *Tale of Tereus* beside her with the leaf turned down 'where Philomel gave up'. What attraction could this particular tale hold for a character as pure as Imogen? Is it too conjectural to view Imogen's fascination for it as Shakespeare's attempt to express the ironical paradox which occurs when a virtuous heroine possesses both saintly and sensual qualities – when a virtuous wife harbours a saint's preoccupation with martyrdom? Later in the play Imogen is likened to a martyr or sacrifice; wrongly persecuted, but willing to die for her love and faith in Posthumus: 'The lamb entreats the butcher' (III.iv.98).

In a superficially pagan play, as is sometimes the case in Shakespeare's works, Christian traditions are surprisingly apparent; yet Gombrich's argument that Christianity linked the spiritual world with the terrestrial through the mystery of the Incarnation and the doctrine of Revelation, is relevant to the portrayal of Imogen's character in a Renaissance context: 'The Logos became flesh and God speaks to man not only through the Scriptures, but through the whole of Creation and the whole of History. Symbolism, as we read in Giarda, is this form of Revelation that God in His mercy created to make the Ideas that dwell in His mind known to Man.'[12] In this tradition, nature, as in the later Puritan practice, was full of signs which, rightly read, confirmed and supplemented the Scriptures. Imogen has many signs of the saint or Christ figure about her. She is frequently associated with the image of a lamb (signifying innocence and sacrifice) and, apart from the religious connotations in II.ii already mentioned, she is also the subject of an apparent resurrection: 'Is not this boy reviv'd from death?' (V.v.120). At I.vii.3–4, her words:

> O, that husband,
> My supreme crown of grief!

could be linked with the burden of her royal birth which caused their separation, but it is also related to the idea of a saint suffering martyrdom as, according to Anne Lancashire, the winning of crowns by virgin martyrs is emphasised in many of their stories.[13] Behind both these images is the original crown of grief in the Christian tradition – the crown of thorns.

In relation to the martyr aspect of Imogen, it is significant that her virtue is constantly linked with blood: at I.v.53 the Frenchman describes a former occasion when Posthumus talked of Imogen, saying:

It was much like an argument that fell out last night, where each of us fell in praise of our country mistresses; this gentleman at that time vouching (and upon warrant of bloody affirmation) his to be more fair, virtuous, wise, chaste, constant,

> I.v.53–7

The 'bloody affirmation' implied is that of the supposed slanderer, but in the practice of the test, Posthumus is led to believe that Imogen's blood is shed at his request, and the bloody cloth he later carries becomes, for him, the 'bloody affirmation'.

Sexual passion and religious martyrdom are also linked. Clifford Leech comments on the sexual elements in 'Hark, hark, the lark' – of Phoebus's steeds watering at springs on 'chalic'd flowers' – and remarks: 'chalic'd may link the eroticism with the Eucharist'. He relates this to the bedchamber scene immediately preceding it and the crimson drops in the bottom of the cowslip: 'In this instance there is an interesting inversion: the flower's chalice is related to the girl's breast; the idea of concavity is insisted on throughout the song.' He continues: 'the "crimson" not only deepens the eroticism but, if I am right about the reverberations of "chalic'd", links the erotic with Christ's blood'.[14] This argument could be pursued, for II.ii and II.iii, in particular, seem to stress the conflicting, yet here, strangely compatible notions of human sexual passion and Christ's Passion.

Theodore Spencer stresses the development of realism and emphasis on emotion in religious devotion in the Renaissance. He traces this back to St Bernard of Clairvaux (1095–1155) who first stressed the sufferings of Christ, and therefore influenced medieval and subsequent attitudes. St Francis also emphasised this philosophy and had the marks of Christ's suffering on his own body. Even when *Cymbeline* was written, an audience would be aware of the tradition which still survives today in the Catholic Church, and which Hopkins expressed so well in *The Wreck of the Deutschland*:

> Five! the finding and sake
> And cipher of suffering Christ ...
> Stigma, signal, cinquefoil token
> For lettering of the lamb's fleece, ruddying of the rose-flake.
>
> Stanza 22

In the possible sources for *Cymbeline*, the mole which Shakespeare describes as:

> cinque-spotted: like the crimson drops
> I' th' bottom of a cowslip.   II.ii.38–9

appears as a black wart (Fredryke of Jennen) and a mole surrounded by golden hairs (Boccaccio). Why should Shakespeare be so specific about five crimson marks which do not appear in the sources unless they have further significance? The sign may be related to the idea which Gombrich expounds – that symbolism 'is this form of Revelation that God in His mercy created to make the ideas that dwell in His mind known to Man'. Saints often carried the marks of the stigmata on their bodies, and on Imogen such marks are compressed into the unusual expression of an adornment rather than a sign of suffering. They are, however, a sign of purity and it is ironical that this particular 'proof' should be used to condemn her for adultery.

If the mole and the five crimson spots are associated with the blood of Christ, they also give an insight into Iachimo's account to Posthumus:

> I kiss'd it, and it gave me present hunger
> To feed again, though full.   II.iv.137–8

Behind the idea of a bird of prey is a parody of the Eucharist, linking with Leech's inverted 'chalic'd' flower of Imogen's breast – under which the mole lies. Iachimo's supposed participation in such a sensual Eucharist is a further condemnation of his soul (in Christian terms) for Article 29 of the 1562 Articles of Religion reads: 'The Wicked, and such as be void of a lively faith, although they do carnally and visibly press with their teeth ... the Sacrament of the Body and Blood of Christ, yet in no wise are they partakers of Christ: but rather, to their condemnation, do eat and drink the sign or sacrament of so great a thing.' This would be known to most people familiar with the Book of Common Prayer of the time, and still

appears in it today. It also relates to the sacrilegious connotations of
Iachimo taking the bracelet from the arm of a monument or religious
image, and a reference to his fears for his soul can be found in his parting
words:

> I lodge in fear;
> Though this a heavenly angel, hell is here.   II.ii.49–50

Imogen's purity seems to ensnare him even more than her beauty and
his fears could be more than merely those of being discovered in her
bedchamber if his words are considered in relation to *Titus Andronicus*.
Here the quarrel between Chiron and Demetrius over Lavinia results in an
actual rape, and once the plan has been made, Demetrius says:

> *Sit fas aut nefas*, till I find the stream
> [be it right or wrong]
> To cool this heat, a charm to calm these fits,
> *Per Stygia, per manes vehor.*
> [I am borne through the Stygian regions, i.e. I am in hell] II.i.133–5

This comparison with the earlier play implies that Iachimo's words are
associated with a similar lust to that of Demetrius, and it provides another
link with the *Tale of Tereus* which is enacted in *Titus Andronicus*, but
avoided in *Cymbeline*.[15] However, it is only just avoided if Cloten's plans
are seen as an extension of Iachimo's desires:

> With that suit upon my back, will I ravish her: first kill him, and in her eyes;
> there shall she see my valour, which will then be a torment to her contempt. He on
> the ground, my speech of insultment ended on his dead body, and when my lust
> hath dined (which, as I say, to vex her I will execute in the clothes that she so
> prais'd) to the court I'll knock her back, foot her home again. She hath despis'd me
> rejoicingly, and I'll be merry in my revenge.   III.v.138–47

These lines suggest a comparison with Chiron's words in *Titus
Andronicus*:

> Drag hence her husband to some secret hole,
> And make his dead trunk pillow to our lust.   II.iii.129–30

which are probably themselves related to Nashe's *The Unfortunate
Traveller* – 'Her husband's dead bodie he made a pillow to his abomi-
nation'. Neither Chiron nor Cloten actually carry out these threats, but
the related events in *Titus* provide a dramatic precedent and are sufficiently brutal to cause a contemporary audience concern for Imogen's
well-being once the comparison is apparent.

Cymbeline, therefore, includes authentic ingredients of the earlier
tragedy, but the tragi-comic mode which Shakespeare adopts in the play

prevents them from being fulfilled – except in a way which stresses the differences between *Cymbeline* and tragedy: it is not Posthumus who is killed, but Cloten; and Imogen, by mistaking his identity, uses him as a pillow – but in relation to love, not lust:

> Who is this
> Thou mak'st thy bloody pillow?   IV.ii.362–3

The tragi-comic nature of the drama invites experimentation on Shakespeare's part. There is a striking affinity between Cloten and Iachimo – the former attempting physical violation and going unrepentant to his death, does not succeed; whereas the latter, speculating only mental rape, manages to steal her honour for the sake of a wager (superficially a far less serious design) using words alone, but producing far more harmful and far-reaching consequences. Ironically, he who does the most actual damage lives to repent and make amends. These two planned assaults on Imogen balance each other in degrees of intended and actual harm.

Cloten and Iachimo seem to alternate in pursuing a very similar plan. Iachimo's assault on Imogen's honour in II.ii is followed by Cloten's *aubade* of II.iii and it seems that Imogen inspires the same blend of religious and sexual fascination for Cloten as she did earlier for Iachimo: both Iachimo and Cloten are linked to the Eucharist parody. In addition, Cloten attempts to bring about a resurrection scene from the death-like sleep Iachimo invoked in, 'O, sleep, thou ape of death, lie dull upon her'. In II.iii, the song 'Hark, hark, the lark' is linked with death through the reference to heaven's gate, but it calls for an awakening: 'my lady sweet arise'. In relation to Imogen's paradoxical appeal, 'Mary-buds' (II.iii.24) has connotations of both the Virgin Mary and of the former prostitute Mary Magdalen, who arrived first at the tomb on Resurrection Day. Similarly, 'my lady sweet arise' is linked not only to a spiritual return to life in the religious sense, but also to Cloten's bawdry and wordplay associated with a sexual awakening:

Come on, tune, if you can penetrate her with your fingering, so: we'll try with tongue too: II.iii.13–14

Cloten's exit with his cry after Imogen, 'I'll be reveng'd' (154) is followed immediately by Iachimo achieving a surrogate revenge for him in II.iv, by lying to Posthumus about his wife. Also, Iachimo's account of feeding on Imogen's body (II.iv.136–8) is recalled in Cloten's later plans – 'and when my lust hath dined' (III.v.143). Both characters, therefore, share similar characteristics, and often appear as two faces of the same coin which is tossed as Shakespeare sees fit. If doubling of parts did occur in the original staging of *Cymbeline* it can be argued that there would be dramatic advantages in the same man playing both parts, as well as the doubling solving obvious practical necessities involved in a large cast.[16]

Throughout *Cymbeline* stage action seems to comment, often ironically, on the text. Imogen's plea:

> To your protection I commend me, gods,
> From fairies and the tempters of the night,
> Guard me, beseech ye!   II.ii.8–10

is immediately followed by the stage direction: '*Iachimo from the Trunke*' (Folio). This is an old technique, previously used in *A Midsummer Night's Dream* when, after the fairies' song – expressing similar sentiments – Titania wakes to fall in love with Bottom. In *Cymbeline* the technique is adapted and used to express one of the many ambiguities which abound throughout. A. C. Kirsch, in particular, has drawn attention to *Cymbeline*'s deliberate self-consciousness as a work of art, and these juxtapositions of text and stage actions can be seen as elements of this theme. Similarly, in IV.ii the chanted dirge over Fidele's body ends with:

> No exorciser harm thee!
> Nor no witchcraft charm thee!
> Ghost unlaid forbear thee!
> Nothing ill come near thee!
> Quiet consummation have,
> And renowned be thy grave!   IV.ii.276–81

Not only is this immediately followed by Belarius laying Cloten's headless body beside her, but her 'quiet consummation' takes the form of a frantic, distracted lament when she wakes.

However, probably the most striking juxtapositioning of seemingly incongruous elements occurs in the portrayal of Imogen herself – part saint or chaste goddess and part sensual woman. Wind discusses the tradition of a hybrid figure – Diana and Venus merged – which has been mentioned in relation to *Pericles* and is also a probable basis for Imogen's portrayal: it may shed light on the way a contemporary audience would have reacted to her. This theory also helps to explain the unlikely combination of Cleopatra, chaste Dian, and cupids in the decorations of her bedchamber – if, indeed, they are meant to exist outside Iachimo's fertile imagination: however, even if this was the case, they are not likely to have been represented on stage.

Wind cites a design by Giovanni degli Albizzi of a huntress carrying a bow and arrow, wearing a winged crown on her head and heavy boots on her feet, standing on a small cloud which covers the sun, but allows its

11   The Royal Shakespeare Company in *As You Like It* (1985/6), directed by Adrian
Noble: the dream landscape of Arden. Roger Hyams (Silvius) and Colin Douglas
(Corin). Photo: Joe Cocks Studio

rays to be seen around it. An inscription accompanies it which is a verse
from the *Aeneid*, in which Venus appears disguised as a nymph of Diana:
the goddess of love as a devotee of chastity: '*Virginis os habitumque gerens
et virginis arma*' (*Aeneid* 1.315). Wind says of this figure, 'In her the Renaissance Platonists thought they had found a fine poetical confirmation for
their doctrine of the union of Chastity and Love.' The design was apparently a popular ornament on Florentine marriage cassoni, but was developed more fully in France and England than in Italy. Imogen's composite
figure may even have had a counterpart in the late Queen Elizabeth:

In view of the Italian sources of Elizabethan imagery, perhaps the question is not
unjustified whether the worship of Queen Elizabeth as Diana was not also a cult of

Venus in disguise. Among the portraits of the queen by Isaac Oliver there is one that bears ... an inscription which ... refers to the verse in Virgil:

Virginis os habitumque geris, divina virago.[17]

This composite figure suggests that chastity is a weapon of Venus, 'arousing the passions it professes to restrain'. The weapons of Diana are also the weapons of Cupid: 'While the arrow flies and hits blindly like passion, the bow, held steadily in its place, is used with a seeing eye; and because its strength resides in its tension, it is a symbol of restraint.'[18] The notion of chastity being a compelling force of attraction helps to illuminate the magnetic appeal Desdemona instigates in Cassio, Iago, and Othello and the desire Angelo has for Isabella. It also relates to Imogen's power to attract both Iachimo and Cloten, while professing to love only Posthumus. Imogen's purity, as well as her beauty, attracts these men, and in the case of Cloten, it is her professed chastity and devotion to Posthumus which goads him into plans of murder and rape. Imogen is associated with the chastity and death themes of popular dramatic tradition through the undercurrents of these ideas running throughout the play, but her character also includes remnants of the saint tradition from miracle drama, and most strikingly, characteristics of a human Venus and a vulnerable, sensitive young woman in the Viola mould.

Imogen's composite character probably seems stranger in a twentieth-century appreciation of the play and much more difficult to portray than it might have been in the seventeenth century when living people were constantly blended with tradition and symbol. Queen Elizabeth had been such a figure, and in James's court, masque characters were less charismatic equivalents. However, although a contemporary audience would have been familiar with the concept, Shakespeare still needed a means of blending the disparate elements involved. One of his methods in *Cymbeline* is his use of the dream medium.[19] This not only helps to integrate symbol and reality in character portrayal, but also blends these elements throughout the play in imagery and stage actions.

The medium of dream is particularly appropriate as an atmospheric setting in *Cymbeline* when Gombrich's words are considered: 'In our dreams we all make no difference between the metaphorical and the literal, between symbol and reality.'[20] The Royal Shakespeare Company's 1985/6 production of *As You Like It* (directed by Adrian Noble) demonstrated the dramatic effectiveness of dream effects in that play. The Forest of Arden was reached through a dream-like journey and was portrayed as a transformed version of the court. The key phrase in the programme was, 'within the forest: the forest within', which emphasised the psychological and surreal approach. Imogen's journey in III.ii could be portrayed in a similar fashion, as could Posthumus's later experiences.

Imogen seems to take part in many dream sequences – the most obvious being II.ii (the bedchamber scene), and it is interesting that the dream atmosphere is evoked in the waking world of which Iachimo is a part, while only a hint of the nature of Imogen's dreams is given by the *Tale of Tereus*. That she does dream is implied in the next scene (II.iii) in Cloten's, 'Let her lie still and dream' (64); and in III.iv she admits to having 'fearful' dreams for Posthumus (44–5). However, all these are an undercurrent and it is clear that it is the dream-like qualities of the waking world which are prominent and which help to blur the boundaries of dream and actual experience, leading up to Posthumus's vision in v.v. This sequence possesses that most complex combination of characteristics of both worlds – seeming to be a dream, yet leaving the tablet as proof that it occurred.

The first Gentleman's words in the first scene seem to set the tone for the rest of the play, 'Howso'er 'tis strange … Yet is it true, sir' (1.i.65–7). A dream atmosphere suits the romance elements in the play, such as the lost princes living a pastoral life in Wales, waiting in a cave like Glendower until they are called to defend their country and take up a new life. At the other end of the scale, nightmare qualities surround the wicked queen and these become clearer as the play proceeds, e.g. when her order,

> Whiles yet the dew's on ground, gather those flowers;
> Make haste …   I.vi.1–2

is considered in relation to Belarius's comment that flowers and herbs,

> that have on them cold dew o' th' night
> Are strewings fitt'st for graves: IV.ii.284–5

Dream qualities help to blend mythology with reality as in Iachimo's evocation:

> Our Tarquin thus
> Did softly press the rushes, ere he waken'd
> The chastity he wounded.   II.ii.12–14

and they also convey the flexing lens effect, switching from magnification of minute detail to diminution of large objects – as in Imogen's impression of the diminishing figure of Posthumus on deck 'As little as a crow' (1.iv.15).

As a prominent theme in *Cymbeline* is death and rebirth, the links between dreams, sleep, and death are important. In the *Iliad*, Homer speaks of the 'twin brethren, Sleep and Death' (XVI.671) and Hesiod gives:

'Night indeed brought forth hateful Fate and black Doom and Death, and brought forth Sleep and gave birth to the race of Dreams' and also, 'the other one, destructive Night, veiled in musky mist, in her hands Sleep, the brother of Death'.[21] Shakespeare was obviously aware of these traditions, judging by the famous lines in *Hamlet*:

> To die, to sleep;
> To sleep, perchance to dream –

and it is interesting that it was the possible nature of these eternal dreams which caused Hamlet concern. According to J. Mandel, the Renaissance commonly accepted a tripartite division of dreams: dreams of natural, diabolical, or divine origin: and these could originate either within or outside the individual consciousness.[22] Interpretation was crucial in deciding to which category a particular dream belonged. In II.ii either two very different dream sequences occur simultaneously (the Iachimo action related to the *Tale of Tereus*, and the possibility that behind her 'heavenly angel' appearance, Imogen was experiencing one of the 'fearful' dreams she mentions in III.iv) or the same dream is shown from two different viewpoints – it is significant that Iachimo uses imagery related to Tarquin long before he spies the tale Imogen has been reading.

Linked with Hesiod's words quoted above, is the image of death resembling a mist, which is not far removed from the world of dreams. In 2 *Tamburlaine*, Zenocrate is seen, 'all dazzled with the hellish mists of death' (II.iv.14),[23] and in Shakespeare's works death is likened to a journey – at the end of *King Lear* Kent says, 'I have a journey, sir, shortly to go.' These associations all play a part in Imogen's journey to Milford Haven. On these travels, Posthumus believes she meets her death when, in fact, she only dies metaphorically (through changing her clothes and her identity); but she does also undergo a state of apparent death, a burial ritual and a later resurrection.

Linked with the *Tamburlaine* reference to the 'hellish mists of death' is Imogen's vision of her contemplated journey in III.ii – a way through a dense fog:

> I see before me, man: nor here, nor here,
> Nor what ensues, but have a fog in them,
> That I cannot look through. Away, I prithee,
> Do as I bid thee: there's no more to say:
> Accessible is none but Milford way.   III.ii.79–83

Imogen is blind to all but her love for Posthumus, but in retrospect, the dream image of death surrounding her path seems obvious – especially in view of Posthumus's plans for her and her ironical comment, 'Why, one that rode to's execution ... Could never go so slow' (III.ii.71–2). Similarly, the difficulty Imogen has in pursuing her journey to its end:

> Thou told'st me when we came from horse, the place
> Was near at hand: III.iv.1–2

takes on a new significance if the metaphor of the journey of death is realised – for in the tragi-comic mode, she will not be allowed to complete it, although she may come near.

Death and resurrection form an undercurrent throughout the play, occasionally breaking the surface. They exist on many levels, from the metaphorical or supposed deaths of characters and their eventual rein-statement, to the new life of a nation; and beyond it all are Christian echoes of the resurrection and life after death, implied in the appearance of the Leonati ghosts. In relation to this theme, Belarius's cave takes on a new emblematical significance. Imogen supposedly dies within this cave whose 'gate/Instructs ... how t'adore the heavens' (III.iii.2–3) and, like Christ, her body is removed and a resurrection later takes place. On one level the cave is merely a stage property, similar to those mentioned in Henslowe's diary, or even just a discovery space behind the central doors or curtain; but on another level it relates to the Holy Sepulchre and beyond this to Plato's cave in Book VII of *The Republic*. Between these poles is the medieval phrase, *mors janua vitae* which is represented by death as a gate – an image with which the Renaissance was familiar.[24]

Belarius specifically says, 'this gate' rather than 'this cave' in III.iii, which links the image with the lark singing at heaven's gate in the *aubade* of II.iii and provides a visual representation of the idea. The concept, *mors janua vitae* – death as the gate of life – is particularly interesting in relation to the ambiguities of *Cymbeline*, as Imogen is carried out through the cave's 'gate', supposedly dead, and later returns to life. Pico, writing of the story of Alcestis and Orpheus in Plato's *Symposium*, said: 'Alcestis achieved the perfection of love because she longed to go to the beloved through death: and dying through love, she was by the grace of the gods revived'.[25] Imogen's desire to die as a martyr to Posthumus's love, her assumed death and subsequent revival, all indicate a parallel with this train of thought. However, Posthumus's vindication in the final act is even more closely related, as he achieves his ultimate state of worthiness by courting death in order to atone for Imogen's murder and be reunited with her.

Lorenzo de' Medici further expounded the link between love and death in his commentary on his sonnet sequence in which he celebrated love by starting with a sonnet on death:

He that examines these matters more closely will find that the beginning of the vita amorosa proceeds from death, because whoever lives for love, first dies to everything else. And if love has in it a certain perfection ... it is impossible to arrive at that perfection without first dying to the more imperfect things. This very rule was followed by Homer, Virgil and Dante: for Homer sent Ulysses into the underworld, Virgil sent Aeneas, and Dante made himself wander through the Inferno, to show that the way to perfection is by this road.[26]

It is interesting that Posthumus's last stand is in a lane 'Close by the battle, ditch'd, and wall'd with turf' (v.iii.14), as this is reminiscent of a grave. Later in the scene it is said of Belarius and the two brothers whom he met there, ''Tis thought the old man, and his sons, were angels' (v.iii.85). According to the imagery, Posthumus's search for death leads him right into the grave (as it does Imogen) and then delivers him from it. As he said in v.iii:

> I, in mine own woe charm'd,
> Could not find death where I did hear him groan,
> Nor feel him where he struck.   v.iii.68–70

His purgatory is to live with the knowledge that he has destroyed his love, and because *Cymbeline* is a play concerned with the expression of metaphor, both verbally and visually, imagery and staging combine in v.iv to stress the contrast with earlier happier days. In v.iv the bracelet which he gave Imogen ('It is a manacle of love, I'll place it/Upon this fairest prisoner', 1.ii.53–4) and which Iachimo stole in order to take her good name, is recalled by the manacles the gaoler puts on him. A figure of speech has become a literal interpretation, just as Cloten, earlier in the play, related Imogen's figure of speech, 'his meanest garment', to a realisable act. In v.iv Posthumus's manacles are a manifestation of the manacle of love image, but they are also a metaphor for his state of mind:

> My conscience, thou art fetter'd
> More than my shanks and wrists: you good gods give me
> The penitent instrument to pick that bolt,
> Then free for ever.   v.iv.8–11

He seems to be referring to his earlier thought, that 'Death' was 'the key/T'unbar these locks' (6–7).

Love can be seen as an important element in the Renaissance philosophy of death, and Wind points out that Renaissance humanists argued that Thanatos and the funerary Eros were one – depicted by the same winged figure on death monuments. Fincino remarked: 'Love is called by Plato bitter (*res amara*) and not unjustly because death is inseparable from love (*quia moritur quisquis amat*). And Orpheus also called love γλυϰύπικϱου, that is, *dulce amarum*, because love is a voluntary death. As death it is bitter, but being voluntary it is sweet.'[27]

The relationship between the components of this tradition is very apparent in the vision of v.iv. Posthumus wishes to commune with death in order to reach Imogen, and in this scene death finally comes to him – not as he expects, but in the guise of his dead family. Atmospheric elements are important and John H. Long's suggestion[28] that the music may have grown louder to show that Posthumus was asleep and to signify the start of the vision, seems feasible.

In this scene a knowledge that the emblems of love and death both lack eyes is useful. At line 180, the gaoler remarks:

> Your death has eyes in's head then: I have
> Not seen him so pictur'd.

in which he is referring to the eyeless skeleton which symbolised death; and in a different context, Cupid was sometimes regarded as being blind. Among the many arguments relating to a love without eyes is Pico's philosophy that love did not need them because it was above the intellect. Posthumus's love for Imogen, which prompts him to say 'O Imogen/I'll speak to thee in silence' (v.iv.28–9), i.e. through closing his eyes and dreaming, is fused in v.iv with Pico's ninth kind of amorous blindness – a sacred blindness produced by the immediate presence of a deity: 'Wherefore the most profound and divine theologians say that God is better honoured and loved by silence than by words, and better seen by closing the eyes to images than by opening them.'[29] It can be argued that the vision is an integral part of the play's design, and far from being, in Granville-Barker's phrase, 'A pointless pageant that he sleeps through',[30] does express the culmination of a number of themes in which imagery and stage technique fuse to create a dramatic peak. It is unlikely that this scene is an interpolation when it is considered that it has a precedent in IV.ii – Imogen's mistaken burial ceremony.

In the dirge spoken over Fidele, references are made which augur Jupiter's appearance and the relationship of love and death expressed in v.iv:

> Fear no more the lightning-flash,
> Nor th' all-dreaded thunder-stone.
> Fear not slander, censure rash.
> Thou hast finish'd joy and moan.
> All lovers young, all lovers must
> Consign to thee and come to dust.   IV.ii.270–5

According to Spencer and Strong,[31] the good and the famous had tombs bearing remembrances of their lives because the Elizabethans particularly dreaded being forgotten: future generations had to know that they had lived. In Fidele's dirge, the words: 'And renowned be thy grave' express this sentiment – an idea which is also relevant to the appearance of the Leonati and the tablet Jupiter leaves on Posthumus's chest. Strong writes that for the Elizabethans, fame was connected with family, and amongst the evidence which reflects this is the use of ancestral heraldry and the advent of published family histories. It is possible to view the Leonati in terms of this Tudor tradition: Posthumus is the last of his line, therefore the fate of his family depends on him.

Similarly, the tablet which Jupiter leaves is recognised by Posthumus as a record that he has lived. He does not understand it but declares:

> Be what it is,
> The action of my life is like it, which
> I'll keep, if but for sympathy.   v.iv.149–51

In this context it resembles the tablet laid on Zenocrate's hearse:

> And here this table as a register
> Of all her virtues and perfections.   2 *Tamburlaine*, iii.ii.23–4

However, the reason Posthumus does not understand his tablet is because it relates to his future, not his past life – as Jupiter says:

> This tablet lay upon his breast, wherein
> Our pleasure his full fortune doth confine,   v.iv.109–10

Just as Fidele experienced a mis-placed funeral ceremony in which the dirge was spoken rather than sung, thereby distinguishing it from the real event, so, in v.iv, Posthumus experiences a reversal of a funeral ceremony – a ritual for new life. In one sense the old Posthumus has died and has been replaced by a new self who is now worthy of Imogen's love. This love gives him new life, for, in the phraseology of Lorenzo de' Medici's doctrine, he has first 'die[d] to everything else'. The vision scene is one part of the expression of this metaphor. Another part is present in the reunion of Posthumus and Imogen, and is linked with the property of the bloody cloth.[32]

Posthumus addresses the cloth at the beginning of the final act:

> Yea, bloody cloth, I'll keep thee: for I wish'd
> Thou shouldst be colour'd thus.   v.i.1–2

A few lines later, the words:

> Gods, if you
> Should have ta'en vengeance on my faults, I never
> Had liv'd to put on this: v.i.7–9

could mean that he would never have lived to 'incite (this crime)' as the Arden editor suggests; but it could also relate to the cloth itself and the fact that Posthumus wears it as a constant reminder of what he has lost. His choice of words at v.i.1–2, indicates the reason he carried the cloth – because he believed it to signify Imogen's physical death, after which their only possible reunion would be a spiritual one. Now, because he has undergone a kind of death experience, he has gained access to the plane of love which Imogen already possessed when she said, 'for then/I am in heaven for him' (I.iv.32–3). Presumably this development accounts for the surprisingly beautiful poetry of these lines at v.v.263–4 – poetry which does not tend to occur in Posthumus's former speech.[33]

The union of Imogen and Posthumus is one of many ways of inter-preting the play's final image of the eagle vanishing in the sun's beams. Posthumus is the 'eagle' Imogen chose (I.ii.70), who could behold the sun with a firm eye (I.v.11), and the latter image gains added significance when it is recalled that Imogen is likened to the sun in I.iii.30 and I.vii.86. Beholding the sun implies being distanced from it, so this image gives an insight into their early relationship – perhaps relating to Posthumus's awareness of his inferior social standing at that point, and later, to his disgust at Imogen's supposed moral inferiority. However, in v.v, the eagle vanishing in the sun's beams implies a total fusion of the two characters, beyond the reach of outsiders. Perhaps this is the state of 'beyond beyond' to which Imogen refers, when speaking to Pisanio:

> Then, true Pisanio,
> Who long'st, like me, to see thy lord; who long'st
> (O let me bate) but not like me: yet long'st
> But in a fainter kind. O not like me:
> For mine's beyond beyond: III.ii.53–7

As Rudolf Wittkower shows,[34] the eagle is depicted as the bird of resurrection in Syria from the third century B.C. onwards. The eagle and the sun image is also associated with the early Christian allegory in which the eagle, in its old age, is able to renew its youth in the light of the sun and in the waters of a fountain, which signifies an access to spiritual life through a turning to God and through baptism.[35] This relates to the spiritual elements in Imogen and Posthumus's reunion, but is also relevant to the new-found lives of many other characters, including Cymbeline, Belarius, and Iachimo. Above all, it relates to the play's setting in Cymbeline's reign – the king who ruled Britain at the time of Christ's birth – and appropriately, in Egyptian hieroglyphics, the letter A is represented by an eagle – meaning 'warmth of life, the Origin, the day'.[36] In this respect it implies the coming of a new spiritual life for a whole nation of people and indicates the transition from a pagan to a Christian God – the vanishing eagle could be linked with that of Jupiter which must take away the old god so that the new one may take his place. Such images have multiple possibilities of interpretation and represent a characteristic of the play as a whole.

The different levels on which the image exists relate to Pico's doctrine of three worlds; the terrestrial, the celestial, and the supracelestial – all of which reflect each other. In this doctrine, everything in the higher world can be grasped through its lower counterpart in this world, which suggests a train of thought similar to the one expressed in *Cymbeline*:

Everything which is in the totality of worlds is also in each of them and none of them contains anything which is not to be found in each of the others . . . whatever exists in the inferior world will also be found in the superior world, but in a more elevated form; and whatever exists on the higher plane can also be seen down below but in a somewhat degenerate and . . . adulterated shape . . . In our world we have fire as an element, in the celestial world the corresponding entity is the sun, in the supracelestial world the seraphic fire of the intellect. But consider their difference: the elemental fire burns, the celestial fire gives life, the supracelestial loves.[37]

In *Cymbeline*, the eagle motif is linked with the supracelestial in the image of the eagle vanishing in the sun's beams, but it is also linked with the elevated terrestrial love of Imogen and Posthumus – perhaps moving towards the celestial plane. Similarly, Jupiter's eagle, as an image, evokes the higher plane of the gods, but as a stage property – either the same or very similar to that used in Heywood's play, *The Golden Age*, and in various masques and pageants, it is firmly rooted in the terrestrial sphere. It is not certain whether Shakespeare's play preceded Heywood's or vice versa, so it cannot be proved that Heywood was imitating Shakespeare, or that Shakespeare was commenting on the commonplace sight of a god descending to a public playhouse stage. The only certainty is that both employed the same tradition and used similar theatrical techniques. However, as there are no eye-witness accounts of either scene in performance (Forman's account is mainly narrative), it is not known whether Shakespeare's eagle creaked down like Jonson's criticism of a playhouse throne, deliberately drawing attention to the naive artifice of the moment, or whether it was executed with all the splendour of the contemporary masques and appeared as a spectacle inspiring wonder and admiration. If the latter occurred, the staging would indicate the increased sophistication of the public stage, be an answer to Jonson's criticism, and reflect the merging of public and private playhouse practices, but it seems more likely that the reality may have been a mixture of the two – both self-conscious artifice and awe-inspiring spectacle.

12 A model of the set by René Allio for *Cymbeline* v.iv at the Royal Shakespeare Theatre, Stratford-upon-Avon (1962), directed by William Gaskill. The cage was lifted when Posthumus slept and lowered when he awoke.

The spectacle of Jupiter on the eagle is important as a visual representation of ideas expressed elsewhere in the drama. As Gombrich said in relation to Egyptian hieroglyphics, 'truth condensed into a visual image was somehow nearer the realm of absolute truth than one explained in words. It was not what these images said that made them important, but the fact that what was said was also "represented".' He also wrote that one concrete image or motif may represent one thing, symbolise another, and express yet another – and to us the three levels of meaning remain quite distinct.[38] The eagle used in performance in *Cymbeline* represents the theatrical interpretation of the mythological bird, is associated with the character of Posthumus who is lying before it (both very different sorts of eagle), expresses Shakespeare's use of masque elements and affinity with popular pageantry, recalls the Roman eagle, against whom the Leonati fought and met their deaths, and encompassing them all (according to Ripa) is an image which signifies the union of supreme insight and supreme power.[39]

The eagle was credited with the virtues which Plutarch ascribed originally to the falcon, in *De Iside et Osiride*, 'This bird ... is distinguished by the sharpness of its vision and the speed of its wings.' Wind notes: 'the image of an eye with wings brings to mind the ubiquity of the omniscient God, because the word deus was illustrated in the *Hieroglyphica* (Horapollo) by an eye, while the wings signify celeritas'[40] and Karl Giehlow quoted a passage on hieroglyphics from Diodorus (*Bibliotheca historica* III.iv) in which the eye is associated with justice and the wings of the falcon with speed: he linked this with the 'ever present possibility' of being 'called before the judgement seat of God'.[41] Shakespeare's play gives a novel twist to this interpretation as in v.iv it is the dead who summon the god to judgment, not vice versa. In addition, Wittkower writes, 'as the bird of magic, the eagle is especially significant in the interpretation of dreams'.[42]

In Pliny (*Historica naturalis*) all other birds are frightened at the sound of the eagle and all birds which are birds of prey are so frightened that they stop hunting.[43] The appearance of Jupiter on his eagle coincides with Posthumus's change in fortunes and with Iachimo (the bird of prey)'s repentance in the next scene. However, it is interesting – in terms of the simultaneous existence of different interpretations of the same image – that Iachimo's repentance also occurs after Posthumus (a different kind of eagle) has beaten him in combat, yet has spared his life (v.v.411–13).

The eagle property, like the bracelet, the bloody cloth, or the tablet, is not important in itself, except that in the visual representation, all the threads of earlier associations and images are gathered together. The multi-dimensional nature of the play is stressed through the obvious shallowness of a concrete artifact. The scene (v.iv) where the much mentioned eagle takes shape on stage, indicates the importance of viewing each motif in its correct context while realising that all dimensions exist simultaneously. This view also relates to the Renaissance fascination with trick perspective paintings. The soothsayer in *Cymbeline* does not possess the required ability: he views one level at a time and can only divine that in relation to his own narrow range of experience and professional hopes:

> thus:
> I saw Jove's bird, the Roman eagle, wing'd
> From the spongy south to this part of the west,

> There vanish'd in the sunbeams, which portends
> (Unless my sins abuse my divination)
> Success to th' Roman host.   IV.ii.347–52

Later he made amends his view to read:

> Th'imperial Caesar, should again unite
> His favour with the radiant Cymbeline,
> Which shines here in the west.   V.v.475–7

and in this he expresses yet another terrestrial interpretation of the eagle and sun image which also exists on so many other levels.

Boundaries within images constantly dissolve to reveal new possibilities, which relates to the play's dream-like quality. Similarly, worlds may merge indistinguishably with their opposites, e.g. life and death. It is interesting that the peace which forms the final living world of *Cymbeline* bears noticeable similarities to the description of death in *Titus Andronicus*:

> In peace and honour rest you here, my sons;
> Rome's readiest champions, repose you here in rest,
> Secure from worldly chances and mishaps.
> Here lurks no treason, here no envy swells,
> Here grow no damned drugs, here are no storms,   I.i.150–4

This is a dirge which recalls many of the dangers finally overcome in *Cymbeline* and in the last plays as a whole. In *Cymbeline* a sequence of dream-like journeys lead up to the peace linked with death and these are particularly stressed in the final act by the silent battle scene (v.ii), the image of the narrow lane 'close by the battle, ditch'd, and wall'd with turf' (v.iii.14), the dumb-show of Posthumus's capture (v.iii.95), Posthumus's invocation to death (v.iv.7), and most obviously, the apparitions and the vision. It is as if the peace could only be achieved through confrontations with death and those who survive the experience are, by some means, elevated to a higher plane of existence. The peace in *Cymbeline* is created out of cumulative experiences at last meeting in one body in v.v. This concept is viable because the play is so blatantly a composite artifact and it contrasts with the desperate plea of Marcus in *Titus Andronicus*:

> O, let me teach you how to knit again
> This scattered corn into one mutual sheaf,
> These broken limbs again into one body;   v.iii.70–2

Severed limbs cannot be reunited in *Titus Andronicus* because the events of the drama have worked against the realisation of such a metaphor – the opposite to Shakespeare's technique in *Cymbeline*. In *Titus Andronicus*, the stage direction, '*Enter a messenger with two heads and a hand*'

(III.i.233) shows that it cannot be so easily achieved. However, Cymbeline, described as a Lavinia figure, is capable of being restored:

> The lofty cedar, royal Cymbeline,
> Personates thee: and thy lopp'd branches point
> Thy two sons forth: who, by Belarius stol'n,
> For many years thought dead, are now reviv'd,
> To the majestic cedar join'd; whose issue
> Promises Britain peace and plenty.   v.v.454–9

Even here it is clear that the clock cannot be turned back: too much time has passed and too much has been experienced for life to go on as if nothing has happened between the rift and the recovery. On the contrary, it is apparent that the suffering and loss cannot be forgotten because they are the foundation stones of the recovery – just as Christ's suffering and death form the basis of the Christian faith and the new life it promises. After the experiences depicted in the drama a new level of collective existence is achieved in *Cymbeline* in which characters as different as Iachimo and Imogen are integrated. *Titus Andronicus* possesses no such future: no dramatic transformations took place to make it possible – all that was sought was a return to the past – a hopeless situation, bound to the rules of tragedy. In IV.i, however, Titus's sentiments are those of the Leonati in *Cymbeline*:

> Magni dominator poli,
> Tam lentus audis scelera? tam lentus vides?
>
> IV.i.81–2

[Ruler of the great heavens, art thou so slow to hear and see crimes?]
Seneca, *Phaedra* line 672

Titus also makes a similar appeal to that of the Leonati:

> We will solicit heaven and move the gods
> To send down Justice for to wreak our wrongs.   IV.iii.50–1

but *Cymbeline* possesses traces of the divine – in the potentialities of its characters' better natures; in the assertion of benevolent guidance implicit in the god's appearance; and in the anticipation for the future, linked to the Christian references – whereas *Titus Andronicus* lacks even the most basic assurances of a pagan faith.

The tragedy seems to be based on the assumption that there could be no justice for revenge in a world controlled by ruthless men – a world which even the gods have forsaken: there is no trace of any sort of higher authority beyond man's rule. Titus sent letters on arrows to the gods, but Saturninus received them: justice began and ended with the Emperor. In

Titus Andronicus, the link between Jupiter and the gibbet maker is a pun made by the clown and associated with mis-placed faith, but in *Cymbeline*, Jupiter appears between Posthumus and the gibbet, as if staying the hangman. However, the implication is not that the god intervenes to change the future, but that the future was already set and his appearance merely confirms and reassures.

Cymbeline is a fluid play: boundaries dissolve between the metaphorical and the literal. It is thematic rather than narrative-based, and moments such as the vision of v.iv must be viewed in this light. As *Cymbeline* is a composite play there is a need to fuse some of its many elements together in a particular moment which will cause the audience to recall what has passed, appreciate the spectacle that is occurring, and look forward to what is to come. Even the end hints at a new beginning, right at the start of modern civilisation, so such open-minded moments are the most appropriate.

Viewing the play as an experiment in the dramatic expression of metaphor fused with reality, provides a context for the integration of the various traditions mentioned here and Shakespeare seems to have realised the potential which the romance tradition and the tragi-comic mode offered to his development. Any incongruities can probably be set down to the fact that at this early stage he was still in the process of defining his limits and may have set them too wide. Nevertheless, he successfully integrates many disparate elements: pagan and Christian, religious and sensual, life and death are fused to produce compound effects, and this is achieved by another sort of fusion – that of textual imagery and symbol with dramatic representation. Twentieth-century reactions to the play may be mixed because, lacking the same background of contemporary traditions we, like the soothsayer, fail to recognise the many strata of meaning and take an aerial view rather than a deep cross-section.

6 · Webster and 'The suburbs of hell': *The White Devil* and *The Duchess of Malfi*

Webster's *The White Devil* and *The Duchess of Malfi* have some things in common with Shakespeare's late plays: like Shakespeare, Webster juxtaposes previously established, and sometimes old-fashioned stage techniques with experimental contemporary effects. The most famous of these are the waxworks in *The Duchess of Malfi*, following the precedent of the Lady's effigy in *The Second Maiden's Tragedy*.[1] These plays also contain pageantry, dumb-shows, an echo scene, and other traditional stage pieces: an amalgam of old and new was obviously a common facet of Jacobean drama. However, although the concept was far from unique, Webster applied it in his own individual manner. This chapter will explore the ways in which he adapted traditions to stage particular metaphors crucial to his plays' understanding.

R. W. Dent points out that Webster used an astonishing number of sources in the writing of these two plays,[2] but his originality should not be judged by his compulsive verbal, and occasionally visual 'borrowings'; instead it should be viewed in relation to the creative ways in which he employed them. The echo scene was a well-known device, most recently used in *The Old Wives Tale* (1590), *Old Fortunatus* (1599), *Cynthia's Revels* (1601) and *The Masque of Beauty* (1608), but as a dramatic device it was a peripheral event.[3] In *The Duchess of Malfi*, the echo is not a clumsily superimposed device; it is closely integrated into the dramatic development of both Antonio and the duchess. More often than not Webster's borrowings are given a new context, so a consideration of his staging is concerned not with the repetition of basic materials, but with his individual style.

Prior to 1612, when *The White Devil* was first performed, Webster had written only in collaboration – chiefly with Dekker, and more than once for the Children of Pauls – a fact which helps to account for the similarities which *The White Devil* occasionally manifests to the style of the private theatres. Ralph Berry[4] unconsciously illuminates this in his comment: 'stylistically, the norm is provided by Flamineo's fake suicide. It requires to be played with aplomb and daring'. *The White Devil* expresses the wit and self-conscious daring found in plays like Marston's *Malcon-*

tent which was originally performed by the boys of Blackfriars,[5] but was later adopted by the King's Men at the Globe, for whom Webster wrote the Induction. It is clear that mutual feedback occurred between the private and the public theatres at the beginning of the century: *The White Devil* was performed in the wake of such movement, but certain audiences seem to have reacted more enthusiastically to the changes than others.

Its first unsuccessful reception at the Red Bull suggests that, apart from the unfavourable winter weather and the 'so open and black a theatre', it also deviated significantly from other plays in the Queen's Men's repertoire to which the audience was accustomed. The Red Bull was not the best public playhouse for a play with private theatre tendencies. As John Russell Brown remarks: 'When the plays of the Queen's Men were not boisterous and unreflective, they were usually practical and unsubtle; they had nothing to compare with Flamineo's elaborate cynicism or with Vittoria's courageous pride.'[6] The Globe (where *The Duchess of Malfi* was performed) may have been more receptive to *The White Devil* as it had successfully shared a repertoire with the private Blackfriars theatre (both under King's Men's control) from approximately 1609. Such dissimilar plays as *The Winter's Tale*, *The Maid's Tragedy*, and *The Alchemist* appeared in the King's Men's repertoire 1610–11, but their discrepancies seem minimal as the quality was consistent, compared to the gulf at the Red Bull between *The White Devil* and the continuous spectacle and noisy narrative action of Heywood's *Ages* plays which were performed at the same time.

Webster surely pleased the audience with the fight at barriers in v.iii, various disguisings, and the spectacular fake death of Flamineo in v.vi, but the ghosts of Bracciano and Isabella are, like Banquo's ghost, linked to more complex expressions of the individual imagination, and the play as a whole demands a far more sophisticated reaction from its audience than do the *Ages* plays: at the Red Bull, it seems this response was not forthcoming. Individual metaphors in the play's staging may have been grasped, but it is doubtful whether the audience would assimilate them into an integral experience. In addition, Webster's deliberate policy of favouring multiple viewpoints rather than one in particular, may have left them directionless.

Webster, unlike Heywood, does not provide a chorus figure to instruct his audience how to view the play, and the chorus function which Flamineo often provides is sometimes complicated by opposing contributions – as in I.ii when Flamineo, Zanche and Cornelia view Bracciano and Vittorio's assignation:

Flam. Most happy union.
Cor. [*aside*] My fears are fall'n upon me, O my heart!
        My son the pandar: now I find our house
        Sinking to ruin. Earthquakes leave behind,
        Where they have tyrannized, iron or lead, or stone,
        But – woe to ruin – violent lust leaves none.   1.ii.215–20[7]

These opposing reactions to the same sight may be emphasised on stage
by the different positions from which it is viewed. The carpet with the
couple on it would probably be centre stage with Flamineo reclining at
one side, watching with his accomplice, Zanche, while Cornelia, standing
at a distance on the other side (probably nearest the audience), looks
down on them all from a higher stance – both literally and morally. This
tableau effect and its dialogue recalls the vogue for perspective pictures to
which Inga-Stina Ewbank draws attention, citing *The Oxford English
dictionary*'s definition of perspective: 'A picture or figure constructed so
as to produce some fantastic effect; e.g. appearing distorted or confused
except from one particular point of view, or presenting totally different
aspects from different points.'[8] The similarity between Webster's scene
and a perspective picture may be unintentional, but it seems that he does
intend a diversification of attitudes at this point and it seems likely that he
would seize an opportunity to stress this visually as well as verbally. As
Dieter Mehl observes: 'The visual element is always predominant, even in
the dialogue scenes, so that the spectator does not feel the dumbshows to
be independent additions, contrasted with the character of the play
proper.'[9] In 1.ii Cornelia rudely interrupts the action, which was becoming
absorbing, breaks up the tableau, and puts the audience in a quandary,
since she is obviously a virtuous moral figure opposing a more dubious,
but far more interesting group of characters. Echoes of morality play
technique make the audience further aware of the implications of the
scene for, as Glynne Wickham notes,[10] Webster has placed it simultaneously at court and in a Garden of Eden context – as various comments
stress: 'Never dropt mildew on a flower here,/Till now' (1.ii.272–3) and:

> O that this fair garden
> Had with all poisoned herbs of Thessaly
> At first been planted, made a nursery
> For witchcraft; rather than a burial plot,
> For both your honours.   1.ii.274–8

Furthermore, Flamineo can be identified with the serpent in: 'We are
engag'd to mischief and must on' (1.ii.347) and:

> The way ascends not straight, but imitates
> The subtle foldings of a winter's snake,   1.ii.351–2

Earlier in the scene, Cornelia's words, 'Be thy act Judas-like, betray in kissing' (298) hint that these distorted echoes of a morality play will continue throughout; this is picked up later, after Flamineo's murder of Marcello, by Vittoria's couplet:

> [reads] '*I give that portion to thee, and no other,*
> *Which Cain groan'd under having slain his brother.*'   v.vi.13–14

Apart from the morality tradition, such instances have a more recent precedent in the play-within-a-play in *Hamlet*. Old biblical standards are being invoked in I.ii, as elsewhere, yet Webster's technique diverges from the traditional interpretation and suggests connotations of Marlowe's achievement in *Tamburlaine*, where the audience is placed in the predicament of having to judge a morally undeserving, but dramatically superior figure. Webster offers no straightforward instructions to match those of Homer in Heywood's plays; nor does he temporarily suspend all consideration of standard values in favour of pure theatrical delight, as Heywood occasionally does in presenting the humour and spectacle of the gods' behaviour – instead, Webster forces immoral and moral attitudes side by side, almost as if he does not encourage a judgment of the situation, but an understanding appreciation of its complexity.

In I.ii the Garden of Eden metaphor of the Fall seems melodramatic and Cornelia's outburst, an over-reaction. Here, Webster, as elsewhere in the play, turns traditional associations upside down – this time to condition the audience's reaction to Cornelia. Flamineo tries to dispel her as if she was a threatening evil spirit: 'What Fury rais'd thee up? away, away!' (270); and while the last words could be spoken to Zanche, who immediately exits, it would seem more effective if they were addressed to Cornelia, before whose anger Zanche flees. In this way they would be part of Flamineo's attempted exorcism of the demon. His next words are also more appropriate to something evil than to his virtuous mother:

> I pray will you go to bed then,
> Lest you be blasted?   I.ii.273–4

Here his secular threat is invested with the religious insinuation of Christian prayer and divine retribution. Later, Bracciano further tarnishes the audience's impression of Cornelia's moral outlook by treating her as a malevolent witch (the ability to raise storms and influence the weather was attributed to witches in the seventeenth century, cf. *Macbeth*: Bracciano uses this metaphor):

> Uncharitable woman thy rash tongue
> Hath rais'd a fearful and prodigious storm, –
> Be thou the cause of all ensuing harm.   I.ii.305–7

Returning to the perspective analogy, here it is Cornelia's vision, the traditional moral view, which is portrayed as a distortion. However, in the trial scene (III.ii) this is slightly modified. In this scene, Dent has revealed Webster's application of the old proverb, 'An unbidden guest knows not where to sit [must bring his stool with him]',[11] but he offers no explanation as to how Bracciano's action might be dramatically significant. It may be no more than an indication of his alienation from those judging Vittoria and his affiliation with her, but visually it could be important.

Monticelso's words, 'Forbear my lord, here is no place assign'd you' (1) suggest a prior placement of the other characters on the stage. Their reluctance to include him amongst them and his reluctance to be associated with them would indicate that he sat apart from the official grouping, which would express its opposition most effectively with Vittoria, Zanche, Flamineo, and Marcello entering at one side and the Ambassadors, Francisco etc. at the other, with the lawyer moving between them. This would leave a central position free for Bracciano (possibly upstage) so that when he spread his gown out and sat down on it alone, the audience would immediately be reminded of the carpet in I.ii, perhaps placed in exactly the same position, on which his relationship with Vittoria began, and on which the seeds of the murder, now being tried, were sown through his interpretation of Vittoria's dream.

Cornelia's dire warnings, which seemed hysterical exaggerations then, now, with hindsight, demand more respect. The 'rich gown', the carpet and the 'two fair cushions' are properties which provide a valuable symmetrical effect. When he exits, Bracciano leaves the gown lying on the stage (172–9) where it again mimics the empty carpet of I.ii beside which Flamineo and Cornelia argue when first Vittoria, then Bracciano, have abandoned it. During the rest of the trial scene and Vittoria's spirited denials, it is a constant reminder of the clashes of that first meeting, but now Cornelia's ineffectual protestations have been replaced by Monticelso's harsh accusations.

However, despite the probable justice of Monticelso's words and the fact that Cornelia's fears have proved prophetic, Vittoria's wit and *energeia* win her sympathy. The empty gown, like the empty carpet, hints at Vittoria's and Bracciano's guilt, but both remain ambiguous emblems since their emptiness fails to provide proof – one way or the other. As the title suggests, it is increasingly more difficult to distinguish between good and evil because elements of each exist in the portrayal of the other.

This overlapping of opposite states occurs elsewhere in the imagery and staging of *The White Devil*, especially in relation to death and life, disease and health. Like the religious versus secular connotations of I.ii, it indicates Webster's technique of establishing an atmosphere of precarious instability by turning accepted concepts inside-out, often juxtaposing the actual with conflicting metaphors, e.g. Vittoria, who appears as the beautiful heroine, describes herself as deformed in an attempt to stress the severance of her relationship with Bracciano and her new moral status. Here a contradictory physical metaphor is used to express a physical state:

> I had a limb corrupted to an ulcer,
> But I have cut it off: and now I'll go
> Weeping to heaven on crutches.   IV.ii.121–3

The White Devil even opens in the same manner when the scarcely human Lodovico ('begotten in an earthquake', I.i.27) is straightaway likened to a living corpse, producing a substance which his followers take as medicine, but which proves to be harmful rather than curative:

>   Your followers
> Have swallowed you like mummia, and being sick
> With such unnatural and horrid physic
> Vomit you up i' th' kennel –   I.i.15–18

The reference to mummia, a substance prepared from corpses, is recalled much later when he appears at Bracciano's death-bed in the habit of a Capuchin friar. The uneasy violence of the earlier description is linked with Bracciano's fate when his two ministers reveal themselves:

> *Gasp.* This is Count Lodovico.
> *Lod.*   This Gasparo.
>   And thou shalt die like a poor rogue.
> *Gasp.*   And stink
>   Like a fly-blown dog.
> *Lod.*   And be forgotten
>   Before thy funeral sermon.   v.iii.164–7

Lodovico, associated with storm and earthquake imagery in the play, is the ultimate cause of the physical and mental turbulence in the action which results in the deaths of the protagonists:

> *Lod.* Devil Bracciano. Thou art damn'd.
> *Gasp.*   Perpetually.   v.iii.151

This speech, spoken by men who, in the guise of friars, had just finished speaking of salvation for his soul, immediately evokes the horrors of Judgment Day and temporarily associates Lodovico with the role of God – yet his violent manner and cruel delight simultaneously recall his devilish qualities, previously expressed in his words as he set off on the mission:

Lod.   Now to th'act of blood;
There's but three Furies found in spacious hell,
But in a great man's breast three thousand dwell.   IV.iii.151–3

In typical turnabout fashion, of which Marlowe would have approved
(Tamburlaine; and Lightborn in *Edward II*), the agent of Webster's moral
scourge is not a godly Christian figure, but an agent of the devil – so, once
again, a morally undeserving character, such as Bracciano, invites a
sympathetic response from the audience due to the nature of his attackers.

Lodovico and Isabella seem an unlikely couple (one seemingly evil, the
other supposedly virtuous) until Webster links them through a mutual
affinity for corpses. In relation to Vittoria, Isabella expresses the desire:

> To dig the strumpet's eyes out, let her lie
> Some twenty months a-dying, to cut off
> Her nose and lips, pull out her rotten teeth,
> Preserve her flesh like mummia, for trophies
> Of my just anger: II.i.246–50

She is supposed to be acting a part, but as Joan Lord suggests,[12] her acting
is suspect, since she is far more convincing in this role than in that of the
stoical wife. In a sense the physical violence which occurs on the stage in
the fifth act has its roots in the violence of Isabella's desires which are later
championed by Lodovico on her behalf. Evil and good are once more
inextricably entwined, and the staging emphasises this.

Just as good overlaps evil, and life overlaps death, so the image is
juxtaposed with the living actuality. This follows a less clear design in *The
White Devil* than in *The Duchess of Malfi*, but it is nevertheless an area
which involves the staging of vivid metaphors. The most striking instance
in the earlier play is the dumb-show which portrays Isabella's death and
places Cornelia's words, 'Be thy act Judas-like, betray in kissing' in a new
context.[13]

It is Bracciano's inanimate image – his portrait – which gives the
betraying poisoned kiss,[14] and the suggestion that the portrait was a
substitute for the man himself is stressed both by his earlier refusal to kiss
her and by the incident in v.iii when he prevents a parallel occurrence of
the scene – this time with Vittoria:

> Do not kiss me, for I shall poison thee.
> This unction is sent from the great Duke of Florence.   v.iii.26–7

The Judas image lurks behind all these actions – a reminder of the play's
distorted echoes of the morality tradition, and the religious connotations
of this are present in the dumb-show presenting Isabella's death. This
event stresses the devotional element of Isabella's practice, the picture

being revealed as a kind of altar, before which '*she kneels down as to prayers*'. It may be placed in the discovery space, but it is more likely that this would be required for the entry of the vaulting horse immediately afterwards, so the picture would probably be on the tiring house wall with its own small curtain. The sight also evokes a sense of mourning at a tomb (cf. *The Duchess of Malfi*, 1.i.520–1), thus dramatising the metaphorical death of their marriage and providing a visual irony in that the one who is mourned is the agent of his devoted mourner's death.

Isabella's solemn ritual, presumably accompanied by soft music (construed from the Conjuror's demand for greater volume at the beginning of the second dumb-show) is parodied by Julio and Christophero's earlier ceremony: '*they put on spectacles of glass, which cover their eyes and noses, and then burn perfumes afore the picture, and wash the lips of the picture, that done, quenching the fire, and putting off their spectacles, they depart laughing.*' It may be over-ingenious, but even the choice of their names suggests a black parody of Judas's betrayal of Christ.

Earlier, Isabella associated herself with conjuring and charms when she told Francisco:

> I do not doubt
> As men to try the precious unicorn's horn
> Make of the powder a preservative circle
> And in it put a spider, so these arms
> Shall charm his poison, force it to obeying
> And keep him chaste from an infected straying.   II.i.13–18

The final rhyming couplet resembles a chant as was common in the application of these charms. In the dumb-show, the glass spectacles or masks which protect the murderers provide unnatural ceremonial attire, and the perfumed smoke, the flames of the fire, and their demonical laughter as they depart, suggest that the contrast between their ritual and that of Isabella is one of black versus white magic – the tortures of hell versus the devotion of heaven. The outcome of this scene, the removal of the dead body, is emblematical of the strength of 'his poison' and her failure to 'force it to obeying'; and here the poison is both the actual poison on the picture and the poison of Bracciano's passion which caused its use.

In one sense the figure treated as dead changes places with his mourner: the dead shows signs of life; the living is killed. There are, as Bracciano realises later, no firm barriers between life and death – each intrudes on the other. To Isabella, Bracciano is metaphorically dead, yet he is very much alive and behind the mask of his memorial in his intention to murder her. Later, to Bracciano, Isabella is dead, yet his imagination conjures up her ghost. In *The White Devil*, a fascination with the powers of the imagination and their consequences in reality, seems to be the theme at the forefront of the play's design and Webster's treatment of the associations between life and death seems less well structured.

In *The Duchess of Malfi*, however, his intentions appear clearer in relation to the overlap of life and death. Here, the staging of this metaphor is complete rather than fragmentary. Bosola's words:

> We are only like dead walls, or vaulted graves,
> That ruin'd, yields no echo: v.v.97–8[15]

are proved mistaken by the echo from the duchess's grave (v.iii). This scene is one of the many indications in the play that life and death co-exist – a theme which first occurs in the wooing scene. Here, the duchess's pretence of making her will (an act anticipating death) results instead in a new marriage and a new start in life. When she talks of:

> What's laid up for tomorrow, I did mean
> What's laid up yonder for me ...
>
> > In heaven –   1.i.274–5

she is playing with both the secular and the religious connotations of 'heaven' – a quibble which Antonio seems to take up later when he says of marriage:

> It locally contains, or heaven, or hell;
> There's no third place in't.   1.i.394–5

In iv.i her marriage state is dramatised as a living hell with her exposure to Ferdinand's tortuous device, but, as has been shown, as early as 1.i, characters indicate that life after death and life itself share the same descriptive terms. Their discussion of marriage flits easily across the boundaries of life and death:

> *Ant.* Begin with ...
> > the sacrament of marriage –
> I'd have you first provide for a good husband,
> Give him all.
> *Duch.*   All?
> *Ant.*   Yes, your excellent self.
> *Duch.* In a winding sheet?
> *Ant.*   In a couple.
> *Duch.* Saint Winifred, that were a strange will!
> *Ant.* 'Twere strange if there were no will in you
> To marry again.   1.i.385–92

Here the context of will-making causes ambiguity as to which worlds they are each envisaging. In this stichomythia the duchess jokingly imagines herself dead, while Antonio pictures her alive. Later the imagery is reversed when she chides him:

> What is't distracts you? This is flesh, and blood, sir;
> 'Tis not the figure cut in alabaster
> Kneels at my husband's tomb. Awake, awake, man!　　1.i.453–5.

The juxtaposition continues when their marriage, causing the banishment of the alabaster figure and the revival of the living duchess, is sealed with a kiss which is a bond of living passion, but is described in a phrase applied to death:

> 　　　　　　　　　　here upon your lips
> I sign your *Quietus est*:–　　　　　　　　　　1.i.463–4

The link between love and death in the Renaissance has been discussed in relation to *Cymbeline* and, here, Webster is using associations which would be familiar to his audience and which also occurred, in different contexts, in Shakespeare's last plays. Lorenzo de' Medici's words are as relevant to *The Duchess of Malfi* as they are to *Cymbeline*, 'whoever lives for love, first dies to everything else'.[16] However, the concept of a fusion of life and death is not, in *The Duchess of Malfi*, restricted to the expression of traditional Renaissance ideas: this is only a part of Webster's art. His particular application of the concept forms an integral part of the play's design. This scene (I.i) provides the metaphors which are enacted later in the play – at the duchess's death and afterwards. Antonio's definition of ambition is staged in IV.ii in the masque of the madmen whose individual ambitions have been perverted, and who, although physically living, are dead to sanity and their ambitious hopes:

> Ambition, madam, is a great man's madness,
> That is not kept in chains, and close-pent rooms,
> But in fair lightsome lodgings, and is girt
> With the wild noise of prattling visitants,
> Which makes it lunatic, beyond all cure –　　　　1.i.420–4

Similarly, the duchess's words:

> How can the church bind faster?
> We now are man and wife, and 'tis the church
> That must but echo this:　　　　　　　　　　1.i.491–3

find an ironical answer in the echo scene when the church, which 'echoes' the last moments of their relationship, is in ruins; but the most striking metaphor to be staged is that of the kneeling alabaster statue which the duchess becomes at the point of death (see below).

The Duchess of Malfi is full of instances when boundaries between different worlds are blurred, such as sanity and madness; life and death. One explanation for Webster's apparent oversight in allowing the duchess to leave instructions for the care of children whom she should believe dead, might be, as John Russell Brown suggests, that she has forgotten or rejected the deaths portrayed by the wax images, thus evoking added pathos at her death; or it could be that the confusion arises from her inability to distinguish any longer between the two worlds of life and death. They have been perilously close throughout the play and now, as she stands on the brink of passing from one to the other, it is feasible that she fails to separate the loved ones who are united in her mind, into their life or death division.

If this is the case, her attitude is understandable. Prior to death she is subjected to the confusing experience of the madmen who perform a nightmare sequence, evoking death, doomsday, and hell. Inga-Stina Ewbank suggests that this resembles an anti-masque, popular at contemporary weddings (e.g. that of Princess Elizabeth in 1613), and frequently performed by lunatics,[17] who, as F. L. Lucas stresses,[18] were regarded primarily as an amusement at the time.

In iv.ii the jarring bestiality and incoherence of the lunatics are used to deepen the pathos of the duchess's predicament. Ewbank regards it as 'a contrivance of cruel irony on the part of Ferdinand' that the duchess is mocked with a belated marriage masque leading up to the main masque where she is 'taken out' by Bosola. As she shows, even the duchess's preparations for the laying out of her dead body are ironically associated with those of the dressing of a bride (iv.ii.190).[19] Just as her marriage was linked with death in 1.i, here her death is associated with marriage.

However, the image which most successfully expresses the fusion of life and death is that of the alabaster figure. This is far more significant than Lucas implies: it is not merely a suggestion of the dead and of the duchess's forgetfulness. Kneeling wives and children were popular features of Elizabethan and Jacobean tombs, as Eric Mercer illustrates,[20] and for the duration of the play the duchess exists simultaneously as the figure kneeling at her husband's tomb (expressing the public image which complies with her brothers' wishes), and the figure of 'flesh and blood' – the living duchess who eclipses the image and chooses a personal life outside the rigid confines of her public state.

This dual representation is all the more striking if it is realised that, by an alabaster figure, Webster most probably did not mean a cold, white, remote image, but one which had been carefully painted to resemble the duchess as closely as possible. Although Terence Spencer, in relation to Hermione's statue in *The Winter's Tale*, comments: 'In the churches of

London and throughout England were many charming funerary statues, lying supine or kneeling in prayer. It must be admitted, however, that they were not of such realism that one would speak to them and stand in hope of an answer',[21] such effigies may, in certain cases, have been more realistic than he is willing to credit. Some tombmakers were obviously less skilled as Mercer points out, but he does suggest that: 'It is possible, because of their individual features, that some of the effigies by the early Burton alabasterers are intended as true likenesses,'[22] and he cites the example of Sir Robert Watter (d.1612), buried in St Crux Church, York, with the inscription: 'Here lie the true portraiture of Robert Watter ... and of his wife Margaret.'

Colouring of funeral effigies appears to have been the norm rather than the exception in England at this time, although, as Ben Jonson indicated, it had begun to be unfashionable by 1631, when it was dismissed as 'city taste'.[23] As early as 1584, in *Campaspe*, Lyly drew attention to the fact that, 'Sepulchres have fresh colours but rotten bones.' Katherine Esdaile notes: 'Colouring was usually of the essence, even some of our finest brasses have it introduced by means of enamel, and in the case of alabaster the colour was delicately applied so as not to destroy the translucency of the marble.'[24] The image, therefore, has qualities of a life-like ghost. Esdaile also draws attention to the statue of Hermione in *The Winter's Tale*, which Bergeron and others have likened to a funeral effigy; pointing out that the life-like colouring of the statue plays an important part in the recognition scene:[25] 'colouring and gilding of effigies was a fine art, and very costly, and in many cases, from the sixteenth century onwards, effigies had to be accurate – "cutt graven and colored to the life"'.[26]

The tradition seems important to the impact of the staging of *The Duchess of Malfi* when it is realised that this may considerably affect the audience's visual interpretation of the metaphor in 1.i. The imagined delicate shades of the duchess's alabaster figure contrast sharply with the cruder, blood-stained colours of Antonio's wax figure. Both exist while their originals live, although only one image is prominent at any one time – only the live duchess is visible to Antonio in 1.i, while from iv.i onwards the duchess takes the wax figure to be the sole representation of Antonio. Not until the point of death do the live duchess and the remembered monumental image become one in a brief, visual fusion of image and stage metaphor – an effective expression of the circle in which her life has moved, and of the simultaneous existence of life in death and death in life.

As the duchess kneels to face death she becomes an expression of the image which previously faced death's emblem, the tomb. After kneeling it is feasible that one facing death, who has just talked of heaven, might utter

the invitation 'Come violent death' with her hands together in prayer –
thus posing for her last few lines in a kneeling composure which visually
echoes the 'figure cut in alabaster' which kneels at her first husband's
tomb (1.i.454). This would allow the delicate colours of the alabaster
figure to merge with the life tones of the breathing woman in the minds of
the audience.

In addition, the duchess's words:

> Pull, and pull strongly, for your able strength
> Must pull down heaven upon me:–   IV.ii.230–1

have connotations of the toppling of a monument, or a building, into ruins
– crushed from above by a great force. This recalls Cariola's earlier
prophetic perception that the duchess resembled 'some reverend
monument/Whose ruins are even pitied' (IV.ii.33–4) – a metaphor implicit
in the association of the duchess at the point of death with the funeral
image which is to be pulled down, and one which achieves its final
expression in the voice from the tomb, among the ruins of the echo scene.
As Bergeron notes, by 'ruined monument' Webster may be referring to
any sort of ruined structure, a sepulchre or a carved figure or effigy.[27] The
final parallel between the duchess and the alabaster image is even more
apparent if Bosola's role as tomb-maker is interpreted not merely as that
of one who makes the coffin, but, as he implies himself, of one who forms
and decorates the effigy of the deceased which would traditionally adorn
the tomb – 'My trade is to flatter the dead, not the living' (IV.ii.147).

However, ultimately, it is the duchess herself who moulds her own
monument – refusing to be hysterical, and ironically adopting the very
pose she discarded in 1.ii when she stressed that she was not the kneeling
figure at the tomb. In IV.ii she creates the image of 'sacred innocence'
(355), which impinges on Bosola's mind after death and helps to bring
about his conversion. His role as tomb-maker, with its aspect of painter
'to the life' recurs in his bid to revive her – which parallels the bid of an
artist to recapture the life-like complexion of the dead person comme-
morated:

> Upon thy pale lips I will melt my heart
> To store them with fresh colour: IV.ii.344–5

Yet if he does kiss her here, as his words imply, his human action –
contrasting with the earlier artificial artistry of Ferdinand – is associated
with failure: even the wedding kiss of Antonio and the duchess was a
'*Quietus est*': his attempt cannot achieve the impossible. Later, the same
action of a kiss is to link previous associations with actual death in Julia's

kissing of the poisoned Bible: the organised Church finally appears openly in the Judas role it has taken throughout the play in relation to the duchess and her family.

This underlying current of associated betrayal and evil in a religious context is also staged in the scene of the duchess's death, as her murderers are associated with the killing of a martyr – through her composure and prayers welcoming death; and through her link with a funeral monument at this point, they are also implicated in sacrilegious behaviour. Although only a metaphor here, the toppling or breaking of a church monument was strictly condemned, as John Weever indicated in his book, *Ancient Funerall Monuments*: 'Those (in foregoing ages) which did violate, misuse, or distaine tombes, graves, sepulchers, or any of these funerall Monuments, were punished either with death, perpetuall exile ...'[28] Finally, the wedding ring of I.ii is translated, in IV.iii, to the circle around the duchess's neck which, unlike the Gordian knot of the ring which the Cardinal (like Alexander) removes by force in III.iv, cannot be broken – yet another reversal of Webster's which his characters could neither anticipate nor escape.

The overlapping of life and death not only provides an important demonstration of the instability of states of being in the play, but it also contains a comment on the self-conscious awareness of Webster's characters. Bergeron dubbed Webster 'the supreme tomb-maker'[29] – an aspect of his art which is passed on to his characters in the way they appear to try to mould and direct each other on their ways towards death. This seems to be Webster's individual response to another commonplace dramatic tradition of the seventeenth century – the concept of the world as a stage.

In Webster's art, the emphasis appears to be on the relationship between those controlling the action and those who are controlled; but it is further complicated by the necessity of the latter group to adopt masks and deceit which are alien to their natures, in order to stave off the other roles imposed on them: as the duchess complains,

> O misery! methinks unjust actions
> Should wear these masks and curtains, and not we:–   III.ii.158–9

Just as Bosola sees himself as the director of the duchess's last scene in IV.ii, the duchess is also aware of the situation and looks to him for direction in IV.i:

> Good comfortable fellow ...
>   who must despatch me?
> I account this world a tedious theatre,
> For I do play a part in't 'gainst my will.   IV.i.84–5

She has always played a part against her will because, since the opening of
the play, her private self and her public self have moved their separate
ways, and only at her death are they ironically united.

In *The White Devil*, conscious theatricality is allied to the daring
experimentalism of the private theatre, but as Kirsch shows, in *The
Duchess of Malfi*, Webster manages to: 'convert the self-conscious
conception of drama, essentially characteristic of the comic and tragi-
comic theatre, to the purposes of tragedy'.[30] In *The White Devil* the
metaphor of the stage and life is used to express the dangerous consequences of the characters' uncontrolled imaginations, passions, and
actions. It also provides a distancing effect which occasionally allows the
audience to delight in the characters' affectation almost objectively, with
no restraints placed on them by a conflicting need to sympathise – as in the
staging of the quarrel between Bracciano and Vittoria (IV.ii). According to
Kirsch, although the scene appears to concern the quarrel primarily, its
main focus is on 'Flamineo's stage directions':[31] 'Now for two
whirlwinds' (IV.ii.106), as Vittoria counters Bracciano's anger; or his
command, 'Turn to my lord, good sister' (136), followed by his separate
confidential instructions and encouragement to each (150), which recall a
similar directing role of his in I.ii, between Vittoria and Camillo. In both
these scenes Flamineo is in control, but in v.vi he is rudely awakened to the
activities of an external force which overwhelms his own.

In the scene of his fake death he calculates two possible improvisations,
but fails to anticipate the actual eventuality because it is outside the scope
of his planned performance. However, even then, he cannot discard his
concern for details of staging; and his enquiry about the weapon which is
killing him evokes a mingled reaction of admiration, pathos, and black
humour, providing a distancing barrier between him and the audience
even at the last:

> O what blade is't?
> A Toledo, or an English fox?
> I ever thought a cutler should distinguish
> The cause of my death, rather than a doctor.
> Search my wound deeper: tent it with the steel
> That made it.   v.vi.234–8

He cannot resist attempting to direct his own death, so great is his
obsession; yet he must finally acknowledge his lack of control, 'O I am in a
mist' (260).

This reaction is not unlike that of Bosola (who shares many similarities
with Flamineo) when he is asked how Antonio's death occurred, and
answers:

In a mist: I know not how –
Such a mistake as I have often seen
In a play: v.v.94–6

However, unlike Flamineo, Bosola does not die whilst still trying to direct
those around him, and it is an indication of the greater sophistication of
the later play that he is aware that he was only a tool or agent for more
powerful directors, who were themselves displaced in the end by the
irrefutable controlling force of Webster the playwright. Bosola, like the
duchess, was an actor whose actions were predetermined by his part:

and lastly, for myself,
That was an actor in the main of all
Much 'gainst mine own good nature, yet i'th' end
Neglected.   v.v.84–7

Ultimately it is the futility of the characters' attempts to control their own
fates which strikes Webster's audience most forcibly through the cumulative effects of the 'world as a stage' metaphor – and although the concept
works successfully in *The White Devil*, its influence is limited: in *The
Duchess of Malfi* its expression as an integral part of the tragedy seems a
finer achievement.

In many ways the moulding of characters by other characters reaches a
greater refinement in *The Duchess of Malfi* and moves beyond the bounds
of entertaining burlesque, self-directed deaths, or semi-tragic confusions.
In the later play, the moulding of characters is juxtaposed with the visual
images and representations of effigies, and is therefore firmly involved
with the overlapping of life and death, the natural and the artificial, the
private and the public – themes which have already been cited as
important elements in the play. Webster's method here is not dissimilar to
that of Shakespeare in *Cymbeline*, where an accumulation of images and
associations finally achieves actual representation on stage in the form of
Jupiter's eagle. The technique can also be found in later works; John
Ford's, *'Tis Pity She's a Whore*, for example. Here, textual references and
associations with the heart culminate in staged events involving a representation of a real heart. The waxworks in *The Duchess of Malfi* can be
considered part of this tradition. Often taken to be the play's most
sensational aspect, they are, nevertheless, an important part of its design,
and their significance far transcends mere theatrical effect: like the eagle
or the heart, they are a visual focus for many associations and images.
Above all, they shed new light on the exact nature of Ferdinand's cruelty.

Lucas, among others, indicates possible literary and historical sources
for the idea: he notes the similarity between the waxwork scene and 'the

pretended executions of Philoclea and Pamela in the sight of those dearest to them, in Arcadia III';[32] and later, he also draws attention to the contemporary practice of preparing and exhibiting funeral effigies:

Wax images of the dead were much more familiar to Webster's audience than to us. A year or two before this play was acted, the citizens had watched a wax effigy of the dead Prince Henry borne through the London streets. 'On the evening of that Sunday (Dec. 6th 1612) was brought a representation of the Prince, made at short notice, though extremely resembling him, and apparelled with clothes . . . in short everything he wore at the time of his creation. This figure was laid on its back on the coffin, and fast bound to it; the head being supported by two cushions, just as it was to be drawn along the streets in the funeral chariot with eight black horses' (Birch, *Life of Prince Henry*, 1760, p. 362). The figure subsequently took its place among the other wax-works in Westminster Abbey.[33]

Webster's so-called sensational effect is, therefore, derived from recognisable literary and historical precedents.

According to W. H. St John Hope, King Henry III seems to have been the first king to have been represented by a wax image on his coffin in 1272; and after this the custom became accepted. The details of this first instance are not known, but an image using 300lb of wax was made and Hope assumes it was probably for the king's funeral ceremony.[34] The first display of an effigy at a royal funeral in England which is on record is, as Ernst H. Kantorowicz reveals, that of Edward II in 1327, when the king's embalmed body, accompanied by an effigy, was taken for burial.[35] Hope notes that the last English king for whom a funeral effigy was made was James I, because although Charles II and William and Mary had effigies, these were not used in their funerals and were primarily decorative, later additions; so it seems that Webster was writing in the last days of an era. Apparently it was unusual for anyone other than a monarch to have an effigy made, but Prince Henry was an exception. His popularity, youth, and tragic death, and the fact that he was honoured in this way, may have made an impression on Webster, and he would have had ample opportunity to view other such effigies in a more complete state than we can view them today[36] because the Treasurer's accounts for 1606 contain an advance of £50 as part of the payment to the Dean of Westminster Abbey for dressing the effigies in preparation for a visit by King Christian of Denmark: 'Imprimis, seaven statues of Kinges and Queenes, viz[t] of our late soveraigne Q.Elizabeth, of Henrie the seaventh and his Queene, Edwarde the third and his Queene, Henrie the fifth and his Queene, repayred, robed and furnished at the King's Majestie his charge.'[37]

As Kantorowicz shows, the effigy in the sixteenth century indicated that the royal Dignity never died and that in the image, the king's jurisdiction continued until the day he was buried. In conjunction with this view a new triumphal element was introduced into the funeral ceremony which had been absent in earlier times. This led to: 'a replacement of the simple bier by the triumphal "chariot d'armes" on which henceforth the effigy rode – at first on top of the coffin, later alone and separated from the corpse'.[38] The custom spread to France where, at Francis I's funeral, in 1547: 'the coffin in a black draped chariot went in the van of the procession, while the effigy, in full royal triumph, was carried near the rear, the position of honour'.[39] Bergeron regards Webster's effigies as prophesying the deaths of the children and stressing the inevitability of the duchess's fate,[40] while Lord describes them as, 'a grotesque parody of the ending of *The Winter's Tale*'.[41] Both views are acceptable, yet neither attempts to pinpoint why Webster used this particular mode of expression, nor stresses the originality of his application of an accepted custom.

By tradition, the royal effigy expressed the dignity of the king; it was a memorial of the dead man's public state, stressing his status in a creative manner, and the king's immortal qualities were emphasised over his physical mortality. Webster deliberately twists all these values and associations – not least in the irony that a memorial of a dead man's public state is used to represent a man who, even when living, could never acknowledge or claim his public position. Webster's wax figures express, not dignity, but degradation; they are the propagators of mental anguish and grief, not comfort and triumphant ceremony. They mock any hopes of immortality by impersonating a defeated, mutilated, physical body, thereby linking a symbol traditionally associated with the king, the head of state, to that of a traitor, as was commonly seen hanging on the gallows, or spiked on London Bridge. This interpretation might even be regarded as a variant of yet another well-known tradition – that of the role reversal of the king and the beggar (referred to in *Richard II* and other plays). It would be particularly fitting that Antonio, a subject who secretly became the duchess's husband and, theoretically, ought to have been a ruler, should inspire this cruel, ironical response in her jealous and ambitious brother, Ferdinand.[42]

Effigies were associated with public display and achieved a distancing effect from grief; personal emotion and mourning were confined to the actual body in the coffin draped with black, and did not affect the rich colours of the effigy. In Webster's scene, a split perspective occurs: the duchess, mistaking them for real bodies, feels personal grief for the images, while the triumphal element, with which effigies were traditionally associated, finds expression in Ferdinand's delight that his scheme has succeeded. It appears that Webster may have blended a variation of the historical associations of effigies with Sidney's attempts to terrify in

Arcadia, and the resulting scene has greater legitimate dramatic value than critics will usually credit.

The underlying evocation of the two bodies, united in the living king, but separated at his death – which is present in the use of effigies – also has reverberations at the duchess's death, where the opposite sequence is shown. As has already been demonstrated, the two bodies, separate in life, finally come together in death. However, it is not merely the tableau of the effigies which relates to the rest of the play's design, but also the duchess's response to them.

The scene is a concentrated expression of Ferdinand's perverted cruelty and her subsequent torture and suffering. The depth of the duchess's despair is stressed by her declaration:

> There is not between heaven and earth one wish
> I stay for after this: it wastes me more
> Than were't my picture, fashion'd out of wax,
> Stuck with a magical needle and then buried
> In some foul dunghill;   IV.i.61–5

which indirectly draws attention to the nature of Ferdinand's exploits. The duchess likens the sight to a cursed wax image of herself stuck with pins and, although she does not know it, her analogy is frighteningly appropriate, for Ferdinand has, in fact, made a life-size wax image of Antonio and has, presumably, mutilated it with a dagger or similar weapon, so that it is also a giant-scale black magic property – not, however, acting on its original but, as the duchess confirms, on his wife. Such practices were not uncommon at the time according to Lucas, and Reginald Scot, in his *Discoverie of Witchcraft* (1584) devotes Chapter 16 of Book XII to: 'A charm teaching how to hurt whom you list with images of wax.&c.'

As M. C. Bradbrook states in 'Two notes upon Webster',[43] the dead man's hand which Ferdinand gave to the duchess earlier in the play is also part of witchcraft rites, being, 'a powerful charm which was also used in the cure of madness but which as the "Hand of Glory" or *main de gloire* was an essential ingredient in the more deadly practices of the Black Art'. Ferdinand's use of witchcraft, however fraudulent, nevertheless expresses the depth to which he has stooped, for as John Weever declared:

the most execrable and hellish abuse of all others offered to the dead, is effected by witchcraft, incantation, and Art-magicke; an art saith Quintilian, Declam. 15 which is said to disquiet the Gods, to trouble and displace the starres, to search into the graves and sepulchres of the dead, to mutilate, dismember, and cut off, certaine parts of the carcases therein inhumed, and by those pairings and cuttings, together with certaine horrid enchantments, charmes, and spels, to bring to passe strange, diabolical conclusions.[44]

The scene, therefore, dramatises two nadirs – that of the duchess's spirits, and that of Ferdinand's behaviour. From here it is feasible that his practices lead him to her murder and his own madness.

It is not only the death of the duchess which might have affected a contemporary audience: the deaths of her children would also have been important. The display of the strangled children is significant because it indicates the first stage of Bosola's compassion and subsequent remorse. Like the audience, he is moved by the sight: Ferdinand, however, is lost:

> The death
> Of young wolves is never to be pitied.   IV.ii.258–9

The duchess, lying beside her dead children, is now provided with another means of attracting sympathy. Not only does she resemble an innocent martyr, but she is also a faithful mother, and as Mercer reveals: 'there was ... a religious sanction ... to praise of fruitfulness. It is well illustrated by the brass at Sherfield-on-Lodden, Hants, to Mary Palmes, who died in childbirth in 1595 at the age of 32 and having borne ten children, with its revealing quotation from the first Epistle to Timothy – "Not withstanding through bearinge of children she shalbe saved".'[45]

There is an obvious echo of *Macbeth*, with its on-stage killing of Macduff's son and the implied off-stage murders of Lady Macduff and her other children, but in *The Duchess of Malfi* this series of events functions in the development of the duchess's character, and in those of her persecutors, as well as in its appeal to the audience. The parallel between the earlier display of wax images and the actual children helps to deepen the pathos of the situation. This point supports Kirsch's view that, 'In the last acts of *The Duchess*, the artificial and the natural become inter-changeable,'[46] and seems particularly relevant to R. B. Graves's argument that artificial light rather than darkness, suits the play towards its conclusion.[47] In the Revels edition, John Russell Brown argues that IV.i – the waxwork scene – could only have been effective in a darkened theatre, and that the play must have been written with Blackfriars in mind because there the auditorium could be darkened by covering the windows.[48] However, Graves points out that the title page of the 1623 first edition reads, 'Presented privately at the Black-Friers and publiquely at the Globe' and goes on to show that even with windows wide open, there would have been little natural light to illuminate the Blackfriars performance, for:

Had the performance begun even as early as 2 p.m., I do not see how the effect could have taken place much before 4 p.m. – just the time of London's winter sunset. The diminution of light was unique neither to Blackfriars in particular nor to the indoor theaters in general. The early winter sunset managed the effect all by itself.

The play is known to have been performed in December 1614[49] so wherever it was enacted at that time, twilight would have been the norm for the closing acts. If it was performed at the newly opened Globe after the summer months, then semi-light would, presumably, have sufficed for, despite its rebuilding 'fairer than before',[50] lighting was not a feature of that playhouse. However, as Graves shows, while twilight would also have been available at Blackfriars, it is unlikely to have been exploited:

Far from being darkened, the artificially lit Blackfriars stage would have appeared brighter in relation to the rest of the auditorium at the end of the play than when daylight flooded through the windows at the beginning. As the daylight waned and darkness gathered – the apparent brightness onstage would have increased because the stage candles would have contributed a greater share of the total illumination.

At Blackfriars, therefore, the torture of the duchess by Ferdinand – the dead hand, garish waxworks, and the madmen – would be emphasised by the brightness of the hundreds of candles burning in the theatre. Accordingly, the duchess could not escape her undesired lime-light; nor could she rely on semi-darkness to weaken the impact of the horrors upon her, but was obliged to confront them in their harsh, illuminated state.

Opposites could be used to evoke each other, so, just as in the open public theatre where torches would be carried in daylight to indicate symbolic darkness, at Blackfriars, the artificial light could be used to draw attention to the characters' individual conceptions of darkness – both physical (as the duchess feels her way across the stage to her brother), and spiritual (as she reacts to his cruel tricks):

> Duch.   yon's an excellent property
>   For a tyrant, which I would account mercy.
> Bos.   What's that?
> Duch. If they would bind me to that lifeless trunk
>   And let me freeze to death.
> Bos.   Come, you must live.
> Duch. That's the greatest torture souls feel in hell –
>   In hell: that they must live, and cannot die.   IV.i.65–71

Her last lines express her longing for lasting darkness which is purposefully denied at this point; and at Blackfriars these words might be spoken in an unrelenting brightness which would echo the metaphor of hell.

Actual or implied darkness is an important feature of both *The White Devil* and *The Duchess of Malfi*. Graves draws attention to the fact that Webster was the only dramatist of the period to stage the removal of lights for scenes involving illicit love. As a rhetorical figure, the idea was well-known, but as a dramatic action, it was previously untried. In *The*

White Devil such symbolism is obvious, e.g. the meeting of Bracciano and Vittoria in I.ii:

> 'tis his pleasure
> You put out all your torches and depart.   I.ii.8–9

but in *The Duchess of Malfi*, its application is more subtle, being confined to undertones suggesting Ferdinand's possible sexual response to his sister, which is implied by lines such as:

> Methinks I see her laughing –
> Excellent hyena! – talk to me somewhat, quickly,
> Or my imagination will carry me
> To see her, in the shameful act of sin.   II.v.38–41

The darkness of their meeting in IV.ii is engineered by Ferdinand's vow never to see her again – a vow made in a state of passion after a heated confrontation concerning her marriage. Darkness, in this play, has functions other than the symbolic representation of moral blackness found in *The White Devil*. Here, the evocation of darkness is also used to produce a hell-like atmosphere whose prime significance is not religious expression, but that of individual states of mind.

In both plays Webster is concerned with exploring tricks of the imagination – both in relation to the characters on the stage and the audience's response. To differing degrees, the exploration is also allied to the art of the theatre, and this conscious awareness of the play's world performing within a larger world outside is an aspect of the contemporary drama which Webster shares with many other playwrights.

The contemporary audience would be aware that the Conjuror in *The White Devil*, who so vehemently denounces false conjurors is, in fact, just such a person – being an actor taking the part of a conjuror. There would be no doubt that it was a theatrical portrayal of magic, brought about by the actors' craft which conjures visions by enacting them. It is this craft which directs the imagination of members of the audience during the course of a play – changing the scene in their minds rather than through the use of elaborate scenery. When the Conjuror tells Bracciano, 'We are now/Beneath her roof' (II.ii.50–1), the audience also readily believes him.[51] Similarly, in *The Duchess of Malfi*, Delio draws attention to the theatrical trick of speeding up time – almost as if Webster was embarrassed at the considerable leap he had made:[52]

> Methinks 'twas yesterday: let me but wink,
> And not behold your face, which to mine eye
> Is somewhat leaner, verily I should dream
> It were within this half-hour.   III.i.8–11

In both plays the audience is aware of such necessary tricks and of the fact
that the drama encourages individuals to use their imaginative faculties to
the full. It is, therefore, not strange that Bracciano should be able to
conjure up Isabella's ghost merely by thinking of her, and the apparent
products of *his* imagination are visualised so that everyone can share his
exact experience – a technique Marlowe employed in *Doctor Faustus*. *The
White Devil* also suggests similarities with *Macbeth* in respect to Bracciano's performance, as Shakespeare had already successfully portrayed the
effects of guilt on an active mind; and both dramatists are employing an
accepted theatrical tradition – particularly common in revenge drama.

The power of the imagination is an important force in both plays, but
this is particularly so in *The Duchess of Malfi*, for the horrific effect of the
waxwork scene hinges on the fact that the duchess believes it to be real,
and the most plausible explanation for her ready belief is the supposition
that her imagination leapt behind the traverse immediately Bosola began
to draw it aside. The sight, then, was a realisation of a nightmare she had
long dreaded; and because her mind had harboured such an eventuality, it
would take only the slightest show of realistic effect to convince her that it
had taken place. If the audience is aware of this it is even more closely
tuned to the turmoil of the duchess's mind.

Just as the duchess's fears and imagination make her vulnerable to Ferdinand's cruelties, so his guilt triggers his imagination to cause his own disease
and madness. He does not look like a wolf on the stage – this is no parody of
A Midsummer Night's Dream – but he acts like one and, most importantly,
he believes in it. Part of Webster's concern is to stage the development of his
characters' states of mind. In Ferdinand's wolf transformation he is staging
the recurrent metaphor of the brothers' predatory qualities:

> Go tell my brothers, when I am laid out,
> They then may feed in quiet.   IV.ii.236–7

These are disturbing lines. If there is a link between this play and
Beaumont and Fletcher's *The Maid's Tragedy*, as Mario Praz suggests,[53]
then Webster may even have adapted Melantius's reply to his sister, 'I'll be
a wolf first', and staged a metaphor from another contemporary play.

Similarly, in the echo scene, a facet of Antonio's imagination is allied to
a recurrent theme in the play, so that the duchess, who was described as
resembling:

> some reverend monument
> Whose ruins are even pitied.   IV.ii.33–4

hears Antonio pitying the ruins and speaks from her grave – a dislocated
voice to match the dislocated ruins. Both Mario Praz and John Russell

Brown cite the similarity between the scene and iv.iv of *The Second Maiden's Tragedy* where a lighting effect being used at Blackfriars would have been employed to produce the 'great light' which appears in the midst of the Lady's tomb and might also have supplied the 'clear light' which presented Antonio with 'a face folded in sorrow' (v.iii.44–5). Although neither critic mentions it, such an effect would not have been confined to Blackfriars. No evidence is available for any performance of *The Second Maiden's Tragedy* and, being a King's Men's play, it is likely to have been staged at both the Globe and Blackfriars. A 'blazing star' was staged at the Globe – probably in v.iii of *The Revenger's Tragedy*, and a similar stage direction occurs in the second part of Heywood's *If You Know Not Me, You Know Nobody* (1605).

In *The Duchess of Malfi*, this effect, if it occurred, would not only visualise Antonio's 'clear light', but would also recall other instances of dislocated parts in the play – the dead man's hand, which parodies the sacredness of the wedding ceremony in which she, figuratively, gave her hand to Antonio; or Ferdinand's desire to make her bleeding heart into a sponge to erase his memory.

In both plays Webster is concerned with the staging of metaphors, but his art achieves greater sophistication in *The Duchess of Malfi*. In *The White Devil* he cleverly plays on the pun 'jewel' and its associations with chastity, honour and love; but its counterpart in the later play – the ring – involves greater complexities and is more thoroughly treated. The wedding ring is simultaneously a band of love and a circle of death. Its recurrence throughout the play charts the progress of the duchess's fortunes. In i.i it is likened to the Gordian knot 'which let violence/Never untwine' (480–1) – a comment which gives added significance to the Cardinal's later action (iii.iv.36–9). However, it is not the Cardinal who next uses the ring, but Ferdinand:

> I come to seal my peace with you: here's a hand
> > *Gives her a dead man's hand.*
> To which you have vow'd much love; the ring upon't
> You gave.   iv.i.43–5

and finally, the relationship between the duchess's ill-fated marriage and death is made explicit after her murder when Cariola's executioner offers her a noose with, 'Here's your wedding ring' (iv.ii.249).[54]

M. C. Bradbrook points out that 'a wedding ring was itself a sacred object possessed of virtuous powers',[55] so in all these instances parody and distortion are important elements – and perhaps it is more illuminating to put them in perspective with the many other instances in both plays where familiar scenes or traditions are manipulated to create striking, but disturbing, dramatic effects.

This seems to provide a key to understanding Webster's almost obsessive borrowing. He alludes to well-known and easily recognisable dramatised situations or characters, such as the play-within-the-play in *Hamlet* (*The White Devil*, 1.i), the mad lamentings of Ophelia or Kyd's Isabella in *The Spanish Tragedy* (Cornelia), the wounded saintliness reminiscent of Beaumont and Fletcher's Aspatia (Isabella), the Iago-like characteristics of Bosola – yet he alludes to them, not to infer similarities with his own creations, but to stress the important differences between them. Bosola is *not* Iago; like him, he is associated with a devil, but unlike him, he is repentant – and it is his repentance and final sympathy with the duchess, not, as it is in Iago's case, his unrelenting villainy, which helps to intensify the heroine's tragedy.

Parody and distortion (not necessarily with any disrespect implied to that which is parodied or distorted) are powerful dramatic tools. In both plays they facilitate the staging of metaphors and the expression of ambiguities – such as the overlapping states of innocence and guilt; life and death; health and disease; good and evil. They are used in the outward dramatisation of inner states of mind, and above all, they contribute to the over-riding sense of insecurity and instability which, it seems, was Webster's intention.

Although, today, we have highly sophisticated theatres and effects, plays like these seem to pose more of a challenge than ever. Philip Prowse's 1985 National Theatre production of *The Duchess of Malfi*[56] demonstrated some of the issues confronting a modern director and designer. The principal setting, with its glass cases and crucifixes (removed at a significant point in the play), suggested a pallid, stark crypt: the Duchess, at first, so obviously a lively, sensuous woman, was immured there as in a religious museum. The play opened with tolling bells and a lengthy funeral procession which moved mechanically across the front of the stage, and it was noticeable that Antonio, Delio, and Bosola were not restricted to its ranks, but had the freedom of outsiders to comment and interrupt. All of this was atmospherically effective but, today, it seems difficult to know how far to go when assisting an audience's imagination.

Webster creates a powerful atmosphere in words and gestures and death's presence is probably most powerfully felt because it is sinister and hidden, though undeniably and uneasily close throughout the play. At the beginning, the duchess is a silent presence on the stage long before she speaks (she enters at line 148, but does not speak until line 214) and this is paralleled in the way her presence is felt long after her death, through the

13   The National Theatre production of *The Duchess of Malfi* (1985), directed and designed by Philip Prowse. Eleanor Bron (the Duchess), Laurence Rudic (Death) and Jonathan Hyde (Duke Ferdinand). Photo: John Vere Brown.

words and actions of other characters. It might have seemed strange, therefore, to some of the audience that the National Theatre's director felt the need to invent additional roles – the hooded figure of Death, present from the beginning, and the ghost of the Duchess (who was always accompanied by Death). The personification of Death, who accompanied various characters (notably the Duchess) at particular times, like a mute monk, led the production back to medieval drama on one hand and, when accompanied by the persistent screech effects (of peacock, owl, or raven) at ominous moments, approached melodrama on the other. The long, coffin-like property over which Death was bowed as the play opened, seemed an almost too explicit use of symbolism compared to the far more effective use of the property at 1.i.361 when the Duchess directed Antonio to sit at it to write her will. Despite some good performances by the actors,

Death's presence could be seen as hindering the (often suffocating) intimacy they were trying to create, and perhaps overplayed hints of mortality and doomed fate.

The duchess's early disappearance (she dies in iv.ii) has often been considered a flaw, and it is easy to understand attempts to keep her on the stage; although it is more difficult to explain why, in this production, more was not made of the one opportunity where the text would have easily accommodated such an appearance – the 'face folded in sorrow' which Antonio thinks he sees among the ruins in v.iii. This image would have preserved the ambiguity Webster creates concerning his characters' uncertainty as to where death will lead them: like Antonio, we cannot be sure of what we see. On the other hand, a stage ghost in a diaphanous gown who appears frequently, yet has no place in the text, denies this mystery. Although a fresh approach to an old play is always welcome, there seems so much within Webster's text which could be exploited visually and atmospherically – in terms of symmetry (the alabaster figure and the duchess's death), and in relation to contrasts and distortion (the wax figures – which Prowse also omitted, the dislocated hand, the wedding ring and mock celebrations, the duchess's ghostly disembodied face) – that perhaps we have not yet reached the stage of needing to invent new material or characters to supplement Webster's efforts. His own skills may still prove to be effective, despite the gap in time.

Both *The White Devil* and *The Duchess of Malfi* reveal the playwright's manipulation of his audience through his handling of the characters – and references to the works of other dramatists emphasise this (although a modern audience cannot necessarily be expected to see these links) – but Webster takes manipulation one step further in allowing his characters to attempt to control themselves and each other. Their failure to do this is both a dramatic and a non-dramatic comment; it indicates the very precariousness of the venture (and in the case of *The White Devil*, perhaps resultant dramatic weaknesses) while at the same time demonstrating the tragic inevitability of their lives. In *The Duchess of Malfi*, the technique is most effective and Webster reached a peak of sophistication and expression which gave him success in both the public and private theatre: a success which is even more of an achievement if, as Chapman implied in 1610,[57] tragedy was no longer the mode.

His power over his audience is linked to the 'security' which, as Bosola said,

> some men call the suburbs of hell,
> Only a dead wall between.   v.ii.337–8

John Russell Brown glosses 'security' as 'confidence that one is secure'.[58] Webster's uneasy attraction depends greatly on denying members of the audience any such confidence by manipulating, and often frustrating, what their knowledge of the various traditions he exploits had led them to expect.

7 · Conventions and improvised rituals in *The Changeling, 'Tis Pity She's a Whore,* and *The Broken Heart*

The Changeling by Thomas Middleton and William Rowley was licensed on 7 May 1622 and was performed in the last years of James I's reign, yet it recalls the traditions and techniques of much earlier drama, and was one of the last Jacobean plays to include a dumb-show. John Ford wrote *The Broken Heart* and *'Tis Pity She's a Whore* in the early years of Charles I's reign (*c.*1625–33)[1] but he, too, looked back to the Elizabethans and early Jacobeans in many respects. These two dramatists might be considered to have sounded the last post for Elizabethan and Jacobean dramatic traditions.

The sub-plot of *The Changeling* can almost be construed as a development of the play-within-a-play function of earlier drama, where the internal play comments on the lives and actions of some of the main characters in the external play – as is the case in *Hamlet*. The sub-plot of *The Changeling* is far more than a humorous device; it is also emblematic. The madmen are linked with similar characters in *The Duchess of Malfi*, whose chaotic minds provide a terrifying ritual and an evocation of hell. In *The Changeling*, a similar association occurs in the sub-plot: it is deliberately submerged and takes the form of a seemingly coincidental, ironical comment on the fates of Beatrice-Joanna and De Flores, which anticipates the independent staging of their final state. In contrast, the image of hell staged in *The Duchess of Malfi* is directly related to the heroine, who is also an integral part of the effect.

In *The Changeling* a direct moral association, in the medieval tradition, of the lives of the main characters with hell is not made until remnants of the old tradition have been subtly implanted in the minds of the audience through the parallel, but separate sub-plot. The insinuations cannot be ignored, but the audience is not asked to swallow them as unpalatable, didactic moralisings: on the surface, hell is only part of the Barley-brake game. I do not believe that Middleton and Rowley's prime intention in the madhouse scenes was to satirise the Bethlehem hospital and Dr Helkiah Crooke.[2] The mad folk of *The Changeling* are seen as entertainers: in the seventeenth century Bedlam seems to have been regarded as an equivalent of the circus or London Zoo by the smugly unafflicted. In the play the madmen are used in this vein at Beatrice-Joanna's wedding celebrations. Their costumes of birds and beasts are similar to those which were used in the celebratory masque for the wedding of Katharine of Aragon and Prince Arthur in 1501, and although this may only be coincidence, it is interesting that the unconsummated marriage of Beatrice-Joanna and Alsemero should be celebrated in the same manner as one of the most famous unconsummated royal marriages in recent history. However, although the fantastically dressed madmen are ultimately harmless, supposedly comic figures, their inner states and outward appearance also suggest more sinister connotations, and illuminate the theatrical presentation of Beatrice-Joanna and De Flores.

Madness and eccentricity were commonly associated with demonic possession in the sixteenth and early seventeenth centuries, and the vocal and visual resemblances of the madmen to birds and beasts not only contribute to this association, but also invoke their affinity with the lowest form of life on earth. In 1586, Timothy Bright wrote:

Other some, that is to say the animals, hee drewe wholly from the earth at the beginning, and planted seede in them onely, and food from other creatures: as beasts, and man in respect of his bodie: the difference only this: that likely it is, mans body was made of purer mould as a most precious tabernacle and temple, wherein the image of god should afterward be inshrined: and being formed as it were by Gods proper hand, received a greater dignitie of beautie, and proportion, and stature erect.[3]

According to this philosophy, man only differs from animals in degree rather than kind. Man has a soul and a greater degree of sophistication, but he can never rid himself of his animal nature – it can only be controlled and sublimated. The madmen in *The Changeling* represent the absence of this restraint.

Ugliness associated with beasts has a long tradition of being used symbolically to depict evil. M. D. Anderson gives examples of pigs' snouts or faces which contribute to the portrayal of gaolers or executioners in early church windows,[4] and this relates to Beatrice-Joanna's view: 'Blood-guiltiness becomes a fouler visage' (II.ii.40) as she thinks of De Flores as the obvious choice for a murderer, in preference to Alsemero. Beast-like characters are also firmly linked to the portrayal of devils; there is a boss in Norwich Cathedral which depicts a demon with an over-all garment of shaggy wool and a human face, partly masked by a curved beak. A demon at Gayton (Northants) has a hooded, but personable face, although his body is clothed in feathers and wings and his hands and feet have triple talons.[5] Similarly, the Chester plays mention, 'The devill in his feathers, all ragged and rente'.[6] Even Spenser, in *The Faerie Queene* I.viii

(46–9), links Duessa's evilness with her true physical characteristics which include a fox's tail, one eagle's claw, and a bear's paw.

De Flores's ugliness is still that of a man, but the madmen may well have portrayed bestial ugliness in its crudest fashion. Only later stage directions imply that the madmen merely imitated animal noises (Dyce and Bullen) – the original quarto reads, '*Madmen above, some as birds others as beasts*'. The descriptions of devils given above did not only apply to church architecture or medieval cycles: not long before the date of *The Changeling*, John Melton wrote, in 1620, of a performance of *Doctor Faustus*: 'a man may behold shagg-hayr'd Devills runne roaring over the stage'.[7]

The costumes for *The Changeling* are not known; perhaps the madmen had complete costumes of wool or feathers and masks with snouts or beaks, or perhaps even animal heads. If not full costumes, masks alone may have been used, and again, there is a long tradition of animal masks. Anderson gives an illustration of a beast mask carved on a misericord of St David's Cathedral: it has a veil which can be fastened to the forehead with a pin, so that it covers the back of the wearer's head, and the following is also relevant:

The Roman winter festivals of the Saturnalia and the Kalends, when every sort of license was permitted and all authority inverted, persisted in spite of all efforts to suppress them, and even penetrated into the churches in the Feast of Fools or festum asinorum. The lowliest sub-deacon then took command of the services, receiving the baculum, or staff of office, from the Precentor as the words of the Magnificat were sung: 'He hath put down the mighty from their seats and hath exalted the humble and meek', and the custom, which may have begun as a symbolic reminder of the need for humility among the leaders of religious communities, degenerated into an unseemly riot when the clergy parodied the Holy Offices while disguising themselves with the masks of animals.[8]

I do not suggest that Middleton or Rowley intended this particular link to be made, but an equally striking inversion is insinuated in the notion of mad people, whose attire recalls the stage portrayal of devils, performing a part in the revels of a rich noble's Christian wedding.

The game which has previously been associated with them is Barley-brake (III.iii.165), described by R. W. Bond as, 'a game … in which two players, occupying a marked space called "Hell" in the centre of the ground, tried to catch the others as they ran through it from the two opposite ends, those caught being obliged to replace or reinforce them in the centre'.[9] N. W. Bawcutt, the Revels editor, adds to this: 'The game was played by pairs of men and women, who held hands and were not usually allowed to separate, and went on until each pair had taken its turn at occupying "Hell".'[10] In many ways this game reflects the medieval attitude to courtship when it was portrayed as one of the deadly sins and was associated with animal lust: 'Two lovers embrace on a bench-end at Wiggenhall St German (Norfolk) but they stand within the jaws of Hell, and, on a roof boss in Lincoln Cathdral, it is a devil who draws together the heads of a man and a woman who kiss.'[11] The association of these madmen in their strange dress with Beatrice-Joanna's wedding revels, now seems even more significant in view of her liaison with De Flores, to whom she is inextricably bound – like one of the couples in Barley-brake; especially when the object of the madmen's game has been to, 'Catch there, catch the last couple in hell!' (III.iii.165).

However, the madmen do not appear on the stage with Beatrice-Joanna and De Flores; they are segregated to the last, but the segregation helps to emphasise the way the sub-plot comments ironically on the main action. Just before the end of the penultimate act, the stage direction reads, 'The Madmen and Fools dance' (IV.iii.212) which presumably recalls their previous game which has, once again, been set in motion. The audience is left to question who will be the last couple caught in hell, and as if to answer this, the final act opens with Beatrice-Joanna and De Flores in a state of desperation, their suspense heightened by the quickly chiming clock (also used in Cymbeline) which signifies that time is rapidly running out as they await Diaphanta.

The sub-plot has pursued a parallel course up to this point, continually underlining the main Beatrice-Joanna and De Flores action – in III.iii Lollio, seeing Isabella with Tony, and knowing that she already has a husband, reacts in a manner similar to that of De Flores, who says of Beatrice-Joanna and Alsemero:

> I have watch'd this meeting, and do wonder much
> What shall become of t'other; I'm sure both
> Cannot be serv'd unless she transgress; happily
> Then I'll put in for one: II.ii.57–60

In III.iii Lollio actually tries this tactic:

> Lol. Come, there are degrees, one fool may be better than another.
> Isa. What's the matter?
> Lol. Nay, if thou giv'st thy mind to fool's-flesh, have at thee!
>   III.iii.220–3

Isabella's reaction, 'You bold slave, you!' (224) is very similar to that of Beatrice-Joanna, which occurs when De Flores attempts a parallel assault in the next scene. By this point he has already hinted at his intention:

> Bea. Thy reward shall be precious.
> De. F.   That I have thought on;
>   I have assur'd myself of that beforehand,

And know it will be precious, the thought ravishes. II.ii.130–2

Considered in the light of these words, Lollio and Isabella's encounter should indicate a precedent to the audience, so that it will be aware of De Flores's intentions and will view Beatrice-Joanna's predicament with the insight of those who do not share her innocence or incredulity.

Lollio and Isabella are innocent counterparts: they do not become entangled. De Flores's argument recalls that of the Physician in *A Fair Quarrel* who demands that Jane becomes his mistress in return for his secretly disposing of her baby. Both scenes exhibit similar misunderstandings of intentions, but in *The Changeling* Middleton's earlier comedy scene has been rewritten: Jane braves infamy and does not give in, whereas Beatrice moves in the opposite direction, towards a tragic conclusion.

In the sub-plot, the serious implications of the main plot are safely controlled in a kind of game – just as the madmen confine the concept of hell to the game of Barley-brake. Lollio keeps Isabella chaste by threatening to 'put in for my thirds' if she is not. Isabella understands the rules of the game and treats it lightheartedly:

> *Isa.* The first place is thine, believe it, Lollio;
>   If I do fall –
> *Lol.* I fall upon you.
> *Isa.* So.   IV.iii.38–41

Isabella is never in danger. Both her husband and Tony are still alive – the plot contains parallel components, but in this case they are safely defused. Once they are activated, as Beatrice-Joanna and De Flores show, there is no stopping on the road to destruction.

When Isabella encourages Tony in III.iii, the madman's voice which conveniently causes Lollio to go off and leave them alone together, significantly calls out, 'Catch there, catch the last couple in hell!' (165); but it is clear that the threat is not to Isabella and Antonio. It occurs in a comic context and is no more than a voice from within – the actual game is going on elsewhere. The end of the fourth act and the beginning of the fifth at last throw light on the locality of 'elsewhere'. The game is out on the stage in the madmen's dance at the end of Act IV and the couple who appear on stage when the madmen leave, is that of Beatrice-Joanna and De Flores – perilously near to being discovered.

Again, this staging prefigures a later event: they are not yet condemned, although it is imminent. De Flores finally draws attention to their ultimate state in language which matches the symbolic staging:

> Yes; and the while I coupled with your mate
> At barley-brake; now we are left in hell.   V.iii.162–3

In a different way, Alibius's act of locking Isabella up with Lollio (who poses a comic threat to her chastity) is parodied in the final scene by Alsemero when he confines Beatrice-Joanna to his closet (presumably the discovery space) and sends De Flores to her. The parody stresses the contrast: no harm comes to Isabella because madmen, warder, supposed madman, and wife are all innocent; however, both Beatrice-Joanna and De Flores are guilty, and the result of the main plot is death.

On the discovery of her guilt, Alsemero accuses Beatrice-Joanna: 'Oh, thou art all deform'd' (v.iii.77). This implies that De Flores's ugliness was matched, throughout the latter part of the play, by Beatrice-Joanna's inner deformity which prompted her to seek her first lover's murder. Alsemero later points out the discrepancies of disguise and indicates a major theme in the play when he rejects the feigned madmen as candidates for the murderer, and says of Beatrice-Joanna and De Flores:

> I have two other
> That were more close disguis'd than your two could be,
> E'er since the deed was done.   v.iii.127–9

Neither the madmen, in the devilish disguise of birds and beasts, nor the courtiers disguised as madmen were really manifestations of evil: they were all harmless innocents – despite appearances. The true villains were 'honest' De Flores and the beautiful Beatrice-Joanna.

This reversal can be viewed as a way of stating, dramatically, that threats now take different forms – or that these threats demand a new dramatic portrayal. The straightforward days of medieval drama are past, when a feathered devil, however comic, still epitomised evil. Now, as Webster indicated in *The White Devil*, the portrayal of evil is more ambiguous. Shakespeare also realised this in *Macbeth*, where aspects of the morality tradition are juxtaposed with the psychological exploration of characters.[12] In *The Changeling*, the infiltration of medieval concepts is subtle so the climax of the tragedy can stand a direct moralistic declaration such as De Flores's reference to Barley-brake and hell: the play is strengthened by an image which achieves dramatic unity by drawing together the many ironical images and emblematic actions it contains. These include (apart from the sub-plot), the references to De Flores as a serpent, recalling Eden (part of a long dramatic tradition from the medieval cycles, also found in *A Midsummer Night's Dream*, *Hamlet*, and *The White Devil*) and his words to Beatrice-Joanna, 'You talk of danger when your fame's on fire?' (v.i.34) which, when linked to his method of quenching this fire by another, off-stage blaze which destroys Diaphanta, is reminiscent of purgatorial imagery.

The play-within-a-play function of the sub-plot seems vital to the total effect of inversion and reversal which exists on many levels – from the simplest application, which demonstrates how easily comedy is turned to tragedy – to the wider implications of distinguishing between exterior guise and internal motive. Despite problems of ascertaining authorship, or criticisms of inferior writing, consideration of this aspect of *The Changeling*'s staging leads me to defend the sub-plot's existence and maintain that, although, as has been suggested, the main plot can stand alone, the sub-plot is not, as was once suggested, 'Silly and only fortuitously connected'.[13] The main action requires the distanced allusions from the world of Lollio and Isabella for the impact of much of its dramatic anticipation and its ultimate climax.

However, the sub-plot is not only an important source of visual allusion, but also draws attention to visual effects in the main action. As Normand Berlin's article shows,[14] a short verbal exchange between Alibius and Lollio illuminates an important visual expression of Beatrice-Joanna and De Flores's relationship:

> *Alib.* I would wear my ring on my own finger;
>   Whilst it is borrowed it is none of mine,
>   But his that useth it.
> *Lol.* You must keep it on still then; if it but lie by, one or other
>   Will be thrusting into't.   I.ii.27–31

The connection between keeping a ring and the chastity of a wife is likened to the possession of a ring (recalling the sexual pun on 'jewel') and implies the simultaneous possession of the woman. This exchange between Alibius and Lollio can be seen as the key to the change in Beatrice-Joanna and De Flores's relationship – from deliberate detachment to inseparability. At the beginning of the play Beatrice-Joanna's hatred of De Flores and his passion for her are established, but an incident at the end of I.i shows De Flores anticipating a change in the relationship in a visually symbolic expression, which is later clarified and reinforced by Lollio and Alibius's verbal imagery.

At the end of the first scene Beatrice drops a glove[15] which De Flores picks up and offers to her, but rather than touch something which she now considers to be contaminated, she throws down the other glove too, and leaves; whereupon De Flores declares:

> Here's a favour come, with a mischief! Now I know
> She had rather wear my pelt tann'd in a pair
> Of dancing pumps, than I should thrust my fingers
> Into her sockets here, I know she hates me,
> Yet cannot choose but love her:

No matter, if but to vex her, I'll haunt her still;
Though I get nothing else, I'll have my will.   1.i.231–7

Berlin's argument is sound: the event is both 'dramatically effective' and 'symbolically significant' because De Flores connects Beatrice-Joanna's act with sexual symbolism. Here, 'thrust' has the sexual connotations which Lollio implies in 1.ii, and sexual violence is inherent in the act of defiance when De Flores plunges his fingers into the glove's sockets. This is underlined by the verbal pun, 'I'll have my will', which anticipates his later speech and actions. Berlin could have pursued his argument further. The act is also important because it expresses the irony of the consequences of the murder: unwittingly, Beatrice-Joanna has given De Flores the means to do what she most abhors – to come close to her. His hand inside the gloves she has recently taken off achieves an intimacy by proxy.

At this stage in the play it is the least disagreeable alternative to her. Her careless discarding of the gloves, which De Flores views as the first step in a sexual conquest, is paralleled later when she gives him Alonzo's ring. Again, this is an image of giving herself to De Flores by proxy and, therefore, remaining untainted, which demonstrates her naivety in believing that both moral standards and sexual commitment can be encountered safely on a superficial level. Murder cannot be committed without incurring guilt, and sexual incitement cannot be stayed by the material worth of a ring, rather than by the sexual and spiritual possession it symbolises.

The glove in 1.i provides a striking reversible image associated with both protagonists. In relation to the symbolism of sexual possession it is associated with Beatrice-Joanna, but this is reversed during the murder plot when she decides to wear De Flores like a glove to enact the deed. His ugliness shields her, apparently innocent, beauty. Her hand is the motivating force inside the glove which is, thereby, freed from direct contact with blood and, as a mere glove, she believes that De Flores can be discarded easily – just as she discarded the tainted glove in the first scene. Her naive attitude can be traced back to this point, which serves both as a precedent for her later plans, and as an ironical comment on the differing complexity of the later situation, which cannot be as easily resolved.

The glove incident may be recalled again in 11.ii when Beatrice-Joanna not only masters her revulsion of De Flores sufficiently to approach him, but she actually touches his face: 'Her fingers touch'd me!' (11.ii.81). This is the beginning of the reversal of the image: Beatrice-Joanna is no longer the glove into which De Flores thrusts his hand, but has become the fingers reaching out to find a glove. His intentions do not belie his appellation 'honest De Flores' here, as his innuendoes and obvious desires never hide his motives from the audience, or from Beatrice-Joanna, who exploits them mercilessly. She, however, woos only to procure a murderer, forcing herself to overcome her revulsion by thinking of his usefulness. The moment of tension as she overcomes her horror can be expressed visually as a fascination with the ugliness she formerly repelled, and parallels her later attitude to murder, immortality and deceit. She probably reaches out to touch De Flores tentatively, enacting the conflicting impulses of repugnance and attraction, and this tentative approach is easily interchangeable with that of a lover. The motivation in each case is different, but the visual appearance is the same. The link is made by De Flores, who instantly interprets the action as a sexual advance and, as Berlin notes, sees the fingers as a symbol of the whole act:

> Oh my blood!
> Methinks I feel her in mine arms already.   II.ii.146–7

They are no more than fingers to Beatrice-Joanna: they act out a part and are only a symbolic gesture to create the illusion of sexual interest. She deals solely in emblems or abstracts, using them to maintain her detachment. De Flores, however, is associated with the actualities behind them. Beatrice-Joanna seems to be concerned, not with symbols – which imply multiple interpretations, but with emblems – which suggest only one; for example, she believes that to De Flores, 'Gold tastes like angels' food' (126) and will satisfy his greed – she does not realise that to him 'food' has other connotations:

> Hunger and pleasure, they'll commend sometimes
> Slovenly dishes, and feed heartily on 'em,
> Nay, which is stranger, refuse daintier for 'em
> Some women are odd feeders.   II.ii.150–3

As Berlin indicates, the lines which follow provide an important insight into the act of cutting off Alonzo's finger on stage. Before the murder De Flores says,

> Here comes the man goes supperless to bed,
> Yet shall not rise tomorrow to his dinner.   II.ii.154–5

The association of eating with sexual appetite recalls Shakespeare's technique in many plays including *Antony and Cleopatra* and *Troilus and Cressida*, but here Alonzo goes 'supperless' to bed and never marries or possesses Beatrice-Joanna. The betrothal ring was married to his finger, as De Flores tells Beatrice-Joanna:

> He was as loath to part with 't, for it stuck
> As if the flesh and it were both one substance.   III.iv.37–8

so not only does De Flores break the engagement by killing Alonzo and removing the ring, but he also severs the finger, emphasising Alonzo's impotence in death to consummate the marriage. This indicates the significance of the appearance of Alonzo's ghost in Act IV where he comes, like Banquo's ghost, at the end of the procession, startling De Flores and 'showing him the hand whose finger he had cut off'.

However, the severed finger also has other connotations. When De Flores shows the finger to Beatrice-Joanna, she is horrified at the reality of the mutilation because she can no longer distance herself from the deed. At last she is forced to realise that abstract ideas involve practical realities – in one sense the finger does stand for the man and must be buried. De Flores associates it with the finger of a 'greedy man thrust in a dish at court', which relates to the eating imagery used earlier, and lewdly links Alonzo with himself. Alonzo was not a man who would have attempted such an unmannerly assault – be it at table or with Beatrice-Joanna, yet he pays the price while De Flores uses Beatrice-Joanna's complicity in exacting the penalty, to allow him to commit the crime himself, unchecked.

The ring is offered to De Flores voluntarily, as a partner in crime, and replaces the glove which he had to stoop to pick up. Now, despite Beatrice-Joanna's attitude, there is an element of equality in their relationship and the ring still possesses symbolic qualities associated with betrothal. De Flores tells her that the deed has 'made you one with me' (III.iv.140). As they leave together their intimacy can no longer be avoided. The ghost at the dumb-show appears to De Flores because he is his murderer, but also because he, and not the bridegroom, is truly sexually and spiritually bound to Beatrice-Joanna. Berlin draws attention to the final extension of this image which occurs when the ring grows to become the circle of hell in the game of Barley-brake, in which the couple cannot be separated.

The severing of the finger has, therefore, like Webster's waxworks and dead man's hand, a justification which transcends accusations of mere sensationalism. However, as the biting out of Hieronimo's tongue in Michael Bogdanov's 1982 production of *The Spanish Tragedy*[16] showed, and as Giovanni's entrance with his sister's bleeding heart on the point of his dagger in John Ford's *'Tis Pity She's a Whore* also illustrates, there is invariably a tension between gory stage property and the poetic metaphors or deeper meaning behind them.

Both the dead man's hand in *The Duchess of Malfi* and the severed finger in *The Changeling* suggest similar problems of staging. One possible solution is highlighted by Anderson's discussion of the mystery plays.[17] She reproduces a drawing in the *Holkham Bible picture book* which suggests a staging possibility for the miracle of the midwife whose hand was disfigured and then subsequently healed. In the drawing a glove is attached to her right wrist by a ribbon and Anderson remarks that it is 'an effect I have not seen elsewhere' which may be a record of, 'some markedly discoloured artificial hand which she donned after impiously touching the Blessed Virgin and slipped off again as she announced herself healed, after taking the Child in her arms'. It was obviously, at this stage, a very crude device, but it is possible that the technique developed a greater degree of sophistication and may have been used in the public theatre in later years. A cast of a wax hand which enabled Ferdinand to wear it like a glove would be far easier to execute on stage than attempts to hide a stage property up his sleeve. In *The Changeling*, the device could easily be adapted to provide a cast like the finger of a glove which could be slipped off with frightening realism, complete with ring, as De Flores appears to cut it off. This would underline the hand and glove imagery of the play, and provide a theatrical trick which the audience might recognise with delight.

Prompting the audience to take delight in recognisable, but nevertheless dramatically effective pieces of staging may be an important aspect of Middleton and Rowley's technique in *The Changeling*. Nicholas Brooke argues that, in this play, 'the Castle and the House are derived from their medieval and renaissance significance as emblems of both the world and the human body.'[18] This may be true,[19] but the significance of De Flores, with a bunch of keys, leading Alonzo through the castle, talking of bells 'At great men's funerals' (III.ii.12) is, to me, due to its association with *Macbeth* and 'Remember the porter'. As Glynne Wickham has shown, hell, on the medieval stage, was represented by a castle or dungeon within a castle, and entry was obtained through a porter – a comic figure, usually portrayed with a bunch of keys.[20] De Flores brings wry humour to Alonzo's death with his words:

> Do you question
> A work of secrecy? I must silence you.   III.ii.16–17

and while the scene is far removed from the old morality tradition and almost as far from *Macbeth* (a play with which *The Changeling* has been associated by Howard Felperin and others), it seems, nevertheless, a striking dramatic twist if De Flores combines associations of both Macbeth and the porter – both the tragedy's protagonist and a source of comedy.

The possibility that the porter scene in *Macbeth*, or the tradition on which this was based, is a faint, but deliberate echo, seems to be borne out by the scenes in the madhouse where Lollio is yet another variation of the porter at hell gate. The implication that the madmen are possessed by devils, the associations of their appearance with devils' costumes, and the inhuman noises, reminiscent of souls in hell or of demons, substantiate this parallel – as does the lewd, witty Lollio, who presumably also carries keys, as he gives one of these to Isabella in iv.iii. The confusion in v.i as people awake and come onto the stage summoned by the clanging bell and cries of 'Fire' rather than of 'Murder', also recalls an aspect of the porter scene. The most obvious explanation for these allusions would be that the dramatists intended to exploit their differences.

De Flores is obviously not merely an imitation of Macbeth. When he sees Alonzo's ghost for the second time, he coolly confronts it:

> Ha! What art thou that tak'st away the light
> 'Twixt that star and me? I dread thee not;
> 'Twas but a mist of conscience. – All's clear again.   v.i.58–60

The imagery of taking away the light recalls the fall of Lucifer from Heaven, but De Flores's practical nature mentions this unconsciously. Unlike Macbeth, he is in control of both mind and conscience and does not even entertain the thought of the supernatural. He will not be destroyed by giving himself away: it is clear that his fall will be determined by an outside agency.

Similarly, although the ghost leaves 'a shivering sweat' upon Beatrice-Joanna (v.i.63), this terror is quickly superseded by the more practical 'terrors' of being disovered outside her husband's bed, with De Flores. It seems that she is not a Lady Macbeth. De Flores and Beatrice-Joanna are outside the range of Shakespeare's play and, by alluding to *Macbeth*, the dramatists are able to stress this fact. This view disputes the attitude of Bawcutt who, in the Revels edition, quickly dismisses the relevance of Shakespearean allusion. *Macbeth* is not the only Shakespearean play to be invoked – nuances of *Othello* are also present and Howard Felperin points out that Alsemero is, from the beginning, associated with Othello, whereas De Flores is linked to Iago. However, as in the case of the *Macbeth* allusions, it is not the similarities, but the differences which matter.

Alsemero lacks Othello's passionate intensity. The emotional decision that the loss of the handkerchief and Iago's unsubstantiated lies can be conclusive evidence are countered by Alsemero's cool attempt at supposedly rational scientific investigation when he reacts to doubts of his future wife's chastity by resorting to the virginity test. This is ultimately as unreliable as Othello's methods, but on the stage it provides yet another example of the failure of external means of judgment to reveal interior deceit – this time in a comic manner. Alsemero lacks Othello's emotional depth: at the end of the play he is sufficiently distanced from his wife's fate to be able to announce:

> justice hath so right
> The guilty hit, that innocence is quit
> By proclamation, and may joy again.   v.iii.185–7

The most obvious difference between the two plays is, of course, that Beatrice-Joanna and De Flores are guilty and that Beatrice-Joanna's associations with the innocent Desdemona mock her, rather than Shakespeare's heroine. Similarly, when, in the final scene, Alsemero ushers De Flores in to Beatrice-Joanna with:

> I'll be your pander now; rehearse again
> Your scene of lust,   v.iii.114–15

he is left with only a hollow remnant of Othello's part. De Flores began to steal elements of his role from him much earlier, and now takes over completely – mortally wounding Beatrice-Joanna before killing himself. It is an act of mutual destruction, but also of love, and provides a new possibility for an *Othello* in which a guilty Desdemona dies with an unvindictive Iago, whose sole motive has been his desire for her. The final image of their relationship is the nightmare of being trapped forever in the madmen's game of Barley-brake – inseparable in hell as in life. Their ignoble deaths contrast with the final dignity of those in *Othello*. In *The Changeling* there are no eulogies afterwards; there are only further denunciations over the bodies:

> Here's beauty chang'd
> To ugly whoredom; here, servant obedience
> To a master sin, imperious murder;   v.iii.197–9

Although Beatrice-Joanna does ask to be forgiven, she does not necessarily repent: she merely accepts the consequences of her actions: ''Tis time to die, when 'tis a shame to live' (v.iii.179). De Flores does not even ask forgiveness. He has achieved his life's desire and seems to feel that it was worth the risk of damnation:

> Yes, and her honour's prize
> Was my reward; I thank life for nothing
> But that pleasure: it was so sweet to me
> That I have drunk up all, left none behind
> For any man to pledge me.   v.iii.167–71

He possesses Othello's jealous love but does not fear death for, unlike Othello, whose possible damnation threatens to separate him from Desdemona forever, hell poses no such threat of separation for Beatrice-Joanna and De Flores.

Images of hands, of gloves, and of rings binding them together – both the betrothal ring which De Flores may still wear, and the ring of hell in the game of Barley-brake – culminate in the enactment of their deaths, which follow each other so closely that they can almost be considered as one death. The contrast with *Othello* contributes one more level to the impact of this final portrayal of inseparability, and indicates that the nature of the dramatists' use of Shakespeare's work was not a debt of characterisation, of plot, or of verbal echoes – but a source of contrasts which would highlight the originality of their own technique.

The Changeling differs greatly from Middleton's earlier work which also alluded to Shakespeare – though this achieved a totally opposite effect. He borrowed extensively from *Romeo and Juliet* for *The Family of Love* (1602). As David L. Frost remarks, in this early play 'The allusions to *Romeo and Juliet* stand out like a wallflower on a bombsite; a reminder of better things'.[21] There is no question of imitation on a lesser scale, or of parody in *The Changeling*, but it was left to John Ford in *'Tis Pity She's a Whore* to use *Romeo and Juliet* as Middleton and Rowley may have used *Othello* and *Macbeth*. Frost sums up the nature of Ford's borrowing: 'It cannot, I feel, be maintained that he could hope to use Shakespeare's plot as a scheme on which to perform variations, without his audience being aware of the borrowing. Indeed, Ford seems rather to multiply the parallels, as if intending that they be seen.' He continues: 'It is not for its interpretation, but for its full emotional effect, that *'Tis Pity She's a Whore* is dependent on *Romeo and Juliet*. The parallels are there to provide the audience with novel shocks; the enormity of a crime which no-one defends being treated in the terms of a love drama of the previous century.'[22]

As in *The Changeling*, Ford's drama seems to reflect a change in attitude to previously accepted concepts. The friar's image of hell seems only a description linked with the morality tradition – it is no longer universally accepted:

> There is a place – ...
> in a black and hollow vault,
> Where day is never seen; there shines no sun,
> But flaming horror of consuming fires;
> A lightless sulphur, choked with smoky fogs
> Of an infected darkness: in this place
> Dwell many thousand thousand sundry sorts

> Of never-dying deaths: there damned souls
> Roar without pity ...
>   there lies the wanton
> On racks of burning steel, whiles in his soul
> He feels the torment of his raging lust.   III.vi.8–23[23]

Giovanni's living tortures of guilt and jealousy are far more real, and hell to him is personal rather than religious: it is equated with separation from Annabella. Like Marlowe's Mephostophilis, Giovanni seems to prove that:

> Hell hath no limits, nor is circumscribed
> In one self place. But where we are is hell,
> And where hell is there must we ever be.
>   *Doctor Faustus* I.v.124–6[24]

Hell, to Giovanni, is not a possible definition of an after-life as it is to Annabella:

> *Gio.*   could I believe
> This might be true, I could believe as well
> There might be Hell or Heaven.
> *Ann.*   That's most certain.   v.v.33–5

The climax in v.vi occurs because the personal, but immoral heaven which Giovanni and Annabella enjoy is to be transformed to hell by discovery and separation. As in *The Changeling*, the locality of a retributive after-life does not make the greatest impact: it is the inseparability of the protagonists which is most striking:

> Where'er I go, let me enjoy this grace,
> Freely to view my Annabella's face.   v.vi.106–7

This is the couple's sole means of escape from the restrictive world of the play, for not only does the social law of the world outside the theatre forbid such love to flourish, but the drama also imposes its own restrictions. The evocation of *Romeo and Juliet* hints that these lovers are also 'star cross'd' and unable to avoid their fate – a fate which is determined from the outset:

> *Fri.* Cry to thy heart, wash every word thou utter'st
>   In tears, and, if't be possible, of blood;   i.i.72–3

This speech relates directly to Giovanni's final entry with his sister's heart upon his dagger, and the link is strengthened if, as M. C. Bradbrook notes,[25] this act is related to Ferdinand's image of using his sister's heart as a sponge to wipe out his guilt (*Duchess of Malfi*, II.v.15–16). *Romeo and Juliet* is not the only contemporary play to which Ford refers; allusions to Webster's plays are also present.

M. C. Bradbrook's words: 'The idea that Ferdinand's driving impulse is an incestuous fixation on his twin sister opens up a meaning more readily available today. It explains the ceremonial forms his persecution takes; ritual is an effective way of disguising and controlling repressed desires'[26] can also be applied to Giovanni and Annabella's marriage ritual which does not control or disguise repressed desires, but is a vehicle for their expression: finding a mode of expression for forbidden desires is shown to be almost as difficult as disguising or controlling them. In their ritual, the repetition of 'Brother' and 'Sister' juxtaposes the sacredness of the marriage commitment with its immoral reality.

Bradbrook notes that the improvised marriage ceremony in *The Duchess of Malfi* might have been the model for Ford's ritual. She does not comment further, but in both cases the couple kneel, the ritual is quickly improvised in an atmosphere of tension, and a kiss plays a significant part in the ceremony. If Ford is deliberately recalling Webster's scene, the kiss with which Giovanni and Annabella seal their relationship can also be seen as a *Quietus est* – not only sealing their relationship, but also their doom. In both plays the ceremony is a way of convincing each other and the audience of the actuality of an unreal situation: it is a means of stressing their commitment and of indicating that the fantasy of their seemingly impossible desires has come into the open and will be enacted to its conclusion.

A kiss ends the stage ritual of their marriage ceremony and marks the beginning of their new relationship: in v.v, when Giovanni kisses Annabella again, it is clear that this is the beginning of another ritual:

> *Gio.* Pray, Annabella, pray; since we must part,
>   Go thou white in thy soul, to fill a throne
>   Of innocence and sanctity in Heaven.
>   Pray, pray my sister.
> *Ann.*   Then I see your drift;
>   Ye blessed angels guard me!
> *Gio.*   So say I.
>   Kiss me.   v.v.63–8

A comparison of the two instances reveals a contrast in Annabella's portrayal; she is no longer likened to the pagan goddess Juno, who married her brother Jove, but is transformed by Giovanni's imagery into a Christian saint and martyr. An atmosphere of tension is created on stage, like that of the former scene, but now it is more intense because the outcome, previously only implied, is now imminent. The words of their earlier vow are evoked: 'Love me or kill me, brother' (1.ii.256) and when Giovanni asks Annabella's forgiveness in the manner of an executioner, she replies, 'With my heart' – an answer he is to take literally. His last kiss coincides with her death wound and is an enactment of a well-established metaphor which associates the act of death with the act of love. It recalls the art of 'dying' of Cleopatra; it is the *Quietus est* of the Duchess of Malfi; it is Death the lover in *Romeo and Juliet* and *Measure for Measure*. Ford fuses metaphor and stage action in a reversal of Othello's 'Killing myself, to die upon a kiss' (v.ii.360). In *'Tis Pity*, Giovanni stabs Annabella 'To save thy fame, and kill thee in a kiss' (v.v.84) which recalls the friar's words to Annabella, describing hell:

> Then you will wish each kiss your brother gave
> Had been a dagger's point;   III.vi.27–8

In the friar's speech the heart is at the centre of repentance:

> But soft, methinks I see repentance work
> New motions in your heart;   III.vi.31–2

Giovanni's last actions are inextricably associated with notions of Annabella's redemption at his own expense: in I.ii he was willing to forfeit his place in a pagan heaven – 'I would not change this minute for Elysium' (I.ii.264), and in v.v, by killing her, he risks losing his place in her Christian heaven.

Throughout the play, the many connotations of blood have been illustrated – among them, blood as an expression of passion and sexuality: Richardetto says of Annabella:

> I rather think
> Her sickness is a fulness of her blood –
> You understand me?   III.iv.7–9

The spilling of her blood by Giovanni is both a perverse act of love and a symbolic purging. This is more than an inevitable tragic conclusion; it is an enactment of a metaphor.

The concept of the heart as the home of truth and the centre of the emotions occurs at many points in the play –

> Gio.   And here's my breast, strike home!
> Rip up my bosom, there thou shalt behold
> A heart in which is writ the truth I speak.   I.ii.209–11

and

> Enough, I take thy word; sweet, we must part:
> Remember what thou vow'st; keep well my heart.   II.i.31–2

In the first example Giovanni offers Annabella a dagger with which to stab him to be certain of the truth of his feelings, but this is accepted as an extravagant, though sincere dramatic gesture; Annabella would not risk putting it to the test. She values Giovanni far more than she values Soranzo, and mocks the metaphor when applied to him:

> Sor. Did you but see my heart, then would you swear –
> Ann. That you were dead.   III.ii.23–4

Soranzo, in turn, threatens to enact it in his passionate attempt to discover the name of her lover:

> I'll rip up thy heart
> And find it there.   IV.iii.53–4

and had Vasques not intervened, the implication is that he would have killed her – without discovering the truth. Soranzo, in trying to grasp at a truth which is hidden in the heart, reaches for the physical embodiment of that truth which he can grasp, but which will never be more than an empty symbol, as Giovanni's later action shows. The organ of the heart, divorced from the body, has no meaning or identity:

> 'tis a heart,
> A heart my lords, in which is mine entombed.
> Look well upon't; d'ee know't?   v.vi.26–8

As M. C. Bradbrook and others have noted, Giovanni's action can be seen as a parody of the devotional worship of the sacred heart[27] and recalls Vittoria's words:

> Behold Bracciano, I that while you liv'd
> Did make a flaming altar of my heart
> To sacrifice unto you; now am ready
> To sacrifice heart and all.   The White Devil v.vi.83–6

However, it is also a dramatic parody of a literary metaphor which carries the parodies in Shakespeare's Sonnets or of Phebe's:

> Now I do frown on thee with all my heart,
> And if mine eyes can wound, now let them kill thee.
>   As You Like It III.v.15–16

to a tragic and extreme pitch. His act, like Phebe's, is one of defiance. He thrusts the speared heart before their faces and asks them to read the truth which is, by tradition, clearly written on it – knowing that they can never do this: they do not even recognise that it is Annabella's heart. The flexibility of conventional language and its retractibility is contrasted with the irreversible reality of the action. It is an effective dramatisation of Giovanni and Annabella's dilemma throughout the play: their love was beyond the range of that particular society's conventions and the inability of the onlookers to penetrate and understand the tragedy of the couple's relationship is matched by Giovanni and Annabella's inability to control their unconventional passion. Both moved in opposite directions and this confrontation with the disembodied heart, dramatises the gulf which now exists between the two groups.

The contrast with *Romeo and Juliet* is particularly poignant. The discovery of their forbidden relationship also occurs when it is too late to save it, but their deaths bring about understanding and reconciliation between the two families. In *'Tis Pity* the opposite occurs – a previously loving father dies renouncing his children in horror. The circumstances of his broken heart differ greatly from the reported death of Romeo's mother in the final scene of that play. Giovanni and Annabella's tragedy cannot evoke sympathy and pity from the bystanders on stage: only the audience can comprehend the tragic complexity of the situation. Not only is it impossible totally to condemn Giovanni because he breaks the moral laws of a society shown to be corrupt in other ways (the Church seizes the family's wealth before they are even buried), but it is also difficult to condemn a man who is so obviously a victim of conventional circumstance.

As the doomed lover of his sister, he fights against unyielding moral conventions, and it is clear that he cannot win because of the precedents of other conventions which have trapped him throughout the play. In I.ii he is, according to Annabella, an example of the pathological state, melancholy-adust, described by Robert Burton in *The Anatomy of Melancholy*, and manifests all the symptoms which Orlando lacks in *As You Like It* (III.ii.366–76). As late as v.v Giovanni conforms to a set pattern of behaviour when he declares:

> why, I hold fate
> Clasped in my fist, and could command the course
> Of time's eternal motion;   v.v.11–13

He may have been believable as a stereotype of Burton's melancholic lover, but this time he appears to have tragically misconstrued his role: the conventions of the *Romeo and Juliet* tradition will not allow him to play the part of Tamburlaine which he would like to adopt. Later in the scene he stabs Annabella, declaring, 'Revenge is mine; honour doth love command' (v.v.86) and the audience may take this as an indication that he is now a victim of another tradition – the revenge drama.

This final phase involves the stabbing of Soranzo and the exchange of his heart for Annabella's (an ironical comment on Soranzo's earlier words, 'My heart is fix'd', v.vi.2). The sequence culminates in Giovanni's own death at the hands of the banditti – which recalls the contrasting spectacles of similar stage actions ranging from the death of the tyrant Piero in Marston's *Antonio's Revenge* to the more noble deaths of Caesar or Coriolanus. This may be considered an unusual end for a character associated with Romeo; but it is not strange for a figure who is trapped between dramatic traditions – love tragedy and revenge drama – and also between dramatic roles: noble hero or immoral villain.

Giovanni is not only a victim of moral deviation; as the stage action reveals, he is also a victim of dramatic manipulation, and in this he resembles some of Webster's characters. However, unlike Webster's creations, he seems unconscious of the fact. He does not possess the self-awareness of a Bosola or of a Flamineo, who openly acknowledge their desires and, using theatrical terms, recognise their inability to direct their own parts. Giovanni's situation is particularly tragic because he acts as if he can control his fate, when it is apparent to the audience that he cannot escape such long-standing traditions so easily. At the same time, the incident with Annabella's heart indicates the inadequacy of existing conventions to express the psychological reality of the play. This suggests that the best way to express the concept on stage would be to use a property heart which, as closely as possible, resembles an unidentifiable human organ. Nicholas Brooke's suggestions fail to acknowledge this:

It can be done with a sheep's heart dripping real blood, which makes the horror apparent, but if it is taken too literally it is apt to be too small to be clearly recognisable enough for its symbolic value to register. If, as is sometimes done, a large cardboard heart is used, the symbolic point is clear but the shocking actuality is lost.[28]

The point is, surely, that the symbolic value does not register. Giovanni goes to great pains to show that it is a meaningless symbol. A 'sheep's heart dripping real blood' would seem to be the better suggestion – but not for the reasons Brooke gives: the physical reality is significant because it is the opposite of the symbol, and not because its prime function is to convey 'horror' alone. A large cardboard heart is very unlikely to have been used at a contemporary performance and would certainly have defeated the whole purpose of this very important dramatic action if it was used.

'Tis Pity was a Queen's Men's play, known to have been performed at the Phoenix Theatre, or the Cockpit in Drury Lane – which was also one of the venues for *The Changeling*. The steep galleries of this converted cockpit would not only bring the audience close to the action, but would place them, from the beginning, in an elevated position. In view of the point that the audience comprises the only group of spectators who can appreciate the complexity of the characters' dilemma, this physical feature

(although coincidental) seems particularly appropriate: the actors would have moved in the depths from which they could not escape.

Unlike G. E. Bentley,[29] I do not believe that the physical characteristics of a Jacobean theatre would influence a playwright to the extent that he would write with a particular theatre in mind – be it Blackfriars or, in this case, the Cockpit: the necessary adaptability of the drama for more than one venue would seem to refute this. (Although *The Changeling* was performed at the Cockpit, it is first recorded as being performed at Whitehall on 4 January 1623/4.) However, it is interesting that certain venues may, unconsciously, have exploited particular psychological approaches to the drama more than others. In more recent years, the Royal Shakespeare Company demonstrated that a production of *Macbeth* (directed by Trevor Nunn; with Judi Dench and Ian McKellen in the leading roles) varied in atmospheric intensity at different places of performance – not because of a few minor adaptations, or because of a discrepancy in the standard of acting, but primarily as a result of the audience's relationship with the drama, which was obviously intensified in the small, claustrophobic settings of The Other Place (Stratford) and the Donmar Warehouse (Covent Garden), and was diffused to some extent in the much larger, less intimate main Stratford theatre. Perhaps the Globe was not the most suitable stage for Shakespeare's play after all – although this obviously had no effect on its success. Occasionally, even if it was purely by chance, the atmosphere of a play and the setting of a theatre building may then, as sometimes occurs today, have coincided to create additional impact. The claustrophobia of the worlds of *The Changeling* and *'Tis Pity* is more akin to the enclosed setting of the Cockpit than to the open stage of the Globe.

In terms of time, Ford might be expected to be a long way from the Elizabethan and early Jacobean theatre and, if the old morality tradition is evoked by the staging of *'Tis Pity*, it is a pointed adaptation rather than a facsimile of the original. Annabella's abrupt repentance must be accepted dramatically because the play demands it, but this does not imply that it is psychologically satisfactory. The tableau effect which opens III.vi comprises the traditional theatrical effects of a repentance scene – the friar with Annabella at his feet, wax lights on an altar, and the melodramatic stage direction, '*She weeps, and wrings her hands.*' This does not accord with her spirited defiant replies to Soranzo which she exhibited the last time the audience saw her – in III.ii. Is Ford deliberately sacrificing decorum – consistency of character – to achieve a particular dramatic effect? Or could it be that Annabella, like Giovanni, is a helpless victim of a different set of conventions?

Annabella and Giovanni commit the first crime because society and religion cannot, or simply do not offer an effective solution to their abnormal passion. This elaborately staged repentance scene is the response of religion and society to conceal such misfits and their offspring under the guise of normality, and emphasises the straitjacket they impose on any deviant set of values. It stresses concealment rather than honesty and implies hypocrisy. It is also a ritual based on fear rather than on love and contrasts with Giovanni and Annabella's own improvised ceremony earlier. In addition, the repentance scene, which ends in tears, leads immediately into a rushed, insincere wedding – so rushed that, it seems, neither party has time to kneel.

The ritual of repentance is staged so exaggeratedly that the element of imposition cannot be ignored; so it is not necessarily an inconsistency to learn that Annabella has not given up Giovanni after her marriage: her conflict with Soranzo in IV.iii is a more dangerously spirited taunting than that of III.ii. Like the friar, Soranzo tries to elicit a response from her through fear, but this time she will not succumb and tells Vasques:

> Pish, do not beg for me, I prize my life
> As nothing; if the man will needs be mad,
> Why let him take it.   IV.iii.93–5

It is not fear but the love which Soranzo expresses (albeit in the conventional metaphors which are now suspect) which causes her second, and most genuine, repentance. The images, both verbally and visually, recall the earlier repentance scene and also the ritual with Giovanni. Annabella's heart is, in all three, a subject of the discourse, and in all three cases there is talk of wounding or killing her. Annabella's second repentance is a visual contrast with the scene involving the friar because in it she kneels to Soranzo who, unlike the friar, will not let her continue, but raises her up and sends her away. The friar's repentance scene possessed all the traditional properties and indulged in elaborate gesture and language, but could not sustain genuine feeling once the properties were removed. In the later scene, Soranzo, who is, significantly, a fellow sinner, cuts off an improvised repentance scene which is genuine. Moral values seem to be restored by words of love and censure from another culpable human being, and not by the inadequate apparatus of religion. However, the apparatus of religion and convention is all that Annabella has at her disposal in her imprisonment:

> That man, that blessed friar,
> Who joined in ceremonial knot my hand
> To him whose wife I now am, told me oft
> I trod the path to death, and showed me how.   V.i.24–7

It is because she knows no other way that she resorts to tradition – expressing repentance in 'This paper double-lined with tears and blood' (v.i.34), which also invokes a long theatrical tradition that includes Bel-Imperia in *The Spanish Tragedy*. It is invested with new significance in a play where blood is believed, literally, to be the currency of truth.

Ford's characters are more helpless than even those of Webster: they are an unacceptable by-product of the hypocritical society in which they are trapped in various conventional dramatic roles. Their tragedy is expressed by the gulf between their personal situation and the rigid application of convention by a society with equally misplaced values. Ford does not give the audience a norm by which they can judge degrees of deviation: there is no firm ground in the world of the play from which judgment can be made, so the members of the audience are, in this respect, detached observers. However, the intensity of Giovanni and Annabella's relationship cannot fail to involve and impress them – both emotionally and dramatically – so, in this respect, they are drawn into the action.

Kirsch[30] mentions the 'peculiar blend of engagement and detachment' in conditions of performance in the private theatres (in relation to Middleton) and it would seem that in *'Tis Pity*, Ford adopted some of these characteristics and, like Middleton, learned to apply them to a wider audience. Perhaps he was aided at certain performances by the physical characteristics of the Cockpit which would distance the audience by elevating them above the players, while at the same time keeping them at an intimate proximity. In a sense, the steep-sided theatre, where spectators look down on the actors below, is reminiscent of the Renaissance anatomy theatres; and it is not inappropriate to think of Ford's characters as human specimens trying to dissect each other, while under the scrutiny of an audience attempting to make sense of the various components of character and tragic situation.

Another means of achieving a blend of detachment and involvement within the drama is the masque-like inset used by both Middleton and Ford. In *'Tis Pity* Hippolita's masque distances the audience with its symbolic entertainment of music and dance by virgins in white – an ironical comment on Annabella, whose marriage feast it is – but it also involves the audience by associating the event with treachery and death, and the play's now familiar, portentous imagery:

> Take here my curse amongst you: may thy bed
> Of marriage be a rack unto thy heart –
> Burn, blood, and boil in vengeance; O my heart,

> My flame's intolerable! – May'st thou live
> To father bastards, may her womb bring forth
> Monsters, and die together in your sins
> Hated, scorned and unpitied! –   IV.i.94–100

The reiteration of 'heart', the references to blood, passion, and vengeance, the hint that Annabella's child will be discovered, and the linking of their deaths (Giovanni exchanges Annabella's heart for Soranzo's) are all omens which prefigure the final actions of the play. However, there is never any suggestion that this is due to Hippolita's curse. Her prophecies come true in ways which she never envisaged and their course was set long before she spoke. Her masque stresses, as if by chance, the predicament of the other characters. Her action highlights Soranzo's own guilt, and therefore modifies the audience's condemnation of Annabella, while at the same time emphasising her deceit by contrasting her with the virgins in white. The device also plays a significant part in Ford's manipulation of audience expectations, for the friar's words:

> I fear the event: that marriage seldom's good,
> Where the bride-banquet so begins in blood.   IV.i.110–11

may later be recalled in relation to Soranzo's:

> My thoughts are great, and all as resolute
> As thunder; in mean time I'll cause our lady
> To deck herself in all her bridal robes,
> Kiss her, and fold her gently in my arms.
> Begone – yet hear you, are the banditti ready
> To wait in ambush?   v.ii.9–14

which suggests a revenge act with overtones of *Othello*. Giovanni's action in v.v, therefore, takes the audience doubly by surprise – not only because of its own extremity of expression – but also because the audience was prepared for a very different outcome, which Giovanni's performance upstages.

In *The Broken Heart*, Ford goes one step further and brings the manipulation of audience expectations to its conclusion during the masque device, which can be viewed as the emblematic climax of the whole play. Bradbrook remarks that the action has a precedent in the tradition of Ganelon, the Senecal man of *Charlemagne* (1600), who, when banished, received the news with a caper (usually an expression of joy) to show how little it affected him;[31] but it seems likely that the original source was, as R. Jordan suggests,[32] Plutarch's *Life of Agesilaus*, in which he tells of the disastrous Spartan defeat at the battle of Leuctra. This occurred suddenly and was an emotional shock to a hitherto self-confident people: Plutarch emphasises the arrival of the news at Sparta and the way it was received by the Spartans who refused to interrupt their festal dance then in progress, even in the face of disaster.

Ford set *The Broken Heart* in ancient Sparta and this incident stresses Calantha's great strength of mind, which will ultimately culminate in her ability to will her own death. It is a strength which enables her to enact a literary convention – the broken heart – and in the enactment, to juxtapose an emblem of emotion with a theatrically presented actuality. Ford seems to bring together the symbol and the reality so that they validate each other, and in this he seeks an opposite effect to that achieved by Giovanni's action with his sister's heart.

By setting the play in ancient Sparta, Ford has ensured that the conventions of the society represented in it reinforce the heroine's response to her situation. Ford can be criticised for imposing a Spartan setting on an otherwise Jacobean society in order to make the dramatic climax he desired more meaningful. Calantha relives the Spartan reception of death news, but Armostes, Bassanes, and Orgilus reflect the audience's response of surprise, and therefore stress Calantha's solitary position.

The dance, with its significantly loud music, can be performed as a powerful expression of emotion controlled by ritual. Calantha's comments, 'To the other change' and 'Lead to the next' suggest a formal patterned movement. Whether she shows total control of her feelings, or whether she uses the movements of the dance to express her grief silently, depends on individual interpretation. There is a remote echo of the Dance of Death (known to have been represented as an actual dance in 1393)[33] where, one by one, members of the dance leave the floor and do not return. In *The Broken Heart* the deaths occur elsewhere, perhaps while the dance is going on. Although the audience has already seen the dead Penthea and Ithocles, the time sequence is not clear and the opening words of v.ii could suggest simultaneous events:

> *Calantha* We miss our servant Ithocles, and Orgilus.
> On whom attend they?
> *Crotolon*   My son, gracious princess,
> Whispered some new device, to which these revels
> Should be but usher; wherein I conceive
> Lord Ithocles and he himself are actors.
> *Calantha* A fair excuse for absence. As for Bassanes,
> Delights to him are troublesome. Armostes
> Is with the king?
> *Crotolon*   He is.   v.ii.1–8[34]

Penthea is probably included in the reference to Bassanes, so all missing people are located in relation to the dance. The various messages which come, one after the other, can be equated to the actual bodies leaving the dance floor in the Dance of Death. The messages are associated with changes in the dance pattern – which might also apply to the original Dance of Death, as the dance would need to adapt itself to the loss of more than one dancer. The outbursts of Armostes, Bassanes, and Orgilus steadily increase in theatricality to reach the pitch: 'Brave Ithocles is murdered, murdered cruelly' (v.ii.16) and Calantha's cool, detached response is belied by the loud music which she orders to be increased in volume, 'How dull this music sounds! Strike up more sprightly' (v.ii.17). The resultant staging could produce a disturbing but powerful contrast between the deafening music (which may almost drown Orgilus's remark) and the quiet dignity of the dance. Like those taking part in the banquet scene in *Macbeth*, the members of the court here are forced to go along with the whims of their ruler, and are unable to respond to the situation as they might think fit: the only dancer who can show self-possession throughout is Calantha herself.

Calantha maintains the ritual after the dance has ended, through her formal questions and remarks. Her apparently callous, business-like manner provides for Orgilus's execution and immediately moves on to deal with her coronation. The play is an effective example of how one ritual may be exchanged for another. In IV.iv Chrystalla and Philema relate the circumstances of Penthea's death to Orgilus and show that it took the form of a ritual starvation: it was a death ceremony enacted with considerable theatrical precision:

> *Philema*   She called for music,
> And begged some gentle voice to tune a farewell
> To life and griefs. Chrystalla touched the lute.
> I wept the funeral song.
> *Chrystalla* But her last breath sealed up these hollow sounds:
> 'O cruel Ithocles, and injured Orgilus!'
> So down she drew her veil; so died.   IV.iv.4–10

This description prefigures the action of v.iii when Calantha, crowned and dressed as a bride, dies at the end of a song which could also be said to 'tune a farewell/To life and griefs'. Between this almost symmetrical description and corresponding action are the deaths of Ithocles and Orgilus – both of which are performed with almost mechanical observance to ritual. Ithocles dies fastened in a chair beside the dead Penthea, to an accompaniment of stylised speeches which take the form of a duet between Orgilus and himself. Orgilus, the 'bloody relater of thy stains in blood' (v.ii.77), chooses to bleed to death: a ritual which may be seen as a symbolic purging. The harsh contrast of revelry and death has a long theatrical history and is also linked with the sexual connotations of revelry and banqueting which Ford exploits in *'Tis Pity* when Annabella tells Giovanni:

> And know that now there's but a dining-time
> 'Twixt us and our confusion: v.v.17–18

In *The Broken Heart*, the revelry of the dance infiltrates Orgilus's execution with grotesque results. His blood is said to 'sparkle[s] like a lusty wine new broached' (v.ii.125), and gives a new slant to the remark, associated with successful revels, that wine flowed like water.

The marriage in v.iii can also be seen as a funeral ceremony and, according to Bradbrook,[35] there was a theatrical precedent for funerals in white (John Mason's *Mulleases the Turk*, 1607–8) and a historical precedent of white mourning dress through Mary Queen of Scots (who was painted in this manner while mourning Francis I). The colour symbolised that the marriage was not consummated and is, therefore, appropriate in *The Broken Heart*. Calantha's language brings the two opposite ceremonies together – as is the case in the wooing scene of *The Duchess of Malfi*. Bassanes points to the reversal:

> This is a testament
> It sounds not like conditions on a marriage.   v.iii.53–4

When Calantha has put her ring on Ithocles's finger, and kissed him in imitation of the wedding rites, she bids those at the altar sing the song which she chose to accompany her death. Although the stage directions do not mention another throne, it seems likely that she does sit by Ithocles, and so visually substitutes herself for Penthea, by whose side he died earlier.

The whole play can be staged as a unity of shifting symmetries and rituals. This chapter began by indicating the function of the sub-plot in *The Changeling*, and likened its emblematic characteristics to a development of the play-within-a-play device which is developed in yet another direction in *Women Beware Women*. Hippolita's masque in Ford's *'Tis Pity* fulfils a similar function to that of *The Changeling*'s sub-plot, although on a much smaller scale – and its obvious limitations make it less dramatically effective. Elsewhere in *'Tis Pity*, traditional rituals or recognisable dramatic roles from other dramas are, as is occasionally the case in *The Changeling*, evoked or enacted in order to obtain added dramatic effect from the contrast between the original situations and the positions of the characters in the later plays. In *The Broken Heart*, Ford seems to have extended the emblematic ritual of the play-within-a-play to the whole drama. However, although Ford's ultimate achievement in *The Broken Heart* can be considered a success in the staging of a unified design, the rigidity of that design, coupled with his formalised characterisation, tend to stifle the dramatic life of his characters and rob them of *energeia*. In both *'Tis Pity* and *The Broken Heart*, Ford's characters are easily viewed as slaves to the dramatist's intentions, and it seems to be *The Changeling* – with its old fashioned dumb-show and shrewd emblematical sub-plot, which comment surreptitiously on the main action – which allows its main characters the psychological freedom of expression necessary for the staging of great drama. Such a judgment is, perhaps, unfair to Ford, whose strength is his artistic self-consciousness and whose unique voice as a dramatist explores the dubious legacy of Elizabethan and Jacobean drama, specialising in characters trapped (dramatically and otherwise) by traditions and conventions which they cannot evade.

Notes

The following abbreviations have been used in the notes:

EIC   *Essays in Criticism*
ELH   *Journal of English Literary History*
ELN   *English Language Notes*
ES   E. K. Chambers, *The Elizabethan stage* (4 vols., Oxford, 1923; repr. with corrections, 1974)
HLQ   *Huntington Library Quarterly*
MLR   *Modern Language Review*
NQ   *Notes and Queries*
RenD   *Renaissance Drama*
RenQ   *Renaissance Quarterly*
RES   *Review of English Studies*
SEL   *Studies in English Literature 1500–1900* (Rice University)
ShS   *Shakspeare Survey*
SQ   *Shakespeare Quarterly*
TH   Thomas Heywood, *Dramatic works* (3 vols., New York, 1964)
YES   *Yearbook of English Studies*

Introduction

1 Rosalie L. Colie, *Shakespeare's living art* (Princeton, N.J., 1974), p. 5.
2 Anne Pasternak Slater points to the value of what she calls, 'stage-orientated study of Shakespeare's imagery': *Shakespeare the director* (Brighton, 1982), p. 6. A useful annotated bibliography may be found in the notes to her introduction, pp. 202–4.
3 M. C. Bradbrook, *The artist and society in Shakespeare's England: the collected papers of Muriel Bradbrook* (2 vols., Brighton, 1982), vol. 1, p. 87.
4 Michael Hattaway, *Elizabethan popular theatre* (London, 1982), p. 57.
5 R. A. Foakes, 'Suggestions for a new approach to Shakespeare's imagery', *ShS*, 5 (1952), 81–92.
6 See the works of G. Wilson Knight, C. F. E. Spurgeon, Robert Heilman, etc.
7 Emrys Jones, *Scenic form in Shakespeare* (Oxford, 1971), p. 3. See also Alan C. Dessen, *Elizabethan drama and the viewer's eye* (Chapel Hill, 1977), Chapter 3.
8 Colie, *Shakespeare's living art*, p. 25.

9 David Bevington, *Action is eloquence: Shakespeare's language of gesture* (Cambridge, Mass., 1984).

10 James R. Siemon, *Shakespearean iconoclasm* (Berkeley and Los Angeles, 1985).

11 Bevington, *Action is eloquence*, p. 3.

12 Ibid.

13 Ibid.

14 See Helen M. Whall, 'As You Like It: the play of analogy', *HLQ*, 47 (1984), 33–46.

15 Siemon, *Shakespearean iconoclasm*, p. 251

16 Ibid., p. 29.

17 Ibid., p. 30

18 All references to Shakespeare's plays are to the Arden editions unless otherwise stated.

19 Malcolm Evans, 'Deconstructing Shakespeare's comedies', *Alternative Shakespeares*, ed. John Drakakis (London, 1985), pp. 82–3. See also Malcolm Evans, 'Asterion's door: truth's true contents ...', *Glyph*, 9 (1985).

20 Colie, *Shakespeare's living art*, p. 25.

21 See also Dessen, *Elizabethan drama and the viewer's eye*, pp. 87ff.

22 Roland Mushat Frye, *The Renaissance Hamlet: issues and responses in 1600* (Princeton, N.J., 1984), p. 94.

23 Ibid., pp. 243–53.

24 Peter Kemp reviewing Elijah Moshinsky's production for B.B.C. 2.

25 *Love's Labour's Lost*, directed by Barry Kyle for the Royal Shakespeare Company, 1984.

26 Madelaine Doran, *Endeavours of art* (Madison, Wis., 1954), p. 4.

27 Katherine Duncan-Jones, 'Ford and the Earl of Devonshire', *RES*, 29 (1978), 452.

28 Ibid., 449.

1 Heywood's *Ages* and Shakespeare's last plays

1 Bernard Beckerman, *Shakespeare at the Globe* (New York, 1962), p. 106.

2 *ES*, vol. I, pp. 223–4.

3 Thomas Heywood, *Londoni Emporia, or Londons Mercatura* (London, 1633), B3v–B4.

4 Thomas Dekker, *The dramatic works*, ed. F. Bowers (4 vols., Cambridge, 1955–61), vol. II, p. 257.

5 M. C. Bradbrook, *The living monument* (Cambridge, 1976), p. 71.

6 Pageant arches or masque settings were often obscured by cloths to heighten the impact of their disclosure; see James I's Royal Entry, 1604, *The Masque of Blackness*, 1605, *Lord Hay's Masque*, 1607.

7 François Laroque ('A new Ovidian source for the statue scene in *The Winter's Tale*', *NQ*, 31 (1984), 215–17) suggests a link with Deucalion and Pyrrha rather than Pygmalion.

8 Leonard Barkan, 'Living sculptures: Ovid, Michelangelo and *The Winter's Tale*', *ELH*, 48 (1981), 639.

9 Stephen Booth sees the 'fusion and confusion' of identities in the play as 'of the essence of *Cymbeline*' and discusses the possible doubling of Posthumus

and Cloten in relation to this. See *King Lear, Macbeth, indefinition, and tragedy* (New Haven, 1983), pp. 149–53.

10 Glynne Wickham, *Early English stages, 1300–1660* (3 vols., London, 1959–81), vol. II.i, p. 230.

11 Rosemary Freeman, *English emblem books* (London, 1970), p. 62.

12 Wickham, *Early English stages*, vol. II.i, p. 229.

13 *ES*, vol. I, p. 148.

14 Michael Shapiro, *Children of the revels* (New York, 1977), p. 179 and R. A. Foakes, 'Tragedy at the children's theatres after 1600', *The Elizabethan theatre II*, ed. David Galloway (Toronto, 1970), p. 38.

15 Wickham, *Early English stages*, vol. II.ii, p. 136.

16 See also Andrew Gurr, *Playgoing in Shakespeare's London* (Cambridge, 1987).

17 G. E. Bentley, 'Shakespeare and the Blackfriars theatre', *ShS*, 1 (1948), 38–50.

18 *ES*, vol. III, pp. 109–10.

19 A. S. Venezky, *Pageantry on the Shakespearian stage* (New York, 1951), p. 90.

20 David M. Bergeron, *English civic pageantry: 1558–1642* (London, 1971), p. 61.

21 Thomas Heywood, *An Apology for Actors* (London, 1612), F3v.

22 *TH*, vol. III, p. 239. All references are to this edition unless stated otherwise.

23 Ibid., p. 225.

24 Although probably written in 1613, *The Iron Age* was not published until 1632. See R. A. Foakes, *Illustrations of the English stage 1580–1642* (London, 1985), p. 135, for reproductions of the title pages with woodcuts of the story.

25 *TH*, vol. III, p. 427.

26 Ibid., p. 428.

27 Ibid., p. 394.

28 Ibid., p. 385.

29 Ibid., p. 423.

30 Bergeron, *English civic pageantry*, p. 26.

31 Wickham, *Early English stages*, vol. II.i, p. 225.

32 *TH*, vol. III, p. 155.

33 Ibid., pp. 27 and 133.

34 Ibid., p. 306.

35 Allardyce Nicoll, *Stuart masques and the Renaissance stage* (London, 1937), pp. 187–8.

36 Wickham, *Early English stages*, vol. II.i, p. 226.

37 J. L. Styan, *Shakespeare's stagecraft* (Cambridge, 1967), p. 123.

38 See D. E. Landry, 'Dreams as history: the strange unity of *Cymbeline*', *SQ*, 33 (1982), 68–79.

39 Emrys Jones, 'The Stuart *Cymbeline*', *EIC*, 11 (1961), 84–99.

40 Leo G. Salingar, *Shakespeare and the traditions of comedy* (Cambridge, 1974), p. 59.

41 *TH*, vol. III, p. 122.

42 R. A. Foakes and R. T. Rickert (eds.), *Henslowe's diary* (Cambridge, 1961), p. 320.

43 C. Walter Hodges, *The Globe restored* (London, 1953), p. 74.

44 Wickham, *Early English stages*, vol. II.I, p. 235.
45 Nicoll, *Stuart masques*, p. 94.

2 The multiple roots of symbolic staging

1 Given at Leeds University on 2 December 1981.
2 Marjorie Garber, '*Cymbeline* and the languages of myth', *Mosaic*, 10 (1977), 105.
3 See Dessen, *Elizabethan drama and the viewer's eye*, p. 87.
4 A. P. Rossiter, *English drama from early times to the Elizabethans* (London, 1950), p. 70.
5 See Marjorie Garber, *Coming of age in Shakespeare* (London, 1981) and Slater, *Shakespeare the director*.
6   Look, York: I stain'd this napkin with the blood
             That valiant Clifford with his rapier's point
             Made issue from the bosom of the boy;
             And if thine eyes can water for his death,
             I give thee this to dry thy cheeks withall.   *3 Henry VI*, I.iv.79–83
7 Bradbrook, *The artist and society in Shakespeare's England*, vol. I, p. 171.
8   *Othello*   the recognizance and pledge of love,
             Which I first gave her; I saw it in his hand,
             It was a handkerchief; an antique token
             My father gave my mother.   v.ii.215–18
9 Giovanni Battista Giraldi Cintio 'Gli Hecatommithi' (1566), *Narrative and dramatic sources of Shakespeare*, ed. Geoffrey Bullough (7 vols., London, 1973), vol. 7, p. 246. H. Diehl ('Inversion, parody and irony: the visual rhetoric of Renaissance English tragedy', *SEL*, 22 (1982), 208) discusses Shakespeare's combination of 'two conventional icons' – the strawberry and the kerchief.
10 As Werner Habicht ('Tree properties and tree scenes in Elizabethan theater', *RenD*, 4 (1971), 69–92) shows: 'The tree property ... can assume symbolic qualities and emblematic functions. By the way it is led up to, through the words and gestures delivered in it, and through the visual and verbal images it contains, a tree scene provides the audience's imagination with familiar motifs established by iconographic and literary traditions, the sheer multiplicity and disparity of which account for its ambiguous effects' (p. 81).
11 Ovid, *Metamorphoses*, trans. Arthur Golding; ed. W. H. D. Rouse (London, 1904), Book IV, lines 150–2 (Reprint of a copy of the first edition, 1567, in Cambridge University Library).
12 Ibid., lines 191–5.
13 *Funk and Wagnalls standard dictionary of folklore, mythology and legend* (2 vols., New York, 1949–50), vol. II, p. 759.
14 Neither the *Oxford dictionary of nursery rhymes* (Oxford, 1951) nor Jean Harrowven's *The origins of rhymes, songs and sayings* (London, 1977) list or give an explanation of the source of this nursery rhyme, but the reference to a frosty morning and the ritual of dancing round a tree seem to associate it with spring rites.
15 Philip Stubbes, *The Anatomie of Abuses ... the first part* (London, 1583), M3v–M4r.

16 J. G. Frazer, *The illustrated golden bough*, ed. Sabine MacCormack (New York, 1978), p. 209. The extract quoted is taken from part two of 'Pange lingua gloriosi praelium certaminis' – 'Sing my tongue, the glorious battle': a passiontide hymn. (*Historical companion to hymns ancient and modern*, ed. M. Frost (London, 1962), p. 188.)

17 G. B. Ladner, 'Vegetation symbolism and the concept of renaissance' *De artibus opuscula XL: essays in honor of Erwin Panofsky*, ed. M. Meiss (New York, 1961), vol. I, p. 308.

18 J. E. Cirlot, *Dictionary of symbols* (London, 1971), p. 103.

19 Thomas Kyd, *The Spanish Tragedy*, ed. Philip Edwards, Revels plays (London, 1959), p. 40. All textual references are to this edition.

20 R. E. R. Madelaine remarks that this stage business may have influenced I.i of *The Changeling*, but he does not examine this further. See: R. E. R. Madelaine, *The moral and dramatic functions of stage images and verbal emblems in selected Jacobean plays*, D.Phil. thesis (University of London, Westfield College, 1972), p. 676.

21 Thomas Middleton and William Rowley, *The Changeling*, ed. N. W. Bawcutt, Revels plays (London, 1958; Manchester, 1977), p. 14. All textual references are to this edition.

22 Frank Ardolino, 'The hangman's noose and the empty box: Kyd's use of dramatic and mythological sources in *The Spanish Tragedy* III.iv–vii', *RenQ*, 30 (1977), 335.

23 Ibid., 339.

24 Dora and Erwin Panofsky, *Pandora's box: the changing aspects of a mythological symbol* (London, 1956), p. 7.

25 Ibid.

26 G. Jobes, *Dictionary of mythology, folklore, and symbols* (3 vols., New York, 1961), vol. II, p. 1374.

27 The Luceron relic, *c*.1500, and a window in the church of St Denys, York, among others. A sixteenth-century poet honoured her with two hymns (Butler's *Lives of the Saints*, ed. H. Thurston and D. Attwater (4 vols., London, 1956), vol. III, p. 152).

28 Ibid., pp. 152–3.

29 E. L. Mascall and H. S. Box (eds.), *The blessed Virgin Mary: essays by Anglican writers* (London, 1963), p. 39. See also R. Verstegan, *Odes in imitation of the seaven penitential psalmes*, 1601 (Menston, 1970), p. 44.

30 Garber, '*Cymbeline* and the languages of myth', 108.

31 Ibid., 109.

32 E. E. Stoll, 'Symbolism in Shakespeare', *MLR*, 42 (1947), 10.

33 *ES*, vol. I, p. 244. In 1606 a statute 'to restrain abuses of players' banned mention of the deity on the stage. See: Peter Thomson, *Shakespeare's theatre* (London, 1983), p. 77.

34 M. C. Bradbrook, 'Shakespeare and the multiple theatres of Jacobean London', *Elizabethan Theatre VI*, ed. G. R. Hibbard (London, 1978), p. 104.

3 *Macbeth* and *Lord Hay's Masque*

1 These include the return of the ship 'Tyger' in August 1606 after a 567-day voyage which matches the witches' 'Sev'n-nights nine times nine' (I.iii.22);

the allusions to equivocation and the hanging of traitors, associated with Father Garnet who was tried and hanged earlier in the year for his part in the Gunpowder Plot, and the proposal by H. N. Paul, in *The royal play of Macbeth* (New York, 1950) that the play was part of the entertainment for King Christian of Denmark's visit and was probably performed on 7 August 1606. The latter suggestion has not been proved: the play that was performed at Hampton Court on this date was un-named. Paul links the Danish visit to the fact that, in *Macbeth*, the Danes defeated by the Scots were converted into 'Norweyans' – he suggests, out of courtesy for the Danish King. However, King James I was married to Anne of Denmark and such a change would have been politic, even without his brother-in-law's visit.

2 A possible debt to Marston's *Sophonisba* (Stationers' Register, March 1606) has been plausibly argued by Kenneth Muir (Arden edition, pp. xix-xx) who refutes the earlier idea that the debt may have been Marston's. Tomkis's play, *Lingua*, has been inconclusively related to *Macbeth*, but its performance date is unknown (S.R. 23 February 1607), so even if the connections should be confirmed, it is not impossible that Shakespeare's play preceded it. *The Puritaine*, with a possible allusion to *Macbeth*, was not entered in the Stationers' Register until 6 August 1607, and may have been performed not long before. E. A. J. Honigmann finds echoes of *Macbeth* in Barnabe Barnes's *The Devil's Charter* (*Shakespeare's impact on his contemporaries* (London, 1982), p. 31) but although this play was performed on 2 February 1607, it was not entered in the Stationers' Register until 16 October, as having been 'more exactly revewed, corrected and augmented since by the Author, for the more pleasure and profit of the Reader' (*ES*, vol. III, p. 214). If Shakespeare's play was performed in January 1607, allusions could have been incorporated into the performance and, if not, then they may have been part of the later additions. *The Knight of the Burning Pestle*, which presumably alludes to Banquo's ghost, also refers to the Prince of Moldavia who visited court between September and November 1607, and so could have been written and performed at the end of the year or the beginning of 1608. Plague deaths rose to a maximum of 141 on 2 October 1606 and as the theatres closed when deaths numbered over fifty a week, it seems unlikely that *Macbeth* would have been performed at the Globe soon after it opened in the autumn, as Paul suggests: however, the early months of 1607 seem to have been less affected by plague and court appearances by the King's Men (plays un-named) also occurred in January and February. Stylistically, *Macbeth* has been linked with *Antony and Cleopatra* (S.R. May 1608), which, J. M. Nosworthy (*Shakespeare's occasional plays* (London, 1965), pp. 9–13) believes, is related to the revisions Daniel made to his own *Cleopatra* in 1607 – so a date for *Macbeth*, early in 1607, again seems possible.

3 *ES*, vol. III, p. 286.

4 David Lindley, 'Campion's *Lord Hay's Masque* and Anglo-Scottish union', *HLQ*, 43 (1979), 1.

5 Bradbrook, 'The multiple theatres of Jacobean London', pp. 96–7.

6 See Ralph Berry, *Shakespeare and the awareness of the audience* (London, 1985), pp. 88–108 for a similar argument in relation to Webster's plays.

7 Northrop Frye, 'Romance as masque', *Shakespeare's romances reconsidered*, ed. C. McGinnis Kay and H. E. Jacobs (Lincoln, Neb.; London,

1978), p. 29 and M. C. Bradbrook, *John Webster: citizen and dramatist* (London, 1980), p. 147.

8 Alexander Leggatt, '*Macbeth* and the last plays', *Mirror up to Shakespeare: essays in honour of G. R. Hibbard*, ed. J. C. Gray (Toronto, 1984), pp. 189–207.

9 Other characters, e.g. Duncan, occasionally use the form, but not as persistently as Macbeth. See I.iv.50–3; II.i.60–4; II.ii.41–2; III.i.140–1; III.iv.135–9; IV.i.153–4.

10 W. A. Murray, 'Why was Duncan's blood golden?', *ShS*, 19 (1966), 34–44.

11 All masque line references are to the edition by Stephen Orgel and Roy Strong, *Inigo Jones: the theater of the Stuart court* (Berkeley and Los Angeles, 1973), unless otherwise stated.

12 Macbeth, ed. J. Dover Wilson (Cambridge, 1960), p. 128, note 112.

13 Thomas Campion, *Works*, ed. W. R. Davis (London, 1969), p. 222.

14 According to *ES* (vol. 4, p. 122 and pp. 200–1) the King's Men were employed in *Lord Hay's Masque*, presumably in the four speaking parts, Night, Flora, Hesperus, and Zepherus – two of which, Night and Flora, were to be represented as women.

15 *ES*, vol. 1, p. 205.

16 See Chapter 1. Yet another instance is explored in: Ernest B. Gilman, '"All eyes": Prospero's inverted masque', *RenQ*, 33 (1980), 214–30.

17 M. St Clare Byrne, 'Bibliographical clues in collaborate plays', *The Library*, 13 (1933), 31–2.

18 John Holloway, *The story of the night* (London, 1961), p. 66.

19 Thomas Campion, *Works*, ed. P. Vivian (Oxford, 1909), pp. 70–1.

20 Lindley, 'Campion's *Lord Hay's Masque* and Anglo-Scottish union', 1–11.

21 D. J. Palmer, 'A new gorgon: visual effects in *Macbeth*', *Focus on Macbeth*, ed. John Russell Brown (London, 1982), p. 56.

4 Pericles

1 In addition to that offered by the Arden edition's introduction, pp. lxii–lxiii and Appendix B, pp. 171–80.

2 Wayne H. Phelps, 'Edmund Shakespeare at St. Leonard's, Shoreditch', *SQ*, 29 (1978), 422–3.

3 John Day, William Rowley, and George Wilkins, *The Travailes of the Three English Brothers*, ed. A. H. Bullen (London, 1881), pp. 27–8.

4 The incident is mentioned in *The Knight of the Burning Pestle*, IV.29–30.

5 William A. McIntosh, 'Musical design in *Pericles*', *ELN*, 11 (1973–4), 102.

6 Day, *The Travailes*, p. 70.

7 Ibid., p. 72.

8 Ibid., p. 73.

9 Ibid., pp. 73–4.

10 For an enlightening reappraisal of the various playhouse audiences see Gurr, *Playgoing in Shakespeare's London*.

11 Miguel de Cervantes, *The History of Don Quixote of the Mancha*, trans. Thomas Shelton, 1612 (London, 1896), vol. 1, p. 26.

12 G. Wilson Knight, *The crown of life* (London, 1948), p. 70.

13 *Pericles*, ed. F. D. Hoeniger (London, 1977), pp. lxxxviii–xci.

14 John Gower, *The complete works* ed. G. C. Macaulay (4 vols., Oxford, 1899–1902), vol. III, p. 407.
15 Anna B. Jameson, *Legends of the Madonna*, 6th edn (London, 1879), p. 1.
16 McIntosh, 'Musical design in *Pericles*', 102.
17 Thomas Elyot, *The Boke Named the Governour* (London, 1907), p. 94.
18 Edgar Wind, *Pagan mysteries in the Renaissance* (Oxford, 1980), p. 138. First published London, 1958.
19 E. H. Gombrich, *Symbolic images: studies in the art of the Renaissance*, 2nd edn (Oxford, 1978), p. 32.
20 See Edmund Spenser, *The Faerie Queene*:
> Therefore the antique wisards well invented,
> That Venus of the fomy sea was bred;
> For that the seas by her are most augmented.   (IV.xii, stanza 2)
21 Peter and Linda Murray, *The art of the Renaissance* (London, 1963), p. 10.
22 J. P. Brockbank, '*Pericles* and the dream of immortality', *ShS*, 24 (1971), 109.
23 Thomas Lodge and Robert Greene, *A Looking-Glass for London and England*, 1594, Malone Society Reprint (Oxford, 1932).
24 Gower, vol. III, p. 417.
25 See also Knight, *The crown of life*, p. 44.
26 *Pericles*, ed. F. D. Hoeniger, pp. 48–9, note 119.
27 Ibid., p. 4.
28 Orgel and Strong (eds.), *Inigo Jones*, p. 107.
29 Ovid, *Metamorphoses*, Book I, lines 513–16.
30 Cirlot, *Dictionary of symbols*, p. 22; see also R. R. Cawley, *The voyagers and Elizabethan drama* (Oxford, 1938), pp. 11–33 for the contemporary knowledge of Egyptian rites and practices.
31 Jobes, *Dictionary of mythology*, pp. 126 and 320.
32 Gower, vol. III, p. 419.
33 The words 'One twelve moons more she'll wear Diana's livery' could be read as a riddle: 'One twelve moons more and she will wear Diana's livery.' Similarly, Thaisa does not 'undertake a married life' for a twelve-month, but in a different sense to the one Simonides suggests (II.v.3–4); she is married for less than a year when she becomes a nun in Diana's order.
34 Directors, Declan Donnellan and Nick Omerod.
35 See also Lindley, 'Campion's *Lord Hay's Masque* and Anglo-Scottish union', 8.
36 See Chapter 2.
37 Gower, vol. III, p. 443.
38 This need not even be heard by the audience to be effective. In the Cheek by Jowl production the chimes, gongs, etc. used were part of the stage decoration (see Figures 5–7): sound effects were made openly by the actors. Pericles, alone, seemed to hear music; the audience did not – although, in the background, the chimes could be seen moving as other actors mimed playing them – but no sound issued. Eventually Marina seemed to hear too, and both gazed entranced – set apart from characters and audience.
39 John P. Cutts, 'Pericles in rusty armour and the matachine dance of the competitive knights', *YES*, 4 (1974), 49–51.

40 T. W. Waldo, 'Beyond words: Shakespeare's tongue-tied muse', *Shakespeare's more than words can witness: essays on visual and non-verbal enactment in the plays*, ed. Sidney Homan (London, 1980), p. 173.

41 Brockbank, '*Pericles* and the dream of immortality', 107.

42 Knight, *The crown of life*, p. 107.

43 Leo G. Salingar, 'Romance in *King Lear*', *English*, 27 (1978), 7.

44 Bradbrook, 'Shakespeare and the multiple theatres of Jacobean London', 97.

45 Ibid.

5 The multi-layered quality of *Cymbeline*

1 Anne Lancashire, '*The Second Maiden's Tragedy*: a Jacobean saint's life', *RES*, 25 (1974), 268–78.

2 Now ascribed to Middleton – see *The Second Maiden's Tragedy*, ed. Anne Lancashire (Manchester, 1978), p. 19.

3 Ibid., III, line 255, p. 186.

4 Ibid., IV.iv.42, p. 222.

5 Clifford Leech, 'Shakespeare's songs and the double response', *The triple bond*, ed. J. G. Price (University Park, Pa., 1975), p. 77.

6 Ibid., p. 78.

7 Kathleen Tillotson in G. Tillotson, *Essays in criticism and research* (Cambridge, 1942), Appendix 1, pp. 204–7.

8 Lancashire, '*The Second Maiden's Tragedy*: a Jacobean saint's life', 272.

9 This was dramatised very effectively by Helen Mirren and Robert Lindsay in I.vi of the B.B.C. production of *Cymbeline*, directed by Elijah Moshinsky, 1983.

10 Cyril Tourneur, *The Revenger's Tragedy*, ed. Brian Gibbons (London, 1967; revised 1971), pp. 25–6.

11 Bevington, *Action is eloquence*, p. 51.

12 Gombrich, *Symbolic images*, p. 148.

13 Lancashire, '*The Second Maiden's Tragedy*: a Jacobean saint's life', 278.

14 Leech, 'Shakespeare's songs and the double response', p. 78.

15 See also Ann Thompson, 'Philomel in *Titus Andronicus* and *Cymbeline*', *ShS*, 31 (1978), 23–32.

16 But see also Booth, *King Lear, Macbeth, indefinition and tragedy*, pp. 149–51.

17 Wind, *Pagan mysteries*, p. 77.

18 Ibid., p. 78.

19 See Marjorie Garber, *Dream in Shakespeare: from metaphor to metamorphosis* (New Haven, 1974) and Landry, 'Dreams as history'.

20 Gombrich, *Symbolic images*, p. 179.

21 See Theodore Spencer, *Death and Elizabethan tragedy* (Cambridge, Mass., 1936), p. 90.

22 J. Mandel, 'Dream and imagination in Shakespeare', *SQ*, 24 (1973), 61.

23 Christopher Marlowe, *Tamburlaine the Great*, ed. J. S. Cunningham (Manchester, 1981), p. 249.

24 Spencer, *Death and Elizabethan tragedy*, p. 96.

25 Wind, *Pagan mysteries*, p. 157.

26 Ibid.

27 Ibid., p. 161.

28 John H. Long, *Shakespeare's use of music: the final comedies* (Gainesville, 1961), p. 63.

29 Wind, *Pagan mysteries*, p. 53.

30 Harley Granville-Barker, *Prefaces to Shakespeare: Cymbeline* (London, 1935), p. 238.

31 Roy Strong, *The English icon* (London, 1969).

32 See Chapter 2 and also Marion Lomax, 'The letter of death in Elizabethan and Jacobean drama', *The Swansea Review*, 1 (1986), 14–26.

33 See Chapter 1.

34 Rudolf Wittkower, *Allegory and the migration of symbols* (London, 1977), p. 19.

35 B. C. Southam, *A student's guide to the selected poems of T. S. Eliot* (London, 1968), p. 112.

36 For the Renaissance interest in hieroglyphics see Wittkower, *Allegory and the migration of symbols*, pp. 114–20.

37 Gombrich, *Symbolic images*, p. 153.

38 Ibid., p. 124.

39 Wind, *Pagan mysteries*, p. 232.

40 Ibid.

41 Ibid., p. 234.

42 Wittkower, *Allegory and the migration of symbols*, p. 27.

43 Gombrich, *Symbolic images*, p. 136.

6 *The White Devil* and *The Duchess of Malfi*

1 A link has been made between this play and Ford's *The Broken Heart*: see Shanti Padhi, '*The Broken Heart* and *The Second Maiden's Tragedy*: Ford's main source for the corpse's coronation', *NQ*, 31 (1984), 236–7. However, the corpse of Ithocles was probably represented by an actor, whereas the simultaneous appearance of the Lady's ghost and her dead body in *The Second Maiden's Tragedy* shows that an effigy was used.

2 R. W. Dent, *John Webster's borrowing* (Berkeley, 1960).

3 See also Joseph Loewenstein, *Responsive readings: versions of Echo in pastoral, epic, and the Jonsonian masque* (New Haven and London, 1984).

4 Ralph Berry, *The art of John Webster* (London, 1972), p. 19.

5 *FS*, vol. III, p. 432.

6 *The White Devil* ed. John Russell Brown (Manchester, 1966), p. xx.

7 Ibid., p. 24. All quotations are from this edition.

8 Inga-Stina Ewbank, 'A cunning piece of wrought perspective', *John Webster*, ed. Brian Morris (London, 1970), p. 160.

9 Dieter Mehl, *The Elizabethan dumbshow* (London, 1965), p. 139.

10 Glynne Wickham, *Shakespeare's dramatic heritage* (London, 1969), p. 46.

11 Dent, *John Webster's borrowing*, p. 102.

12 Joan M. Lord, 'The Duchess of Malfi: "the spirit of greatness" and "of woman"', *SEL*, 16 (1976), 305–17.

13 See Berry, *Shakespeare and the awareness of the audience*, pp. 88–108.

14 In *The Second Maiden's Tragedy* the Tyrant dies through kissing the corpse's

lips which her lover has painted with poison, but in *The White Devil* this kiss is only one of many such images.

15 *The Duchess of Malfi*, ed. Brown.
16 Wind, *Pagan mysteries*, p. 157.
17 Inga-Stina Ewbank, 'The impure art of John Webster', *RES*, 9 (1958), 262.
18 F. L. Lucas, *The complete works of John Webster* (4 vols., London, 1927), vol. II, p. 181.
19 Ewbank, 'The impure art of John Webster', 265.
20 Eric Mercer, *English art 1553–1625* (London, 1962), pp. 221–2.
21 Terence Spencer, 'The statue of Hermione', *Essays and Studies*, 30 (1977), 45.
22 Mercer, *English art*, p. 238.
23 Katherine A. Esdaile, *English church monuments 1510–1840* (London, 1946), p. 60.
24 Ibid., p. 56.
25 Ibid., p. 60.
26 Ibid., p. 71.
27 D. M. Bergeron, 'The wax figures in *The Duchess of Malfi*', *SEL*, 18 (1978), 337.
28 John Weever, *Ancient Funerall Monuments within the United Monarchie of Great Britaine* (London, 1631), p. 42. See also: *The Second Maiden's Tragedy*, IV.iii and IV.iv, pp. 60–4.
29 Bergeron, 'The wax figures in *The Duchess of Malfi*', 339.
30 Arthur C. Kirsch, *Jacobean dramatic perspectives* (Charlottesville, 1972), p. 111.
31 Ibid., p. 99.
32 Lucas, *The complete works of John Webster*, vol. II, p. 178.
33 Ibid., vol. II, p. 179.
34 W. H. St John Hope, 'On the funeral effigies of the kings and queens of England, with special reference to those in the Abbey Church of Westminster', *Archaeologia*, 60 (1907), 527.
35 Ernst H. Kantorowicz, *The king's two bodies* (Princeton, N.J., 1957), p. 420.
36 In Middleton's *A Chaste Maid in Cheapside*, ed. Alan Brissenden (London, 1968), Tim Yellowhammer refers to these monuments (IV.ii.85–9). This was probably performed in 1613 and so is close to Webster's play.
37 Hope, 'On the funeral effigies of the kings and queens', 567.
38 Kantorowicz, *The king's two bodies*, p. 423.
39 Ibid., p. 424.
40 Bergeron, 'The wax figures in *The Duchess of Malfi*', 331.
41 Lord, 'The Duchess of Malfi', 312.
42 A similar mockery is made of the duchess's public position in IV.ii. See Alan C. Dessen, *Elizabethan stage conventions and modern interpreters* (Cambridge, 1984), p. 67. Here, he effectively associates her 'last presence chamber' with her coffin.
43 M. C. Bradbrook, 'Two notes upon Webster', *MLR*, 42 (1947), 283.
44 John Weever, *Ancient Funerall Monuments*, p. 42.
45 Mercer, *English art*, p. 222.
46 Kirsch, *Jacobean dramatic perspectives*, p. 111.

47 R. B. Graves, 'The Duchess of Malfi at the Globe and Blackfriars', RenD, 9 (1978), 199.
48 The Duchess of Malfi, ed. Brown, xxiii.
49 ES, vol. III, p. 510.
50 Ibid., p. 104.
51 This is a basic prerequisite of Elizabethan drama. See Philip Sidney, A Defence of Poetry, ed. J. Van Dorsten (Oxford, 1966), p. 65.
52 No such hint of humour was deemed necessary in IV.i of The Winter's Tale a few years earlier.
53 Mario Praz, 'John Webster and The Maid's Tragedy', English Studies, (1956), 257.
54 See Dessen, Elizabethan stage conventions, p. 65.
55 Bradbrook, 'Two notes upon Webster', 283.
56 The duchess was played by Eleanor Bron; Bosola, by Ian McKellen; and Ferdinand, by Jonathan Hyde.
57 Berry, The art of John Webster, p. 6.
58 The Duchess of Malfi, ed. Brown, p. 157, note 337.

7 The Changeling, 'Tis Pity She's a Whore and The Broken Heart

1 Dates are from Alfred Harbage, Annals of English drama 975–1700; revised by S. Schoenbaum (London, 1964).
2 Not Dr Hilkish Crooke as the Revels edition states, and subsequent dramatic publications perpetuate. See Health, medicine and morality in the sixteenth century, ed. Charles Webster (Cambridge, 1979), p. 154.
3 Timothy Bright, A Treatise of Melancholy (1586), Section ii, 'Of the Soule and the Body'.
4 M. D. Anderson, Drama and imagery in English medieval churches (Cambridge, 1963), p. 165.
5 Ibid., p. 169.
6 The Chester Mystery Cycle: a reduced facsimile of Huntington Library MS2 (Leeds, 1980), Section 12, 'Reading of the Banes, 1600'.
7 John Melton, Astrologaster (1620), E4r.
8 Anderson, Drama and imagery, p. 20.
9 John Lyly, Works, ed. R. W. Bond (3 vols., Oxford, 1902), vol. III, p. 536.
10 Thomas Middleton and William Rowley, The Changeling, ed. N. W. Bawcutt (Manchester, 1958). All references are to this edition.
11 Anderson, Drama and imagery, p. 55.
12 See Glynne Wickham, 'Hell-castle and its door-keeper', ShS, 19 (1966), 68–74.
13 The popular school, ed. T. P. Logan and D. S. Smith (Lincoln, Neb., 1975), p. 59.
14 Normand Berlin, 'The "finger" image and relationship of character in The Changeling', English studies in Africa, 11 (1968), 162–6.
15 See Chapter 2.
16 At the National Theatre (Cottesloe).
17 Anderson, Drama and imagery, p. 139.
18 Nicholas Brooke, Horrid laughter in Jacobean tragedy (London, 1979), p. 85.

19 See Anne Lancashire, 'The emblematic castle in Shakespeare and Middleton', *Mirror up to Shakespeare*, ed. J. C. Gray, pp. 223–41.
20 Wickham, 'Hell-castle and its door-keeper', 68–74.
21 Frost, *The school of Shakespeare*, p. 33.
22 Ibid., pp. 158–9.
23 John Ford, *'Tis Pity She's a Whore*, ed. Derek Roper (Manchester, 1975). All quotations are from this edition.
24 Christopher Marlowe, *Complete plays*, ed. Irving Ribner (New York, 1963).
25 Bradbrook, *John Webster*, p. 158.
26 Ibid., p. 157.
27 Ibid., p. 158.
28 Brooke, *Horrid laughter*, p. 124.
29 Bentley, 'Shakespeare and the Blackfriars theatre', 38–50.
30 Kirsch, *Jacobean dramatic perspectives*, p. 86.
31 M. C. Bradbrook, *Themes and conventions of Elizabethan tragedy*, 2nd edn (Cambridge, 1980), p. 22.
32 R. Jordan, 'Calantha's dance in *The Broken Heart*', NQ, 16 (1969), 294.
33 Anderson, *Drama and imagery*, p. 75.
34 John Ford, *The Broken Heart*, ed. T. J. B. Spencer (Manchester, 1980). All quotations are from this edition.
35 Bradbrook, *Themes and conventions*, p. 17.

Index

A Chaste Maid in Cheapside
(Middleton), 193 n.36
A Fair Quarrel (Middleton),
159
*A Looking-Glass for London and
England* (Greene and Lodge), 79,
81–2, 190 n.23
A Midsummer Night's Dream, 8, 34,
36–7, 82, 87, 111, 149, 160
Ages, The (Heywood), 1, 6, 11, 13,
19–33, 70, 79, 82, 121, 128, 185
n.24
Alchemist, The (Jonson), 128
Anderson, M. D., 156–7, 164–5,
194 nn.4–5, 8, 11, 17, 195 n.33
Anglo-Scottish union, 55–6, 58,
65–6, 69, 188 n.4, 189 n.20, 190
n.35
Antonio's Revenge (Marston),
15–16, 27, 174
Antony and Cleopatra, 26, 163,
171, 188 n.2
Ardolino, Frank, 46–7, 187 nn.22–3
Artemis of Ephesus *see* Diana,
goddess
As You Like It, 4–5, 34, 36, 82, 112
(illus.), 113, 172–3
Atheist's Tragedy, The, 99

Barkan, Leonard, 15, 184 n.8
barley-brake (game), 155, 157–60,
164, 167
Barnes, Barnabe *see Devil's Charter,
The*
Bawcutt, N. W., 45, 157, 166, 187
n.21, 194 n.10
Beaumont, Francis *see* under
individual works
Bentley, G. E., 19, 175, 185 n.17,
195 n.29
Bergeron, David M., 20, 138, 139,

140, 144, 185 n.20, 193 nn.27,
29, 40
Berlin, Normand, 161–4, 194 n.14
Berry, Ralph, 127, 188 n.6, 192
nn.4, 13, 194 n.57
Bevington, David, 2–4, 106, 184
n.9, 191 n.11
Blackfriars theatre, 1, 18–19, 74,
101, 102 (illus.), 103, 128, 146–7,
150, 175, 185 n.17, 194 n.47, 195
n.29
blood-stained cloths, 34–43, 107,
119–20, 123 *see also* cloths (stage
properties)
Bond, R. W., 157
Booth, Stephen, 184 n.9, 191 n.16
boy players, 1, 17–18, 30, 127–8
Bradbrook, M. C., 2, 14, 34, 36, 54,
56, 98, 145, 150, 169–70, 172,
178, 181, 183 n.3, 184 n.5, 186
n.7, 187 n.34, 188 n.5, 189 n.7
(Ch.3), 191 nn.44–5, 193 n.43,
194 n.55, 195 nn.25–7, 31,
35
Brockbank, Philip, 79, 97, 190 n.22,
191 n.41
Broken Heart, The, (Ford) 155,
178–82, 192 n.1, 195 nn.32, 34
Brooke, Nicholas, 165, 174, 194
n.18, 195 n.28
Brown, John Russell, 128, 137, 146,
149–50, 154, 189 n.21, 192
nn.6–7

Campion, Thomas *see* under
individual works
cave (stage property), 13, 16, 52–3,
114, 116, 122 (illus.)
Cervantes, Miguel *see Don Quixote*
Chambers, E. K., 10, 19, 56, 184
n.2, 185 n.13, 187 n.33, 188

nn.2–3, 189 nn.14–15, 192 n.5, 194 nn.49–50

Changeling, The (Middleton), 8, 27, 44–6, 155–68, 169, 174–5, 181–2, 187 nn.20–1, 194 nn. 10, 14

Charles I, 155; as Prince of Wales, 33

Cheek by Jowl Theatre Company, 8, 86 (illus.), 87–8 (illus.), 92–3 (illus.), 95 (illus.), 190 n.38

Chettle, Henry and Munday, Anthony, 63 *see also Death of Robert Earl of Huntingdon*

chivalric revival, 17, 74, 99–100

Christian, King of Denmark, 143, 188 n.1

Cinthio, Giovanni Battista Giraldi, 37, 186 n.9

civic pageants *see* pageantry, civic

cloths (stage properties) 84, 93 (illus.), *see also* blood-stained cloths

Cockpit (theatre), 174–5, 177

Colie, Rosalie, 1, 2, 6, 183 nn.1–2, 184 n.20

Comedy of Errors, 71

commedia dell' arte, 46, 53

Confessio Amantis (Gower), 75–7, 79, 80–5, 87, 89

conventions, 4, 8, 14–16, 155–82, 193 n.42, 194 n.54, 195 nn.31, 35

Coriolanus, 12, 96, 174

costume, 7, 10, 12, 19, 29, 55, 57, 60, 64–5, 157, 166, 181

court masque *see* masque, court

Crooke, Helkiah, 155, 194 n.2

Curtain (playhouse), 70

Cutts, John P., 95, 190 n.39

Cymbeline, 2, 6, 12–13, 16, 18–19, 21, 30–1, 34, 37–8, 41–3, 52–3, 63, 76, 88, 96, 99–126, 136, 142, 158, 184 n.9, 185 n.38–9, 186 n.2, 187 nn.30–1, 191 nn.9, 15, 192 n.30

Cynthia *see* Diana, goddess

dancing, in masques and plays, 17, 28, 55, 61–2, 71–2, 77, 87, 95–6, 158–9, 177, 179–81, 190 n.39,

195 n.32; Dance of Death *see* death, dance of

Davis, W. R., 58, 68, 189 n.13

Day, John, ix, 72–3; with Rowley and Wilkins, 189 n.3; *see also Isle of Gulls* and *Travailes of the Three English Brothers, The*

death, and Elizabethan tragedy, 191 nn.21, 24; as a gate, 116; as a journey 115–16; as a mist, 115, 141–2; as a preserver of chastity, 99–100, 105–6, 113; dance of, 77, 95, 179–80; letter of, 192 n.32; life after, 116, 135, 169; love and, 116–18, 120, 136, 150, 167–8, 170–1; personified, 152 (illus.), 153; sleep and, 100–1, 106, 110, 114–15; *see also* life, returns to

Death of Robert Earl of Huntingdon (Chettle and Munday), 99

Dekker, Thomas, 11, 17, 29, 89, 127, 184, n.4

Dent, R. W., 127, 131, 192 n.2, 11

Dessen, Alan, 2, 183 n.7, 184 n.21, 186 n.3, 193 n.42, 194 n.54

Devil's Charter, The (Barnes), 97

devils, portrayal of, 3, 22–3, 27, 51, 156–7, 160, 166

Diana, goddess, 28, 51, 54–5, 60, 68, 81–5, 86 (illus.), 87–91, 94, 95 (illus.), 96, 111–13, 190 n.33

Diehl, H., 37, 186 n.9

Doctor Faustus (Marlowe), 12, 149, 157, 169

Don Quixote, 74–5, 189n. 11 (Ch. 4)

doubling of parts, 87, 110–11

dream, in drama, 6, 15, 31, 97, 112 (illus.), 113–15, 118, 123–4, 131, 185 n.38, 190 n.22, 191 n.41, 19, 22

Duchess of Malfi, The (Webster), 1, 16, 127, 128, 133–53, 155, 164, 169, 170–1, 181, 192 n.12, 193 nn.15, 27, 29, 40–3, 194 nn.47–8, 58

dumb-shows, 21, 26–7, 29–31, 96–7, 124, 127, 129, 133, 155, 164, 182, 192 n.9

eagle, property and symbol, 6,

29–30, 32 (illus.), 33, 99, 105,
    120–2 (illus.), 123–4, 142
Edward II (Marlowe), 133
Edwards, Philip, 35, 43
Elizabeth I, 1, 17, 20, 23, 27, 39, 54,
    89, 100, 112–13, 143
emblems, 2, 10, 23, 26, 37, 42–3
    (illus.), 47, 49, 69, 80, 100–7,
    116, 118, 138, 160, 163, 165, 186
    n.10, 187, n.20, 195 n.19
Every Man in His Humour (Jonson),
    62
Ewbank, Inga-Stina, 2, 129, 137,
    192 n.8, 193 nn.17, 19

Faerie Queene, The (Spenser), 78,
    100, 156–7, 190 n.20
Family of Love, The (Middleton),
    168
Fates, the three, 23, 28–9
flights, in plays etc., 19, 23, 26,
    28–30, 32 (illus.)
Foakes, R. A., 2, 17, 183 n.5, 185
    nn.14, 24, 42
Ford, John, 3, 8, 168–82; *see also*
    under individual works
Frye, Northrop, 56, 188 n.7
Frye, Roland Mushat, 2, 7, 184 n.22

Garber, Marjorie, 2, 34, 52, 186
    n.2, 5, 187 n.30–1, 191 n.19
gesture, language of, 4, 12, 96, 176,
    191 nn.40, 11; *see also* dancing,
    in masques and plays; dumb-
    shows; spectacle
ghosts, in plays, 7, 27, 56, 58, 66–7,
    97, 100, 105, 111, 116, 124, 128,
    135, 138, 152–3, 164, 166, 188
    n.2, 192 n.1
Globe (playhouse), 1, 10, 19, 128,
    146–7, 150, 175, 185 n.43, 188
    n.2, 194 n.47
Gombrich, E. H., 5, 106, 108, 113,
    122, 190 n.19, 191 nn.12, 20, 192
    nn.37–8, 43
Gorboduc (Sackville and Norton),
    30
Gower, John *see Confessio Amantis*
Graves, R. B., 146–7, 194 n.47
Gunpowder Plot, 55, 188 n.1
Gurr, Andrew, 185 n.16, 189 n.10

Hamlet, 7, 27, 71, 82, 115, 130,
    151, 155, 160
heart, property and symbol, 4, 36–7,
    142, 164, 169, 171–4, 176–9
hell, gatekeeper of, 51, 81, 194 n.12,
    195 n.20; Judges of, 23;
    representations of, 27, 29, 109,
    135, 137, 147–8, 155, 157–60,
    164, 166–9
Henry, Prince of Wales, 1, 17, 75,
    100, 143
Henry VI, 3, 34–6, 186 n.6
Henry VIII, 82
Henslowe's Diary, 33, 116, 185
    n.42
Heywood, Thomas, ix, 19–33, 89,
    150, 184 n.3, 185 n.21; *see also*
    under *Ages, The*
Hodges, C. Walter, 33, 101 (illus.),
    102 (illus.), 185 n.43
Hoeniger, F. D., 51, 75, 82, 87, 189
    n.13 (Ch.4), 190 nn.26–7
Holloway, John, 65, 189 n.18
Hymenaei (Jonson), 28–9, 57,
    83

iconography, 2, 34, 103–6, 186
    nn.9–10, 192 n.31
Isle of Gulls (Day), 56

James I, 1, 89, 113, 143, 155, 188
    n.1; and Anglo-Scottish unity, 55,
    58, 65–6; as peacemaker, 23, 29,
    58, 65, 68; Royal entry of, 11,
    184 n.6
Jones, Emrys, 2, 183 n.7, 185 n.39
Jones, Inigo, 1, 17, 19, 32 (illus.),
    74, 190 n.28
Jonson, Ben, 1–2, 17, 19, 54, 56, 74,
    121, 138, 192 n.3; *see also* under
    individual works
Jupiter, 6, 23, 26, 28–32 (illus.), 33,
    96, 99, 118–19, 121–3, 126, 170

Kantorowicz, Ernst H., 143, 193
    n.35, 38
King Lear, 82, 91–2, 97–8, 115, 185
    n.9, 191 n.16
King's Men, the, 1, 14, 18–19, 31,
    61, 69, 128, 150, 188 n.2, 189
    n.14

Kirsch, Arthur C., 111, 141, 146, 177, 193 nn.30–1, 46, 195 n.30
Knight, G. Wilson, 75, 97, 183 n.6, 189 n.12 (Ch.4), 190 n.25, 191 n.42
Knight of the Burning Pestle, The (Beaumont), 70, 74, 188 n.2, 189 n.4
Kyd, Thomas, 11, 16, 39–40, 46–7, 53; *see also Spanish Tragedy, The*

Lancashire, Anne, 99–100, 105, 107, 191 nn.1–4, 8, 13, 195 n.19
Landry, D. E., 185 n.38, 191 n.19
Leech, Clifford, 104, 107–8, 191 nn.5–6, 14
Leggatt, Alexander, 56, 189 n.8
life, returns to (in plays), 14–16, 25, 30–1, 50–3, 78, 83–4, 87, 91, 94, 96–7, 99–100, 106–7, 110, 114–17, 120, 125, 128, 141
Lindley, David, 56, 188 n.4, 189 n.20, 190 n.35
Loewenstein, Joseph, 192 n.3
Long, John H., 118, 192 n.28
Lord, Joan, 133, 144, 192 n.12, 193 n.41
Lord Hay's Masque (Campion), 55–69, 74, 184 n.6, 188 n.4, 189 nn.14, 20, 190 n.35
Lord Mayor's shows, 17, 20, 28, 30, 34
Lords' Masque (Campion), 15
love tokens, symbolism of, 24, 35–7, 43–6, 117, 123, 164
Love's Labour's Lost, 8
Lucas, F. L., 137, 142, 145, 193 nn.18, 32–3
Lucina *see* Diana, goddess
Lyly, John, 28, 138, 194 n.9

Macbeth, 6, 12, 53, 55–69, 70–1, 91–2, 130, 146, 149, 160, 165–6, 168, 175, 180, 185 n.9, 188 nn.1–2, 4, 189 nn.8–9, 21, 191 n.16
McIntosh, William A., 72, 77, 189 n.5, 190 n.16
madmen, in plays, 137, 155–60, 166–7

Maid's Tragedy, The (Beaumont and Fletcher), 128, 149, 194 n.53
Malcontent, The (Marston), 127
Mandel, J., 115, 191 n.22
Marina, of Antioch, 51
Marlowe, Christopher, 24; *see also* under individual works
Marston, John, 11, 15; *see also* under individual works
Mary, Virgin, 52–4, 76, 84, 100, 106, 110, 165, 187 n.29, 190 n.15
masque, court, 1, 4, 11, 13–17, 19–20, 23, 28–30, 32 (illus.), 33, 34, 45, 55–69, 70, 74, 113, 121–2, 136–7, 156, 177–8, 181, 185 n.35, 186 n.45, 188 n.7, 189 nn.11, 14–15, 20, 192 n.3; *see also* under individual masques
Masque of Beauty, 127
Masque of Blackness, 184 n.6
Masque of Queens, 28, 56
Measure for Measure, 68, 113, 171
Mehl, Dieter, 2, 129, 192 n.9
Mercer, Eric, 137–8, 146, 193 nn.20, 22, 45
Merchant of Venice, The, 47–8, 50, 52, 82
Middleton, Christopher, 3, 8, 11, 54, 177, 191 n.2, 195 n.19; and Rowley, William, 45, 155–68, 177, 181–2; *see also* under individual works
Milford Haven, 31, 115
miracle plays, 31, 34, 70, 113, 164–5
moralising, in plays, 13, 20, 22, 24–7, 33, 47–8, 81–2, 91, 129–32, 155, 160, 176, 187 n.20
morality tradition, 3, 75, 79, 97, 129–30, 133, 155–7, 160, 165, 168, 175
Muir, Kenneth, 64, 188 n.2
Munday, Anthony, 17; *see also* Chettle and Munday
Murray, W. A., 57, 189 n.10
music, in masques and plays, 10, 14, 17, 28–9, 62–3, 76–7, 93–7, 118, 134, 177, 179–80, 189 n.5, 190 nn.16, 38, 192 n.28; of the spheres, 14, 76, 94–6

mystery plays, 13, 15, 19, 23, 27,
    156, 164–5, 194 n.6

Nashe, Thomas, 109
National Theatre, 151, 152 (illus.),
    194 n.16
Nicoll, Allardyce, 185 n.35, 186
    n.45
Nosworthy, J. M., 188 n.2

Oberon the Fairy Prince (Jonson),
    14
Old Wives Tale (Peele), 127
Orgel, Stephen, 189 n.11, 190 n.28
Othello, 2–3, 34, 36–7, 82, 102
    (illus.), 103, 113, 151, 166–8,
    171, 178, 186 nn.8, 9
Ovid, 15, 35–6, 38–9, 59, 83, 106,
    109, 114–15, 186 n.11, 190 n.29

pageantry, civic, 12–17, 19–22,
    26–8, 30, 33, 56, 69–70, 121,
    127, 184 n.6, 185 n.19
Palmer, D. J., 69, 189 n.21
Pandora's box, 46–53, 187 nn.24–5
Pandosto: the Triumph of Time
    (Greene), 14
Panofsky, Dora and Erwin, 50, 187
    nn.24–5
Paul, H. N., 188 n.1
Pericles, 2, 14–17, 19, 21, 34,
    47–53, 70–98, 103, 111, 189
    nn.5, 13, 190 nn.16, 22, 26, 38–9,
    191 n.41
plague, effect on drama, 18, 188 n.2
Plato, 53, 105, 116–17
Plautus, 31
Plutarch, 26, 123, 178
Praz, Mario, 149, 194 n.53
processions, 11–12, 34, 68–9, 83,
    144, 151, 164

Queen's Men, the, 128, 174

Red Bull (playhouse), 18–19, 54,
    128
Revenger's Tragedy, The (Tour-
    neur), 106, 150, 191 n.10
Richard II, 80, 144
Richard III, 106
Riche, Barnabe, 63

rituals and rites, 7, 12, 30, 34, 65,
    84, 95, 101, 103, 115, 119, 134,
    145, 155–82
romance tradition, 4–5, 17, 70,
    74–5, 98, 114, 126, 188 n.7, 191
    n.43
Romeo and Juliet, 100–1 (illus.),
    103, 168–9, 171, 173–4
Royal Shakespeare Company, 2, 112
    (illus.), 113, 175

Salinger, Leo G., 31, 97, 185 n.40,
    191 n.43
Scot, Reginald, 68, 145
Second Maiden's Tragedy, The
    (Middleton), 99–100, 105, 127,
    150, 191 nn.1–4, 8, 13, 192 nn.1,
    14, 193 n.28
Seneca, 27, 125
Shakespeare, Edmund, 70, 189 n.2
Shakespeare, William, B.B.C.
    productions of, 2, 98, 184 n.24,
    191 n.9; last plays (as a group),
    4–5, 13, 15, 17, 53, 56, 70, 96–7,
    124, 136, 189 n.8; and masque,
    13–16, 19, 55–69, 123; and
    pageantry, 12–17, 19, 21, 56,
    69–70, 121, 123, 185 n.19; and
    spectacle, 10–19, 30–1, 33, 56,
    69, 79, 100, 121–2, 126; *see also*
    Cheek by Jowl Theatre Company;
    Royal Shakespeare Company; and
    under individual plays
Sidney, Sir Philip, 2, 9, 23, 54,
    143–5, 194 n.51
Siemon, James, 3–4, 184 nn.15–17
Slater, Anne Pasternak, 183 n.2, 186
    n.5
songs, in masques and plays, 28, 68,
    93 (illus.), 94, 96, 107, 110–11,
    116, 180–1, 191 nn.5–6, 14
Sophonisba (Marston), 99, 188 n.2
Spanish Tragedy, The (Kyd), 10, 16,
    34–41, 43–7, 53, 151, 164, 177,
    187 nn.19, 22
spectacle, 2, 6, 9, 10–33, 40, 56, 69,
    79, 100, 121, 126, 130
Spencer, Terence, 137, 193 n.21
Spencer, Theodore, 107, 118, 191
    nn.21, 24
statues and effigies, in masque and

drama, 13–16, 50, 87–8 (illus.),
    94, 104, 127, 136–9, 142–5, 192
    n.1, 193 nn.28, 34, 36–7; see also
    waxworks
Strong, Roy, 118–19, 189 n.11, 190
    n.28, 192 n.31
Stubbes, Philip, 39–40, 186 n.15
Styan, J. L., 2, 31, 185 n.37

Tamburlaine (Marlowe), 10–11, 22,
    115, 119, 130, 173, 191 n.23
Tempe Restored (Townsend), 32
    (illus.), 33
Tempest, The, 19, 80, 82, 189 n.16
Thompson, Ann, 191 n.15
thunder and lightning, 28–9, 31, 33,
    62–3, 79, 118
tilts and tournaments, 17, 19, 33,
    49, 75, 90
'Tis Pity She's a Whore (Ford), 8,
    142, 155, 164, 168–78, 181, 182,
    195 n.23
Titus Andronicus, 27, 82, 109,
    124–6, 191 n.15
tragi-comedy, 2, 6, 27, 34, 109–10,
    116, 126, 141
Travailes of the Three English
    Brothers, The (Day), 70–5, 89,
    97
trees, symbolism of, 37–43, 49, 57,
    65–6, 90–1, 125, 186 n.10
Troilus and Cressida, 163
Twelfth Night, 113
Tyger (ship), 55–6, 187 n.1

Venus, 16, 23, 26–7, 52–4, 76–8,
    88–90, 111–13, 190 n.20
Vision of the Twelve Goddesses,
    The, 28

waxworks, 16, 127, 137–8, 142–7,
    164–5, 193 nn.27, 29, 34, 36–7,
    40
Webster, John, 3, 8, 11, 16, 127–54,
    164, 169–70, 174, 177, 188 n.6,
    189 n.7 (Ch.3); see also under
    individual works
Weever, John, 140, 145, 193 nn.28
    44
White Devil, The (Webster), 101,
    127–35, 141–2, 147–51, 153,
    160, 172, 192 n.6–7, 193 n.14
Whitehall, Banqueting House, 59,
    175
Whore of Babylon, The (Dekker),
    89
Wickham, Glynne, 2, 17, 29, 129,
    165, 185 n.10, 186 n.44, 192
    n.10, 194 n.12, 195 n.20
Wind, Edgar, 78, 111, 117, 123,
    190 n.18, 191 nn.17–18, 25, 192
    nn.26–7, 29, 39–41, 193 n.16
Winter's Tale, The, 13–15, 62, 82,
    128, 137–8, 144, 184 n.8, 193
    n.21, 194 n.52
Wittkower, Rudolf, 120, 123, 192
    nn.34, 36, 42
Women Beware Women (Middle-
    ton), 45, 181